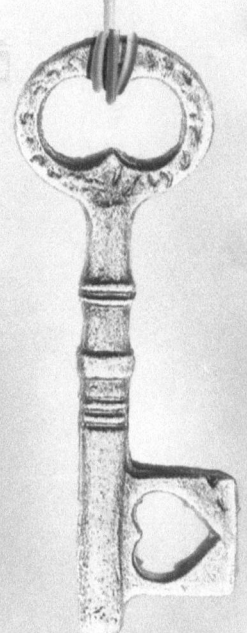

DreamChaser

Dite Coumou

Dream Chaser
— God's Keys for the Night

Published by Arrowz USA, North Palm Beach, Fl
info@arrowz.org
www.arrowz.org

Author: Dite Coumou
Translator: Hope Visser
Art direction and interior design: Ronald Gabrielsen, 3ig.org

ISBN 978 1 951014 13 1 (paperback)
ISBN 978 1 951014 14 8 (ebook)
ISBN 978 1 951014 17 9 (audiobook)

Copyright © 2023 Dite Coumou

Unless otherwise noted, all Scripture quotations are from the ESV® Bible (The Holy Bible, English Standard Version®), copyright © 2001 by Crossway, a publishing ministry of Good News Publishers. Used by permission. All rights reserved.

Scriptures marked NIV are taken from the THE HOLY BIBLE, NEW INTERNATIONAL VERSION®. Copyright© 1973, 1978, 1984, 2011 by Biblica, Inc.™. Used by permission of Zondervan.

Scriptures marked TLB are taken from The Living Bible, copyright © 1971 by Tyndale House Foundation. Used by permission of Tyndale House Publishers, Carol Stream, Illinois 60188. All rights reserved.

The spelling of tetragrammaton and the use of honorific capitals has been changed to match the publisher's house style of this book. Italicization of Bible texts has been added by the author.

For the sake of readability, inclusive language such as 'he or she' and 'his or her' has been omitted and the pronouns 'he' and 'his' have been chosen as neuter terms.

The testimonials in this work have been used with the written permission of the individuals involved. Examples of individuals and their experiences that lack consent have been anonymized.

All rights reserved. No portion of this book may be reproduced, stored in a retrieval system or transmitted in any form, electronically, mechanically, by means of photocopying, recording or otherwise—with the exception of brief quotation in printed reviews—without the prior written permission of the publisher.

*And it shall come to pass afterward,
that I will pour out my Spirit on all flesh;
your sons and your daughters shall prophesy,
your old men shall dream dreams,
and your young men shall see visions.*
- Joel 2:28

I dedicate this book to all those who chase after God's presence in every area of their lives. I pray that you will accept the Holy Spirit's invitation as you read this book. That He would speak to your heart so that you will be inspired, activated and strengthened through his words. That you would increase your ability to live under an open heaven, all of your days and nights.

Table of Contents

Endorsements	11
Foreword	13
The Solomon Generation	15
Supernatural Meetings	19

PART 1 THE NIGHT BELONGS TO GOD 21
Redemption 21
Shadow of Protection 26
God's Night Shift 29

PART 2 THE ORIGINAL PLAN FOR OUR SLEEP 31
The Influence of Sleep 32
The Rhythm of Sleep 34
Sleep Disorders and Problems 36
Sleeping Beauty 38
The Shower of Grace 42
Putting a Good Night's Sleep Into Practice 45
Do's and Don'ts 47
Conquering Insomnia 51
Fantasies 53
Sweet Encounters 57

PART 3 DO I DREAM TOO? 61
Come Closer 62
Do I Dream Too? 63
Turning Your Thinking Upside Down 65
Dreaming Dreams 71
The Dew of the Night 73

Receive Your Gift ... 74
Awakening in God's Safety ... 76
Remembering Dreams ... 79
Stewardship as a Key ... 81
Slumbering ... 83

Part 4 Dreams in the Bible ... 87
Dreams of Direction ... 88
Dreams of Prediction ... 90
Dreams that Provide Insight ... 93
Dreams of Warning ... 94
Encouraging Dreams ... 96
Dream Interpretation ... 100
Visions ... 105
Characteristics of Biblical Dreams ... 108

Part 5 Getting to Work With Your Dreams ... 111
God's Voice as a Compass ... 112
Recognizing God's Voice ... 116
Do You See God? ... 117
Various Kinds of Dreams ... 119
Recognizing God's Dreams ... 123
Interpreting Dreams ... 125
Dreams to Process Things or an Invitation? ... 129
How God Reveals Himself ... 136
Symbolic Dreams ... 139
Missing the Mark With an Interpretation ... 152
Common Dreams ... 154
The Click ... 159
Clean Glasses ... 162
Difficult Dreams ... 163
A Dream With Impact ... 166
How Do You Write Down a Dream? ... 168
I Am Doing Something New ... 170

PART 6 THERE IS ALWAYS MORE WITH GOD   173
  You Are New   173
  Creative Dreams   176
  Dreams in Business   179
  God's Calling   183
  A Symbol of God's Presence   184
  Transforming Word   185
  Heavenly Sounds   187
  Art   189
  Spiritual Warfare in a Dream   191
  Freedom in the Night   200
  A Surprising Awakening   203
  Traveling While You Sleep   207

PART 7 DREAMING IN GOD'S FAMILY   213
  Family   214
  Dreams to Bring Encouragement   216
  Dreams to Pray Through   219
  Healing in Families   223
  Dreams in Your Marriage   225
  Dreams in Friendships   227
  Keys for Deliverance and Healing   229
  Dreams in the Prophetic Ministry   232
  Receiving Messages   236
  Sharing Dreams   239
  Unexpected Response   242
  Dreaming Children   244
  Children and the Supernatural   247
  Teaching Children   250
  Belonging   253

PART 8 WALKING IN GOD'S DREAMS   257
  Wake-up Call   258
  Your Life is a Set of Keys   259

Solomon's Lessons — 264
Step-by-step Plan: From Dream to Reality — 268
God's Fire Over Your Nights — 270

Testimonials — 275
Notes — 281
Acknowledgments — 283
About the Author — 285

Endorsements

In this thought-provoking and highly practical work, Dite eloquently takes us on a journey to reveal both the purpose and the power of the gift God gave us to dream. Her diligence has produced a body of work that will inform and equip you to partner God's super to your natural in a most profound way. As Dite says, "When we sleep, the boundaries of our rational thinking fall away, and God has room to reveal Himself to us in new ways." We would do well to follow her and meet Him there.

– *Mark Appleyard*
Co-founder, Anothen, NC

Since the beginning of humankind, dreams have been an important way through which God communicates with us. But although we know this, there are still too few books on this subject. What I appreciate about *Dream Chaser* is the thoroughness with which Dite Coumou treats the subject. Whether you have been familiar with dreams and their interpretation for a long time, or have little experience with them, this book is a must-read!

– *Dr. Arleen Westerhof*
Co-pastor, God's Embassy Amsterdam,
Founder, Dutch Prophetic Council

Dream Chaser is written from a sincere and pure heart, full of passion and faith in a loving God. This book is a journey of discovery in which Dite has combined her experiences and revelations with the treasuries of God's Word. A book that will change and bring life to everyone who reads it!

– *Albert and Michelle van der Heide*
Senior Leaders, I AM Foundation, Zwijndrecht

I enjoyed being educated in *Dream Chaser*. Much was new to me, although I have been walking with God for a long time and am consciously trying to understand Him. I discovered while reading that God had already spoken through dreams a lot in my life. Dite Coumou shares spiritual principles in an accessible way. This way she makes the spiritual understandable and applicable. Since I began to understand more about God's speaking in our dreams, I have become much more mindful in my sleep, and I started having meaningful dreams more and more often. This includes the explanation of them, and without this education I would not be able to do that. I also recommend this book for families, because children dream about God from an early age!

– *Carla Veldhuis*
Arts Alive, Deventer

God's blueprint for the night has been given to Dite to equip and empower the Body of Christ. I believe this book will open new dimensions of your spiritual life. Dreams are an exciting and often underexposed topic. Dite has translated the precious insights she has received into this wonderful book and additional studies and programs. These insights have been revealed to Dite to distribute around the world. Discover the richness of the different ways God speaks to you!

– *Jan van Meerveld*
Keys Foundation, Veenendaal

Foreword

Throughout the Bible, God speaks to people through dreams. Joseph has dreams and interprets dreams, Solomon receives wisdom in a dream and Daniel interprets the dreams of kings. And that's just the beginning. God still speaks through dreams.

The night belongs to God. When we lay our head on our pillow, we open ourselves to receive revelation from Him. God gives important, detailed strategies from heaven into our minds and spirits. From another dimension He gives wisdom, courage and insight into our earthly existence. When our defenses are down because we're asleep, God can communicate through dreams and we can hear things we might not otherwise be able to hear.

How God speaks to me through dreams is best explained by a dream I once had. In this dream I explained to the people around a table that I loved it when God spoke to me through dreams. "I know God speaks in all kinds of ways," I said, "but it is very meaningful when He speaks to me in dreams. He is always so loving."

– *Ralph Veenstra*
  Bethel Prophetic, Redding, CA

HOW IT ALL STARTED

The Solomon Generation

> Your kingdom come, your will be done, on earth as it is in heaven.
> – MATTHEW 6:10

It was a Wednesday afternoon, at the end of October 2019. I was driving home from Rotterdam just before rush-hour traffic. I remembered that I needed one more thing for dinner and decided to drop by the supermarket first. While I was there, I could also quickly post a package and it would be sent on time. While I was running down a list of things in my mind I suddenly sensed the presence of God in my car. It was like a gentle breeze, my stomach felt warm and my thoughts were silenced. It was as if God had spoken to the storm of thoughts in my mind, and made room so that I could hear what He was going to say. Then I heard God's voice: "Listen, I am raising up a Solomon generation. They will receive wisdom in the night and they will rule as kings from my abundance and goodness. They will build my Kingdom in this land."

I felt how the presence of God touched my head; a tingling sensation moved from the top of my head down to my chin. Then God spoke: "Teach my children what it is like to meet Me in the night."

I started to cry and nodded. Just at that moment a truck passed me on my left. The name "Solomon" was written on the side of the truck in huge letters. What an incredible confirmation!

I knew the story of Solomon. As a young king he had an encounter that changed his life. God appeared to him in a dream and said: "Ask what I shall give you." Solomon asked for "an understanding mind to govern your people, that I may discern between good and evil, for who is able to govern this your great people?" (1 Kings 3:5, 9) Solomon was filled with God's wisdom during this dream. Nothing was too profound for him. No one was wiser than he was. No one was wealthier. He did not keep his heavenly riches to himself, but used them instead to bless the people and transform the nation. While Solomon ruled, the people lived in peace and safety. There was an abundance for all. God's glory was everywhere and his presence was at the center of it all.

The tears streamed down my face as I experienced a small portion of God's passionate desire to meet his children in the night. I was overwhelmed by what was happening and knew deep down inside that the time was now.

From the moment I had come to know God, He would speak to me through dreams. It was a normal part of our relationship. The year before this meeting with God in the car I had had the opportunity to travel to America and to learn more about dreams and dream interpretation. It was during that trip that God put the desire in my heart to pour out over the nations all the things He had taught me through the years. God had already spoken about a book and many other things, a year prior. I just didn't know how to go about it. Thankfully God has perfect timing, and his promises are always yes and amen.

Solomon's story is unusual. But Solomon is also an example of what God wants to do for us. God wants to bring in the great harvest and fill his Fatherly home. He wants to revive, restore and renew; He desires to see the earth filled by heaven. God pours out wisdom over his children so that they can cooperate with heaven and build his Kingdom here on earth.

His wisdom is not just for special super-Christians, but for all of his children. That includes you. God wants to give you the wealth of his wisdom during the day and the night, so that you can live from it and share His abundance and goodness. Let us change the nation together!

PREFACE

Supernatural Meetings

If we believe in Jesus, then we cannot omit the supernatural from our lives. Jesus was also supernatural. He walked on this earth and at the same time He saw what the Father did in heaven. He knew the thoughts of people. He walked over water and changed water into wine. His hands brought about signs, wonders and healing, and just a single word from his lips brought life to that which was dead. Heaven and earth touched each other in Jesus. Through His sacrifice Jesus made it possible for us to live in continual intimacy with the Father and to act from the supernatural. Many people think the supernatural is scary and unfathomable, but if we follow Jesus and hang out with Him, then it is a normal consequence to change to His image and likeness.

Throughout the entire Bible we see supernatural encounters between God and people through dreams and visions. One-third of the Bible actually deals directly or indirectly with dreams and visions. Isn't it strange that we barely talk about dreams and visions today? Has reasoning prevailed over God's creativity?

Many people do believe that God gives dreams, they just don't believe that God gives *them* dreams. But it has always been God's intention and if these are the last days, if the prophet Joel was right (Joel 2:28), then God has already decided how He will speak in these days: Through dreams, visions and prophecy. We should take dreams and visions seriously, so that we are in tune with the ways God shows Himself.

God is doing something new, something that we have not seen before. That is His promise (Acts 2:28; Isa. 43:19). The barrier between the natural realm and the supernatural realm has thinned and we cannot fully understand the times we are living in unless we can see the spiritual realm. God is pouring out His Spirit and more and more people are receiving dreams and visions. God is activating us so that we see who He is, what He is doing and what his plans are for the world.

Here is the good news: this is for you too! You are part of the body of Jesus Christ that He is moving across the earth. Not just inside the walls of the church, but in the heart of society. God wants to give us ideas, strategies and revelations for this. Then the world will come to know Jesus as their Savior and Redeemer. That is why it is so important for us to learn now how God speaks in the night.

Are we going to move with God in what He is doing, or are we going to hang on to what we already know? The choice is ours. I want to invite you to dive into the world of dreams and encounters in the night.

I wrote this book for dreamers and those who desire dreams. For those who are searching and those who feel secure. For the free creative spirits and the rational thinkers. But above all, for those who chase God's presence in every part of their life. This book not only contains teaching from God's Word, but also many personal examples and testimonies. The Bible says that our testimony is the "spirit of prophecy" (Rev. 19:10). That means: What God did for me and others, He desires to do for you too.

My prayer is that this book will awaken you to God's plan for the night and that it will bring redemption to your sleep. That it will give you revelation from God's Spirit and take you on a joyous journey through the wonderous possibilities of sleep. That it will give you tools for your dreams and experiences in the night. But above all I pray that this book will bring you to new encounters with an unimaginably good God.

PART 1

The Night Belongs to God

> He who dwells in the shelter of the Most High will abide in the shadow of the Almighty ... He will cover you with his pinions, and under his wings you will find refuge; his faithfulness is a shield and buckler.
> — PSALM 91:1, 4

It already occurred at the end of the very first day of the world's existence: night came and all grew dark. The sun makes way for the moon and stars; night has come. We think nothing of going to bed to sleep and continuing with life the next day. But have you ever thought about what happens the moment we close our eyes? We no longer have everything under control, and the next day we are unable to tell what happened in the night hours. Is that dangerous? Is the night a playground for the devil and is fear of the dark realistic? What does God actually do during the night? We will take a look at these interesting questions in this first part.

Redemption

> But now thus says the LORD, he who created you, O Jacob, he who formed you, O Israel: "Fear not, for I have redeemed you; I have called you by name, you are mine."
> — ISAIAH 43:1

I grew up in a loving family, without Jesus. When I look back, though, He was always there and there were times when I wondered: Could this be God? But up until ten years ago I did not know Him. It may seem strange, but somehow I always believed that there was Someone who would guide my life. Yet I was afraid of all kinds of things. Afraid of not living life to the full, fear of abandonment, fear of not being enough, afraid of dying, unexpected situations and the dark.

It was not strange that I was afraid of the dark. I had always been a sensitive child with an awareness of the supernatural realm. I searched for answers to the deep questions of life in new age and other religions. I was used to the idea that there was more between heaven and earth than could be seen and I regularly experienced supernatural manifestations in my life. I had heard that if I saw a scary apparition or felt an evil presence, I could send it away. So I did that, but it didn't work. I did not know at the time that only the name of Jesus has authority over the darkness.

Years later, when I was twenty-seven, I heard about a God who speaks to people personally. My cousin shared how he had given up everything to move to Belgium and work in an underprivileged neighborhood with kids. He had immediately quit school and his biggest hobby because God had asked him to. God had a plan for him. I was intrigued by what he told me. What I did not know at the time was this same God would call my name several months later.

I had just met the love of my life, Joost. He asked me to join him at a church service. Joost had been raised with a knowledge of God. At the time he had had some turbulent years, but he was very much aware that a life without God was not an option. He had been in the Armed Forces for fifteen years and seen enough to know that the world did not stand a chance without Jesus. What I did not know at the time, is that he had asked God to send him a woman who loved Jesus. Joost met me and fell in love. However, there was a problem: I had no idea who Jesus was. I was even quite opinionated about Christians. I thought they were hypocritical, condemning and boring people who lived life behind a wall that was called church. But because I was open to every form of spirituality, I decided to go to church with Joost. That is how I ended up in a gym on a Sunday morning, where the Baptist church held their weekly services. They sang and there was someone who spoke, but to be honest I did not even hear what it was about. My heart was open more than my ears.

During the service I felt a hand touch me; it was Jesus and He woke me to life. I was shaking as I sat on my chair and felt goosebumps all over. While my body was shaking uncontrollably, my heart became more stable than ever. I knew I was home! An unknown assurance filled the void inside me. For the first time in my life I heard the gospel, and I was touched deeply by God's overwhelming love for me. From that moment on my whole life was turned completely upside down.

The next morning I heard a voice. It may seem strange, but He sounded like the most familiar voice I had ever heard. He said: "Deuteronomy 5 verse 6". I had never read a single thing in the Bible and had no idea what this meant, so I googled it. This is what I read:

> "I am the LORD your God, who brought you out of the land of Egypt, out of the house of slavery. You shall have no other gods before me. You shall not make for yourself a carved image, or any likeness of anything that is in heaven above, or that is on the earth beneath, or that is in the water under the earth. You shall not bow down to them or serve them; for I the LORD your God am a jealous God, visiting the iniquity of the fathers on the children to the third and fourth generation of those who hate me, but showing steadfast love to thousands of those who love me and keep my commandments."
> – DEUTERONOMY 5:6-10

The words touched me deeply and I cried in repentance. The loving voice said: "I am Life, idolatry will not help you."

I was convinced immediately. I went through the house like a whirlwind, looking for books about reincarnation, gemstones that supposedly had healing powers and images of Buddha from Asian temples. I threw everything into a big box and took it straight out of the house.

As I was cleaning my house I suddenly saw what the enemy had done in my life. It was as if the lights were switched on instantaneously. I recognized the curse that was over our family: the sicknesses, addictions, accidents and death. My first mission with Jesus had started. My family had to get to know Him, so that they too could be free of this curse and could live, truly live!

My sister was the first. Jesus did an incredible work in her, so that within a moment she was freed from years of eating disorders and numerous phycological diagnosis' that she had been labeled with since she was a child.[1]

My brother was next. He had been addicted to drugs for seventeen years and left his old life behind when he met Jesus. Finally, it was my parents' turn, first my mother and later my father. They decisively emptied their home of occult items and broke ties with every form of occultism and idolatry in their lives. Death had to make room for life, for Jesus.

God freed me completely from my old life. I literally felt as though I had been born again! He freed me from the darkness and curses. From the very first day I experienced God as a Father who speaks, both night and day. God started to speak to me through dreams almost immediately; that became a normal part of my relationship with Him.

In spite of this powerful move of God in my life, I still struggled with fear of the dark. Joost and I had gotten married, and whenever he had to go on business trips, I would leave a light on in the bedroom and another in the living room. I made sure the bedroom door was tightly closed. Yet I did not sleep well because of my fear of the night that had formed during my old life and the demonic activity that I experienced then.

One night this all changed. Joost had just told me that he had to go to England for a week on an unexpected business trip. I was honest with him and told him I was dreading him leaving. I had not even finished speaking when the Holy Spirit spoke to my heart: "Read Psalm 3 verse 5." I picked up my Bible and found the Psalms. As I read what it said, it was God Himself who spoke these words to me: "Then I lay down and slept in peace and woke up safely, for the Lord was watching over me" (TLB).

The Holy Spirit lead my gaze to another verse on the same page. Once again the Father's voice sounded, gentle and reassuring: "I will lie down in peace and sleep, for though I am alone, O Lord, you will keep me safe" (Ps. 4:8 TLB).

I was completely focused on what I was reading. Again the Holy Spirit spoke to me: "Look at Psalm 91." I read: "Now you don't need to be afraid of the dark anymore" (Ps. 91:5a TLB). As I read these words, God took away the blanket of fear that had covered me. It was a supernatural experience in which the Word of God cut me free from the lie and from my fear of the dark. Every time the fear tried to re-enter my heart, I read these verses again. I memorized them and I meditated on them when I was lying awake.

This is how God brought redemption to my nights and brought them back into His plan. Instead of fear, sleeplessness and demonic activity, He gave me dreams, encounters and heavenly experiences. You can probably imagine how grateful I am to Jesus for life, deliverance and healing. Now I enjoy the nights. They are just as interesting and full of God as my days are.

When God redeems your life, this does not just apply to the day and the moments you are awake, but also to the night. Many people have been damaged in some way when it comes to the night. A lie worked its way into their lives because of a scary experience or a trauma. Perhaps this has happened to you. God wants to free you from that and bring your nights back in line with his original plan. As you read this book and cooperate with the Holy Spirit, I believe that God will give you freedom and healing and cleanse your nights from injustice and all that is evil. He will fill your nights with new things from his heart and you too will dream dreams. God wants to do for you what He did for me. When you discover his wonderous plans for the night, then sleeping will become one great adventure!

Perhaps you see something of yourself in my story and you do not yet know Jesus. Then you can pray this prayer:

Jesus, I come to You. I have wandered away but I yearn to come home to Your love. Thank You for taking my guilt upon Yourself so that I can be free. I need Your redemption. Will You forgive my sins and wash me clean? I surrender my life to You and I want to get to know You. Amen

Shadow of Protection

> He made darkness his covering, his canopy around him, thick clouds dark with water.
> — PSALM 18:11

When we hear the word "darkness" we often associate that with the devil and his plans. Nightmares, crime, secrets and evil spirits are often directly linked to the night. But that was not God's intention when He created the night! Let's take a look at his Word. The Bible uses the word "darkness" in various ways. Sometimes it is simply a description of the night, the opposite of day. Sometimes it is used to describe what it is like to live a life separated from God. There is an important distinction between literal and spiritual darkness.

We see the spiritual meaning here, for example: "For although they knew God, they did not honor him as God or give thanks to him, but they became futile in their thinking, and their foolish hearts were darkened" (Rom. 1:21). Paul uses the word *eskotisthē* for darkened. This Greek word, derived from *skotízō* means to become dark, obscuring God's light.[2] Their eyes, their thoughts and their minds were darkened. It speaks of people who live without Jesus, and because of that do things that damage themselves and others.

We see literal darkness in creation. When God created the earth, He separated the darkness from the light. "God called the light Day, and the darkness he called Night. And there was evening and there was morning, the first day" (Gen. 1:5). Here God uses the Hebrew word *choshek*. That means: darkness or obscurity.[3] This is the same darkness from which God gave the laws to Moses: "The people stood far off, while Moses drew near to the thick darkness where God was" (Ex. 20:21).

Can you imagine that? A voice coming out of thick darkness. It must have been strange for Moses too. And yet he stepped into this secret place, into the darkness. He trusted God, even in the dark, because he knew His voice. Hearing God's voice is the key to freedom from every form of fear.

Many people, young and old, are afraid of the dark. Chills run down their spines when they are at home alone or if they are walking outside at night. That is nothing to be ashamed of, but it is something that can be dealt with, with the help of God's Word. Just take a look: "And God separated the light from the darkness. God called the light Day, and the darkness he called Night" (Gen. 1:4b-5a). Whoever names something is the one who exercises authority over it. That means there never was a battle between the light and the darkness, because God created both of them.

The idea that the night belongs to satan, and that he can do whatever he wants, is a lie. When we read the Bible, only one verse talks about the night and satan (Rev. 20:10). This verse talks about satan's future and that does not look very good.

Satan can only influence our nights if we give him that authority. But God wants to transform our nights from *skotízō* to *choshek*. He wants our eyes and thoughts to be enlightened, so that we receive revelation and we can see the hope and "the riches of his glorious inheritance" (Eph. 1:18). The night belongs to God. We can rejoice in what God will do during our nights and open ourselves up to this beautiful truth: "He made darkness his covering, his canopy around him" (Ps. 18:11a). God is present even in the darkest night. And even more than that, God makes the darkness his dwelling place: "The LORD has said that he would dwell in thick darkness" (2 Chron. 6:1). And it gets even better! When God named the night during creation, He used the word *layil*. This word means protective shadow.[4]

So if you still think that the night is not in God's hands, then here is your answer. The night was created by God and is named after Him: a protective shadow in which God dwells.

But there is more. The night is not just a protective shadow and dwelling place for the Father. It is a treasure room from which God want to generously share his riches: "I will give you the treasures of darkness and the hoards in secret places, that you may know that it is I, the LORD, the God of Israel, who call you by your name" (Isa. 45:3).

This Bible verse reminds me of digging for buried treasure. God Himself maps out the route for us, and hides the treasures. He gives us directions that will lead us to the treasure and He thoroughly enjoys our joy and wonder when we find those treasures.

Have you ever thought about this? The biggest treasure, Jesus Christ, came to the world in darkness. The light of the world, born in the night. He was revealed by a star shining in the heavens. The star gave the wise men direction; a singing choir of angels caught the attention of shepherds nearby. Both groups went on their way because they believed that there was something special to be found—and they found the greatest treasure in history.

There is an invitation for you too to come and hunt for treasure. God is excited about revealing his riches to you!

God's Night Shift

> Behold, he who keeps Israel will neither slumber nor sleep.
> — PSALM 121:4

God's Word teaches us about his original plan for the night and our sleep. God does not sleep and He does not get tired. He is always available to listen when we share our heart with Him. But if God does not sleep, then what does He do at night?

There are numerous stories in the Bible about this. For example, God answered Gideon by wetting his fleece with dew (Judg. 6:38). He fed his people by raining manna (Num. 11:9). He had a pillar of fire light the way for the Israelites so they would know where to go (Neh. 9:12) and created Eve while Adam slept (Gen. 2:21).

God made the night His workshop and gave it its own beauty. The stars and planets become visible in the dark. God counted them and gave them each their own name. The Bible even calls on all the starts to praise God: "Praise him, sun and moon, praise him, all you shining stars!" (Ps. 148:3). Every star sings a song to the King.[5] The starry expanse makes for an amazing spectacle for those who are awake and a blanket of calming music for those who are sleeping.

Jesus' nights on earth were interesting as well. He often did not spend his nights sleeping. He prayed on the Mount of Olives (John 8:1), spoke to Moses and Elijah (Luke 9:29-32), walked on the water (Matt. 14:25), had time to talk to Nicodemus (John 3:2), and invited Peter to trust Him to a deeper extent (Matt. 14:29).

Jesus reveals God's heart and plans to us. Based on his life we can conclude that God has clear ideas about the night. It seems it was never his intention for the night to pass us by in a blur and that life would not continue until we opened our eyes again. As humankind sleeps and rests from the day, God is working a nightshift to meet us and care for us. Are you ready to discover God's plan for the night?

PART 2

The Original Plan for Our Sleep

> I praise you, for I am fearfully and wonderfully made. Wonderful are your works; my soul knows it very well.
> — PSALM 139:14

God created us so that we cannot exist without sleep. Therefore, sleep deprivation has many negative effects on our body and soul. We can last on average two months without food and about a day or three without fluids, but normally we cannot stay awake for more than thirty-six hours without the use of aids. Everybody sleeps, but sleep certainly does not come naturally to everyone. Struggling to sleep is something of all ages, and it can lead to serious psychological and physical problems.

So sleep is vitally important! During the night, our body is restored so that it can function optimally again during the day. Our soul finds rest and has the time to organize and process all the memories and emotions of the past day. We sleep an average of seven hours a day; that's about 210 hours a month and over 2,500 hours a year. In our lifetime, we sleep about one-third of the time. If you are seventy-five years old, that's twenty-five years of sleep! Take a moment to think of all that God can do in that time!

In this part we will discover what happens in our minds while we are lying down. This makes sleep much more surprising and rich than you may realize. God created sleep as a time of recovery for body and soul and a meeting place for our spirits with His Spirit.

What is the difference between sleep and rest? And how do you rest? What does the Bible say about sleep and what can disrupt our sleep? Let's take a more in depth look at sleep and its effects.

The Influence of Sleep

> And he lay down and slept under a broom tree. And behold, an angel touched him and said to him, "Arise and eat."
> — 1 KINGS 19:5

Sleep is a wonderous phenomenon and an incredible medicine. Often a good night's sleep is all that is needed to get us back to feeling "human" again, making us able to get through our day successfully. Elijah really understood this. He took a nap and what happened afterward changed him from a fearful, exhausted man who was weary of life, into a powerhouse full of energy who traveled forty days in one go (1 Kings 19:3-8). The touch of an angel was a game changer for him. Elijah was encouraged by heaven to remember who he was and what he had been called to do. He slept, ate heavenly cake and went on his way. This is an amazing example of what an encounter at night during a good night's sleep can do for our spirit, body and soul.

Sleeping well is essential for a vital life. It strengthens our immune system, that fights off infections and illnesses. Sleep keeps our blood pressure down and helps prevent diabetes and cardiovascular disease. Sleep restores our blood circulation, organs and hormonal system. Our body is detoxified, helping us to think clearly and feel refreshed throughout the day.

Our responsiveness and energy levels are much better after a good night's sleep, and muscle growth and recovery after exercise happens primarily during sleep. There is a reason why athletes say, "Rest is growth." Research shows that poor sleepers are up to twice as likely to be injured. Sleep deprivation also increases the need for sugars. These provide a quick energy boost, but our blood sugar level quickly drops afterwards. Because our endocrine system does not recover sufficiently when we are sleep deprived, it releases less of the hormone leptin into our body. This little substance makes us feel satiated. So the consequence of sleep deprivation is cravings! Sleeping little can therefore cause weight gain, not because we burn so many calories during sleep, but because it causes us to eat more during the day.

Our sleep affects our long-term and short-term memory and enables us to learn better. Learning new things often requires more sleep so we can store it in our brains. How we function at school correlates directly with our sleep (or lack of it!). And for those of us who are creative: Sleeping actually helps us to work on ideas. Creativity often peaks after an "incubation period"—a period of time in which we are not task-oriented, such as when we are sleeping. The perfect time to write down or execute our ideas is when we have just woken up!

If we need to make some difficult decisions, we often say: "I need to sleep on that." The right decision or solution will often be clear after a good night's sleep. Also, God Himself wants to give you solutions, answers and creativity! And knowing this, that expression gains a whole new meaning!

It is not just our body that needs to rest at night, our psyche does as well. Our mind is working non-stop all day; we achieve various things and process stimuli. If we do not get enough sleep, then we will be exhausted and unable to think clearly. Life can actually seem quite sad at times. The lack of sleep can cause psychological symptoms such as anxiety and depression, while these two in turn can result in us not sleeping well. It seems as though this is a vicious cycle. Our doctors can prescribe sleeping medication so that we get some relief from our symptoms. But our true healing is in the only One who can give us rest, Jesus. He created our bodies; He is the One who can bring us back to his original plan for the night.

The Rhythm of Sleep

God called the light Day, and the darkness he called Night. And there was evening and there was morning, the first day.
– Genesis 1:5

We live in a world with an endless number of stimuli and fleeting interactions. But this is not how God intended it to be. The very first day started with the night; only after night had passed did the morning come. This shows how God placed the most important thing first: sleep. As the One who laid the foundations of the world and as the Creator of humankind He knows that we function best from a place of rest.

Scientific research also shows the same thing; the results correspond with what God has devised for his children. Let's take a look at what we can learn from these scientific discoveries.

First of all: A good night's sleep is divided into several cycles that are made up of various stages. Every night we go through the cycles of these stages a number of times.

The first stage is when we transition from being awake to sleeping. This does not take longer than five minutes. Our muscles relax and our body temperature drops, our eyes move slowly. If we are fighting sleep as we watch a movie, and our eyes roll back, then we are in the first stage of sleep. It is time to go to bed! During this stage we can experience what feels like a jolt or we may think we are falling. This is called a hypnic jerk, a brief and sudden involuntary contraction of our muscles. This is a normal occurrence when our body starts to relax. In this first stage of our sleep sounds or movement will still easily wake us.

The second stage is superficial sleep. This is the beginning of real sleep. This stage lasts for about thirty to forty minutes. On average we will spend half of the night in this stage. Our sleep is deeper and it is less easy to awaken us.

The third stage is deep sleep. Our muscles are relaxed and our breathing and heartrate slow down and become regular. Our body produces growth hormones and starts to recover. This is the stage in which we rest the most. It is difficult to wake up and if we do awaken, then we will initially feel disoriented. As we get older, these stages will not last as long and as a result we will need more sleep in order to feel truly rested. At the start of the night the stage of deep sleep will last a long time, but as the night progresses, the stage will become increasingly shorter.

The fourth stage is REM sleep (REM stands for *rapid eye movement*). This is the stage in which we dream. This stage accounts for a quarter of the night on average, about two hours in total. As the night passes this stage becomes longer. That is why we dream more as the morning approaches. During this stage our brains are active and our eyes move rapidly back and forth behind our eyelids. The large muscles in our body are nearly paralyzed—and that is a good thing. If that were not the case, then we would jump out of our bed in order to act out what we are dreaming. During the REM sleep stage our heartrate and breathing become more rapid and our body uses more energy.

After these four stages we often wake up, just for a moment and almost imperceptibly, before we enter into the next cycle of stages. A cycle takes about eighty to 120 minutes. Normally we will go through four or five of these cycles during a night of seven to eight hours of sleeping. The first three stages together form the core sleep, which determines for a large part how much we will recuperate.

It is an old wives' tale that the hours before midnight count double. However, the first hours of our sleep do determine how rested we will feel when we awaken. Even if we do not sleep until midnight. As the morning nears, during the last few sleep cycles, we often sleep less deeply. These cycles are characterized by a longer stage of REM sleep. We will feel the most rested if we awaken of our own accord at the end of a cycle.

Many people awaken feeling groggy when they have been able to sleep in. This is because we often wake up halfway through the next cycle of sleep. We may have slept longer, but we do not feel rested. If we want to sleep in, then it is wise to sleep roughly one and half hours longer than we normally do. If we sleep longer than that, then we will probably also feel groggy.

Sleeping longer is not better, per se, as our body functions best when there is a healthy rhythm—getting enough sleep on a structural basis. How much sleep that is can differ per person, but usually it is seven to eight hours a night. Do you want to nap during the day? Then do not sleep longer than thirty minutes. You will not fall into a deep sleep, but you will rest. Or you should sleep an entire cycle of roughly an hour and a half. If you sleep longer, then you will probably awaken less rested and your powernap will not profit you much.

Many people today use a sleep app that promises to provide them with insight in their sleep rhythm. Remarkably, many of these app-users report that the app tells them they have had very little or not enough deep sleep. These apps are not reliable. I do not advise using such an app and many experts say the same thing. Incorrect information leads to incorrect convictions. Instead, you want to align your convictions with God's truth.

Sleep Disorders and Problems

> I am the LORD, your healer.
> – EXODUS 15:26

When God created the day and the night, He said it was good. Yet there are those who do not associate the night with good. They have a tough time getting a good night's sleep. Nearly half of the world's population has problems sleeping. This not only disrupts your night, but your day as well. Your physical condition and your general feeling of well-being suffer greatly. When you have a chronic lack of sleep then you can start to suffer from all kinds of physical and mental illnesses such as depression and memory loss, and you are at an increased risk of cardiovascular diseases. And yet, many people just put up with their lack of sleep, or they simply have no idea how to remedy it.

Stress, trauma or an unhealthy lifestyle can disrupt your sleep and can cause increased production of adrenaline and cortisol, the stress hormone. When this occurs, you are always alert. If you get too little sleep then you automatically create this hormone, causing a vicious cycle. You go to bed all stressed out, and your body can hardly relax.

Do you struggle with sleep problems? I really feel for you. It is a real burden to have trouble sleeping and it can make you feel very lonely. God never intended for your night of rest to be like that. Sleep problems and disorders need to be dealt with. Your body needs restoration and healing from a disrupted system. That is why it is good to revert back to God's plan for your sleep. Don't fall for second rate solutions, but go to the One who created both you and the night.

You see, in the back of our head there is an organ called the pineal gland. This gland continually produces melatonin. As soon as it is dark, our eyes send a signal to the pineal gland. It will create an increased amount of melatonin and send it into our bloodstream. Our body is preparing itself for sleep. That is why we start to feel tired when it gets dark outside. God is clearly a good Father, He even thought about our bedtime!

Your melatonin production can become dysregulated after years of sleeping problems. If this is the case for you, then you can ask the Holy Spirit to restore it. We read about how God is our healer in the Bible (Ex. 15:26). He can heal you, even from sleep disorders and problems. Jesus places His hands on the sick; He touches them and they are healed (Luke 4:40). You can do the same by placing your hand on the back of your head, on the spot where your "melatonin factory" is situated, and pray the following prayer:

> *Father, thank You that You have a deep and peaceful sleep for me. Would You touch me with your healing hand and heal my body from the shortages it has suffered because of my sleepless nights? Will you restore my melatonin factory? I want to ask for Your forgiveness because I was angry at my body and I could not rely on it. Thank You, Jesus, for Your blood that cleanses my thoughts from all of the bad memories of sleepless nights. Fill my thoughts afresh with Your truth about me and my sleep. I speak to my hormones: move back into the order of God. I no longer work with the spirit of insomnia; I bind you and send you out of my life in the name of Jesus. Holy Spirit, fill me anew. I give You permission to rule in me – in my spirit, soul and body, during my day and my night.*
>
> *Father, restore my rhythm of sleep as You intended it to be and teach me to enjoy my sleep once again in Jesus' Name.*

Sleeping Beauty

> The eye is the lamp of the body. So, if *your eye* is healthy, your whole body will be full of light ...
> — MATTHEW 6:22

God created us in His image, perfectly known, heard and loved. Holy and pure and completely in connection with the

Father. But due to the fall of humanity, humankind has been bruised and battered. Yet our blueprint has never changed and it becomes fully visible through the sacrifice of Jesus.

Everything we experience, see, hear or do that is not perfect has a negative effect on us. It damages us and sullies us. It is an impossible task to protect ourselves from these imperfect situations. That is why we can always draw near to God's throne of grace, where He cleanses us and comforts us. We can also choose what we allow into our life. Which people do we hang out with? What do we watch on TV or the internet? Which words do we use? What do we do to calm the inner storm?

Our inner storm is one of the most recognizable emotions of this age. Society places a standard at a pace we cannot possibly keep up with—everything moves at breakneck speed and we have to do our very best if we want to keep up. Many people struggle with restlessness, loneliness and a feeling of inadequacy. The feelings also tell us that we do not have time to talk to God and that we cannot achieve what we really want to do anyway.

These feelings lead to many people being addicted to things that suppress negative emotions or give a (temporary) sensation of peace. These things are easy to find and are often socially accepted. Things like alcohol, drugs, pornography, but also Netflix and painkillers, eating too much or too little and spending endless hours on our phone or the internet. It may seem relaxing but it fills us with junk.

These surrogate solutions influence our thoughts, our actions and our sleep. Whatever we fill ourselves with has a huge impact on our physical and mental health. Sleep works like a washing machine for our bodies and souls: we come out refreshed. What would happen if we placed a big shovel full of dirt in our washing machine? Our laundry would come out filthy and our washing machine filter would get clogged. Our washing machine cannot do what it was created to do if it is filled with dirt.

In the Bible we read how what we see influences us: "The eye is the lamp of the body. So, if *your eye* is healthy, your whole body will be full of light ..." (Matt. 6:22). Perhaps you never made the connection between watching horror movies and nightmares that torment you in the night. Or the connection between the hours we spend on our phones and the fact that we sleep so poorly. But this all affects our nights. If our eyes see heavenly light, then our whole body is full of light. If we keep our eyes focused on Jesus, then our body and soul will find rest. He is the only One who truly fulfills us. We can close the door to our bad habits by bringing the unrest and emptiness to Jesus. The Bible says:

> Do not be anxious about anything, but in everything by prayer and supplication with thanksgiving let your requests be made known to God. And the peace of God, which surpasses all understanding, will guard your hearts and your minds in Christ Jesus.
> – PHILIPPIANS 4:6-7

Jesus promises us a peace that is better than the most beautiful imaginings that the world can never give. But we cannot expect God to be the source of our peace when the world is our source of satisfaction. He wants to fill up every empty place so that we are no longer dependent on other means. It will mean we will need to change some of our habits, but it is more than worth it! Once you have experienced His peace, you will want nothing else.

The question is: What do we do when we are angry, sad or lonely? Do we withdraw with our phones or in our jobs, only to discover a few days later that we are "clogged" with our own emotions? Or do we take the time to talk to Jesus about it? We have been made to feel. We have been created in God's image, and God has feelings too. God is emotional, we can see that all throughout the Bible. There is not a single emotion that Jesus did not feel while here on earth. The Bible says He preceded us in everything. That makes Jesus the perfect person to talk to when we need to discuss our own feelings. He understands us fully and He can heal our emotions and make them healthy.

We need to take the time to ponder what we are feeling. Do we feel harried or alone? Then we need to take the time to tell God about this and to receive from His presence what we need, whether it be peace, safety, truth or something else. It can help to write our feelings down. Keep in mind that it does not need to be a literary masterpiece, it is something between us and God. This will create room for our feelings and prevent us from clogging up our emotions that will then overwhelm us.

Let us ask the Holy Spirit to show us where there are things in our lives that He wants to lead us away from. Let's ask Him where He wants to lead us and what that looks like. That will help us to follow Him and to break free from old habits. Then our feelings will no longer dictate our lives, but Jesus will become the King of our emotions.

Dear Father, thank You that I can always come to you, I desire for You to fill me. I am sorry that I have allowed myself to get involved in things that are not good for me. Will You forgive me? I also want to forgive myself for the choices I have made. I close every door that I have opened for the enemy and break his influence in my life in Jesus' Name. I return to You, Jesus. Would You cleanse me with your precious blood? Holy Spirit, fill me anew. Fill my mind with Your thoughts. Make me hungry for You. Let me desire You more than earthly satisfaction, and help me to spend time with You.
Amen

The Shower of Grace

> Let us then with confidence draw near to the throne of grace, that we may receive mercy and find grace to help in time of need.
> – HEBREWS 4:16

There is a big difference between sleeping and resting. Perhaps you recognize this; you have had a good night, yet you do not feel fully rested. Or it is quite the opposite; your night was short, yet you feel refreshed and ready to go. How is this possible? A large part is determined by how you distance yourself in your thoughts and emotions from the things that happened during the day. In the previous chapter we took a look at the external things that influence your sleep. Now we will continue with the internal things that can prevent us having a peaceful, deep and refreshing sleep.

Perhaps your soul is unable to rest because of all kinds of worries and emotion. King Hezekiah describes this:

> *All night I moaned*; it was like being torn apart by lions. Delirious, I chattered like a swallow and mourned like a dove; my eyes grew weary of looking up for help. 'O God,' I cried, *'I am in trouble*—help me.'
> – ISAIAH 38:13-14 (TLB)

Fear and sadness prevented King Hezekiah from sleeping. There obviously is a close connection between our soul and our sleep. Sadness and mourning, both recent and from times past, disrupts our sleep. Our sleep is also influenced by our worries for the day ahead, or when we think about the things that went wrong in the day that lies behind us. Our body creates adrenaline when we are fearful or sorrowful. This sends a signal to our brains to fight or run. This is not exactly the relaxation we need in order to fall asleep.

Bitterness will also prevent us from sleeping. Bitterness often grows throughout the years. It is like a root that hardens our heart and even sickens it (Heb. 12:15). King Hezekiah said: "All my sleep has fled because of my soul's bitterness" (Isa. 38:15 TLB).

We can ask God to help us remove the root of bitterness from our life, so that we can be free and sleep well. We find another negative influence on our sleep in Ecclesiastes, which states: "Sweet is the sleep of a laborer, whether he eats little or much, but the full stomach of the rich will not let him sleep" (Eccles. 5:12).

The word used here for laborer is the Hebrew word *abad*. This means servant or worshiper. The work these people did is focused on God. They worked as if for God Himself, while the rich people in this story were busy protecting their goods that they had gained for themselves. This verse tells us that our sleep is disrupted if we focus mainly on trying to defend our lifestyle and do our own thing. But we will sleep deeply if we leave these things to the Father, who knows better what we need.

It is surprising how much the Bible says about our sleep and what can prevent us from having a good night. Obviously there have always been people who struggle to sleep and God wants to give us insight and solutions. Like here for example: "Be angry and do not sin; do not let the sun go down on your anger …" (Eph. 4:26). This Bible verse states that being angry is not so much the problem, but remaining angry is. It makes our heart bitter and it blocks the flow of God's love in and through us. The key is forgiveness. We can use this key as often as we want.

Worries, stress or sorrow, no matter how small or great, hinder us in our days and our nights. This is reason enough to bring our souls to rest with God before we go to sleep.

The writer of Psalm 131 taught this as well: "But I have calmed and quieted my soul, like a weaned child with its mother; like a weaned child is my soul within me" (Ps. 131:2).

A baby who has just been fed is very peaceful and contented. The child falls asleep in its mother's warm, safe arms, completely satisfied. What a lovely idea that peace like that is available to us every evening. So how do we bring peace to our souls? I would like to share a few tips that you can use as often as you want.

Tips

Prepare yourself for sleep. Take the time to think about your day. You could ask yourself the following questions:

- *Are there things I am worried about? And if so, can I do anything about them right now?*

Yes? Then write this down so it is no longer occupying space in your mind and you can work on it later.

No? Then bring it to Jesus.

- *Is there anyone I need to forgive? Perhaps myself?*

Do this now, do not wait any longer. Forgiving is letting go. Forgive that family member who was impatient with you. Forgive yourself for your unreasonable attitude toward your colleague. We live from a place of grace, and Jesus has forgiven us. This means that we can receive his forgiveness. Talk to Jesus.

> Quick! Get out of it if you possibly can! Swallow your pride; don't let embarrassment stand in the way. Go and beg to have your name erased. Don't put it off. Do it now. Don't rest until you do.
> — PROVERBS 6:3-4 (TLB)

Jesus' mercy is like an endless waterfall. You can be assured that God has forgiven your sin and forgives you every day anew. Ask yourself the following:

- *In which area do I need comfort?*

All kinds of things can occur during the day that leave us feeling upset. Maybe someone said something unkind to us, or we saw something or heard something that is bothering us. It makes our soul restless, and we try to comfort ourselves and bring some peace to the situation without even being conscious of this. If we don't know what to do with our feelings, they can overwhelm and frighten us. The Bible says, "Lead me to the rock that is higher than I..." (Ps 61:2b). I love this verse! Jesus is our Rock. We must ask Him to help us, He understands us and knows what is going on. He is our safe tower; He is always close to us. The Holy Spirit is our Comforter, and He lives in us. He can do right away what He is good at: comfort us and bring warmth. We can ask the Holy Spirit to comfort and fill us; to wash away the day so that our souls can find peace. Let us be showered by His mercy. We will sleep so much better when we have been washed clean.

Putting a Good Night's Sleep into Practice

> If you lie down, you will not be afraid; when you lie down, your sleep will be sweet.
> — PROVERBS 3:24

It can be helpful to hear about other people who have had the same struggles as you. It is comforting to know that you are not alone in this and that you can win this battle.

Helen's story

I was raised in a Christian home. That may sound nice, but I didn't want to have anything to do with God. This was mostly because there was a lot of brokenness in our family: Mental illnesses, fear, depression. It was as if there was a blanket of darkness over our family.

From a young age I could sense the spiritual world. I often felt an evil presence, so I was afraid to sleep. I was also interested in occult things at a young age such as spin the bottle and watching horror movies. I delved into various religions like Buddhism.

Halfway through my teen years I started to have trouble sleeping. It started out as just being awake a little longer than usual, but eventually I was awake all night because of restlessness and darkness. I could not keep up at school and at my job and had to quit both. I ended up in a depression and came to a point where I no longer wanted to live. I felt broken on the inside because of the pain and darkness. I missed attention and love, the things a child needs most growing up.

At that low point I had myself admitted to a Christian clinic for psychological treatment, where I came to faith. Or actually, Jesus came to me. Finally, I could lay all of my brokenness at His feet.

God poured His love and mercy into me during a process that lasted years. I had a lot of pastoral counseling through which God performed many miracles. He freed me from the blanket of death and darkness that lay over my life, and from the dark nightmares that terrorized me. He came into my loneliness and sadness and filled me with His love. Throughout the years He took away my troubles sleeping. I experienced and saw more and more of heaven in my dreams. At some moments I knew without a doubt that I had a dream from God, but I did not know what to do with it. Yet God gave me clarity about this, both to me personally as well as through people around me. He awakened me to what He wants to do in the nights, and I noticed that I have been receiving more and more from Him in my dreams. He will continue, in you and in me, until our nights and dreams are full of His glory and majesty. He will continue to pursue you, no matter how deep or dark it is. I pray for you that you may meet Him through this book, in every kind of way, but most definitely in the night!

Do's and Don'ts

> If any of you lacks wisdom, let him ask God, who gives generously to all without reproach, and it will be given him.
> – JAMES 1:5

Though our body is creating melatonin and is preparing itself for the night's sleep, we want to work and have meetings until late at night. Or we watch TV from bed or check our phone. Good conversations often take place late in the day and in the evening you finally have "you time". Though these all seem like logical reasons to be active in the evening, these things disrupt the whole process of recovery and rest during our sleep. Because in the end we all want to have maximum advantage from our nights. For that some adjustments will need to be made. These tips can help:

- A fixed structure before going to sleep has proven to help us get a good night's sleep. This is used for babies and small children, so that they can tell by the actions, sounds and smells that it is nearly bedtime and they will start to relax. An evening ritual can still help us as adults. What do you like to do before you go to sleep?
- Head outside. An evening walk will give you a dose of light (in the right seasons) and fresh air, which has a positive influence on your night of rest.
- Sports activities just before bedtime is not a good idea, though. The adrenaline will still be racing through our body when we are in bed, and can keep us awake.

- If we get plenty of exercise during the day it will help us sleep at night. It is advisable to keep on getting enough exercise when you are recovering from sleep problems.
- Having a cup of coffee in the evening is not a good idea. Caffeine stays in our bodies for six hours and can make it difficult to get to sleep.
- Reading is a good activity before going to sleep. Those few pages we read will help us to relax. However, if it is a book that is intellectually stimulating, then we need to stop reading on time so that our brains slow down. A nice and peaceful story will help us to relax more.
- Try to fill your head with beautiful, good thoughts; this will have a positive effect on your sleep and dreams. Reading a bit in the Bible or talking to God always helps too. Or tell yourself three things you are proud of or grateful for.
- A nightcap can put you to sleep fast, but alcohol also causes you to sleep lightly. After a pleasant evening with some wine, you often fall asleep quickly, but wake up again after a few hours, leaving you feeling tired the next day. Not to mention the risk of a hangover after too much alcohol!
- Make your bedroom a place of rest. It needs to be a room where you don't work or have difficult conversations. Try to make it dark when it's time to sleep and with plenty of fresh air.
- If your TV is on while you sleep, your brain receives a signal that says it's daytime. So turn off that TV, or better yet, banish it from the bedroom.
- Avoid your cell phone and tablet in the last hour before you go to sleep. This is almost unthinkable these days, but your screen brings restlessness to your eyes and to your head. The light and the stimuli you see are the culprit. If this is a habit, try to break it.

- Put your phone on airplane mode and preferably put it farther away from your bed while you sleep. The frequency of the device can subconsciously influence you. This causes your body to produce the stress hormone cortisol, which makes it harder to get into a deep sleep.
- Playing an old-fashioned board game before going to bed is good for your brain.
- You know how good conversations seem to occur later in the evening? Or that meeting that always drags out? The ten o'clock rule is helpful for your sleep. After ten o'clock (or earlier) try not to conduct difficult or emotional conversations.
- A late-night snack is delicious, but not wise. It's best not to eat anything an hour before you go to bed. If your body needs to process (fatty) food, it can keep you awake.
- Certain herbs have a positive influence on your sleep pattern. Herbal teas with chamomile, rooibos or lavender are not only delicious, but also help you to relax. Or, for example, essential oils in a diffuser or on your skin, or valerian in a capsule. There are all manner of natural things created by God that can help you sleep.
- Did you know that music with a rhythm slower than your heartbeat calms you down? And the reverse is also true: music with a faster rhythm keeps you awake.
- Make sure you have a good mattress that suits your personal needs. Having fresh bedding will also make a difference.
- If you have a more or less fixed rhythm for when you sleep and wake up, it will help a lot. Even if you have a period of less sleep, a fixed rhythm will help you. Going to bed on time and not waking up too late ensures that you get the most rest from your nights.

- Are you an early bird or a night owl? If you know your preference, you can adjust your rhythm accordingly. Are you more active in the evening? Then shift your daily rhythm slightly, so you don't force yourself to function at an unreasonable hour all the time. However, there are limits to this. People who get out of bed at eleven by default will continue to have trouble falling asleep at a normal time. One person goes to bed at 9:30 and gets up at 5:30; another goes to bed at twelve and gets up at 8:30. Adjust your rhythm a bit, if you find yourself deviating from these kinds of rhythms.
- Being awakened by the rising sun and singing birds is optimal, but unfortunately not always possible. Whenever possible, waking up by yourself is best. As soon as your sleep cycle is interrupted by an alarm clock, it makes you feel less rested.
- It can feel really good to hit the snooze button a few times. Yet it makes you feel sleepy longer in the morning. Waking up in a bright room works faster.
- The first cup of coffee in the morning tastes best, and the smell is wonderful! Still, it's better to start your day with a good glass of water. During the night you lose moisture, and that needs to be replenished. Drinking enough water ensures that you get rid of waste products and is good for your fluid balance. It helps you with fatigue, both in the morning and during the day if you haven't slept very well.
- Set your alarm ten minutes earlier. Start your day with peace of mind and feeling relaxed instead of eating your breakfast quickly, or worse: not eating breakfast at all.
- A nice breakfast can also be a good reason to get out of bed. Prepare it the night before and get it out of the fridge in the morning.

- Some people can't wake up without a shower. Make sure your shower is not too hot, and finish with an (almost) cold shower. You will be wide awake!
- Getting a breath of fresh air in the morning and listening to the world awaken is a nice way to start the day. Ask God to open your eyes to the way He speaks through nature.
- Did the Holy Spirit speak during your night or slumber time? Then take a moment to write it down while you are still at rest.

When you know what stimulates you, stresses you or makes you restless, you can start creating an environment that helps you sleep. Write down the things on the list that may help you so you can take steps to get more and better sleep.

Breaking a habit takes time, so allow yourself at least a month to do this. But don't give up! Eventually you will sleep and rest wonderfully.

Conquering Insomnia

> My son, be attentive to my words; incline your ear to my sayings. Let them not escape from your sight; keep them within your heart. For they are life to those who find them, and healing to all their flesh.
> — PROVERBS 4:20-22

As I wrote this book I was suddenly struggling with insomnia. Though I had been able to sleep without any trouble for years, I was now wide awake at night. The enemy clearly was not pleased about this book and knew that he would lose ground. Yet I did not want to focus on what the enemy was doing. I wanted to receive new keys from God for sleep disorders.

I discovered something new in this period: the fear of not sleeping or not being able to function well after a bad night was just as damaging as the lack of sleep itself. This fear actually causes more of the stress hormone cortisol and adrenaline to be produced. This makes us sleep poorly, and have trouble functioning the next day. Our expectation is confirmed, which in turn creates more fear for the following night. We need to practice being at peace in the night, even if that means getting out of bed. Grabbing a cup of tea, listening to peaceful music and talking to God can bring much needed peace. This will create a pattern that our brains can recognize. Our brains will then tell our bodies what to do: relax. This will help us fall asleep quicker and function better the next day.

What we eat, our stress levels and medication all influence our sleep. Of course we are not always able to change these things. It is helpful to look at the context of our life and think about what is possible instead of what is impossible. Let's make changes where we can and be patient with ourselves. Every small step brings us in the right direction. A mistake or a setback is not necessarily something we need to forget right away, but we can learn from them instead. Let's discover what works for us and what doesn't, and apply what has proven helpful.

A powerful key for sleep disorders is the spoken Word of God. It brings life. The Bible says: "Death and life are in the power of the tongue, and those who love it will eat its fruits" (Prov. 18:21). If we speak God's Word over our bodies, it will respond even at a cellular level. Let's bless our bodies, tell ourselves we are safe and give ourselves permission to relax. This is incredibly powerful, especially if we have experienced stress, unsafe situations or trauma. We know that God can free our spirit and heal our souls, but we often forget that our bodies were there the whole time too and need to be healed as well. Speaking words over our bodies can ground us once again in the safety and security that God offers.

And finally, just know that we are connected to the Source of hope that says: "For I know the plans I have for you, declares the LORD, plans for welfare and not for evil, to give you a future and a hope" (Jer. 29:11). We can remind ourselves of His words when sad thoughts overwhelm us, so that joy can fill our hearts once again. And you know what happens then? "A joyful heart is good medicine, but a crushed spirit dries up the bones" (Prov. 17:22).

God's words are always a key to turn a negative situation around. Hearing His tender voice and reading His Word is a powerful medicine.

Fantasies

> Finally, brothers, whatever is true, whatever is honorable, whatever is just, whatever is pure, whatever is lovely, whatever is commendable, if there is any excellence, if there is anything worthy of praise, think about these things.
> — PHILIPPIANS 4:8

Did you know more than half of our brain is used to see things? It has been created by God like a screen onto which images are projected. And that is the very place in which He wants to give us inspiration. That is why what we see with our eyes influences us so much. Our brains are super-fast; they only need 13 milliseconds to register an image. The enemy is out to take control of this screen, and to fill it with images of darkness, because he knows that this has a huge impact on God's beloved. We only have one screen, and we can submit it to God's Spirit so that He can fill it.

Many people like to think of nice things and happy memories before they go to sleep. Our bodies and souls respond to this by relaxing and that is a good thing. Being a movie hero, a successful businessman or professional athlete that the crowd is applauding are fun things to think about.

There is nothing wrong with this, as long as it comes from your own brain and you can stop it when you want. But did you know that fantasies can be inspired by demonic spirits too? A demonic spirit wants to keep your mind occupied, isolate you and exhaust you with images and pictures that continue in your dreams. These fantasies can seem innocent, but can also be full of death and impurity. They will make you feel at home in this fantasy world, more than in the real world. This spiritual door can be opened if you are very involved in movies or games, or if you have taught yourself to escape in your mind when something bad happens.

This does not mean that you will immediately be bothered by a demonic spirit if you do these things. But it could be the case, and if so, you will notice that your fantasy takes over, and this will happen in your dreams too. You will feel like you are continually being sucked into another world, causing you to isolate yourself from the here and now. This can also create a barrier for dreams from God.

If you recognize this, or if you feel convicted by the Holy Spirit on this subject, then I would advise you to pray with someone about this, someone who can help you. Turn away from this so-called fantasy world and do not cooperate with that spirit any longer. Your head is not a trashcan. God has something much better for you. He wants to be the source of the images that you see. You are His child and what He has for you is the very best. That is why the Bible says:

> If then you have been raised with Christ, seek the things that are above, where Christ is, seated at the right hand of God. Set your minds on things that are above, not on things that are on earth.
> – COLOSSIANS 3:1-2

If we want to learn to hear, think, see and act inspired by God's throne, then we need to feel at home near His throne. That is possible through the Bible; it tells us that God's thoughts are what heaven's culture is like. And why should we not be allowed to see and taste what heaven is like? The Bible says: "Oh, taste and see that the LORD is good! Blessed is the man who takes refuge in him!" (Ps. 34:8). In order to taste, you need to draw close and in order to see, you need to look. Yet it seems as though there is a barrier, a red and white tape around imagining what heaven is like. That can be a religious stronghold that prevents you from having a deeper encounter with the Father. If you do want to encounter Him, then simply ask: "God, can I have a tour of Your Kingdom?" You have the code to the door: Your worship of Jesus. You have adhered to the dress code: pure white clothing, washed in the blood of the Lamb. Just tear down that red and white tape, you are more than welcome!

The place where you have been seated in Christ since you first met Him, is open to you. You can discover it and what it is like. The Bible tells us a lot about the Kingdom of God, about heaven and what it looks like. There are many verses that will help you form an inner image of it. You can read about Jesus, the amazing things that God can do here on earth, the buildings in heaven and the materials they are made of: gemstones, gold and crystal. There is water flowing from the throne, and there is a floor made of glass and fire. There are thousands upon thousands of angels that worship God. Just take a look:

> Then I looked, and I heard around the throne and the living creatures and the elders the voice of many angels, numbering myriads of myriads and thousands of thousands ...
> – REVELATION 5:11

Why are we so afraid of letting our imagination run wild when it comes to God's Kingdom, a place of freedom, health and love? Many people believe that God is a critical God, pointing His finger at us in accusation, but God has actually lovingly taken us in. Don't you think that He wants to help us see a different image? An image of a wonderous reality:

> "Behold, the virgin shall conceive and bear a son, and they shall call his name Immanuel" (which means, God with us).
> — MATTHEW 1:23

As God is on the throne in heaven, He also lives among us. And as we walk here on earth, we are also seated with Him in heaven. Let's discover what that is like!

When you give yourself permission to create images in your mind of what God is speaking about, then the Holy Spirit can take over your thought life and take you on a journey of inspiration. Then you can truly see and taste what is there. Are you sliding over the glass floor? Are you discovering the storage rooms of hail and snow? Are your hands caressing the smooth pearls on the gates as you gaze at your reflection in the streets of gold? Using your imagination is not wrong. It is proof that you have been created in God's image. What would you like to do in the place without boundaries that is called God's Kingdom?

> And he who sat there had the appearance of jasper and carnelian, and around the throne was a rainbow that had the appearance of an emerald. Around the throne were twenty-four thrones, and seated on the thrones were twenty-four elders, clothed in white garments, with golden crowns on their heads. From the throne came flashes of lightning, and rumblings and peals of thunder, and before the throne were burning seven torches of fire, which are the seven spirits of God, and before the throne there was as it were a sea of glass, like crystal.
> — REVELATION 4:3-6

When I had just come to know God, I really struggled with closing myself off to my surroundings to talk to an "invisible"

Person. Something that really helped me in my relationship with Jesus was creating an imaginary place in my mind where we would meet each other and speak to each other. I knew what it looked like and which scatter cushions were there. I recognized the fireplace, the colors and even the scent and temperature. It helped me to meet Jesus in a place of peace and safety. If I was at a loss on how to find Him, then in I could go to that place in my mind and I always found Jesus there. Perhaps you think you are too grown-up to have an imaginary cabin in your mind where you go to meet Jesus. That is okay. Yet there are many people who struggle with the same thing I did. Then this tip may help you. Just give it a try!

Sweet Encounters

> But he who is joined to the Lord becomes one spirit with him.
> — 1 CORINTHIANS 6:17

While God promises to be with us always, there are many who know what it is like to be lonely and this creates a deep emptiness and pain. Jesus wants to meet you there where you are, in that emptiness. Just take a look at what this psalmist described who was struggling to sleep:

> When I remember God, I moan; when I meditate, my spirit faints. You hold my eyelids open; I am so troubled that I cannot speak.
> — PSALM 77:3-4

We can also learn from what this psalmist tells us:

> I lie awake; I am like a lonely sparrow on the housetop.
> — PSALM 102:7

The author of Psalm 77, Asaph, experienced what it was like to have sleep disrupted by restlessness and loneliness. This passage was written by someone who felt a distance between him and God ... That is very sad but that separation need no longer be felt. Jesus died carrying that loneliness on His shoulders. God's desire for us is that we experience His presence.

We can choose to lay down in the presence of God the Father when we go to sleep. Laying down in God's presence may sound a bit strange, but God is here, and He wants us to experience His presence. We can open our hands to receive what He has to offer us. By focusing on Him you can experience His presence and you will be reminded of this promise: "... for he has said, 'I will never leave you nor forsake you'" (Heb. 13:5b).

If God is always with us, then we do not need long to seek His presence. In God's presence there is peace, love, joy, and we can hear what He says. Jesus is the High Priest, He is reconciliation, a merging. With just one word He can bring you close from very far away.

We read in the Bible about Samuel as a boy, when he first heard God's voice. This happened in the night. He was sleeping in a remarkable place. While Eli was sleeping in his usual room, Samuel was sleeping close to the ark:

> At that time Eli, whose eyesight had begun to grow dim so that he could not see, was lying down in his own place. The lamp of God had not yet gone out, and Samuel was lying down in the temple of the LORD, where the ark of God was.
> – 1 SAMUEL 3:2-3

The ark was the place where God's presence rested. Samuel must have been hungry for God. He chose the better thing and lay down in God's presence to sleep. That was the place where he first heard His voice.

Ruth is another example of this. She lay down at the feet of Boaz. Boaz is a foreshadowing of Jesus, the Redeemer. And Ruth chose to lie down in his presence:

> But when he lies down, observe the place where he lies. Then go and uncover his feet and lie down, and he will tell you what to do.
> — RUTH 3:4

The highest place is at the feet of Jesus. Can there be a better place to sleep?

God says we will have a wonderful night's sleep: "If you lie down, you will not be afraid; when you lie down, your sleep will be sweet" (Prov. 3:24). The word "sweet" in this Bible verse is *we'areba*[6] in Hebrew. This root of this word has a beautiful meaning: communion. It is a position in which to meet and to receive, a position of deep intimacy. During our sleep we can experience the merging that is between us and the Holy Spirit in an entirely different way than during the day. As we sleep, our boundaries become less clear, because our rational thinking is barely active, but our spirit is all the more active. God's Spirit is awake and therefore so is our spirit. That makes it the perfect moment to receive from Him.

Every night, before you go to bed, you may lay down in the mercy of God. Let go of everything in His presence. He invites you to rest in His loving arms that will protect and warm you. God's peace refreshes your soul and comforts you. His presence, His overwhelming love breaks off fear and worries. This creates room for an intimate encounter. Your head is resting against the Father's chest. Your heart beats to the rhythm of His and you become one with your Maker. This is how He restores your body and renews your strength.

God cleanses you with crystal-clear water and clothes you in a new garment of joy. A smile appears on your lips. Hope fills the depths of your soul and every lack is filled from His abundant majesty. The Father sings a song over you and the power of His words creates new things on the inside of you. He is close, so close, and He will stay there. A deep, peaceful and sweet sleep is your portion.

Night after night you receive a new invitation to merge with the Father, who is crazy about you and cannot keep His eyes off of you.

PART | 3

Do I Dream Too?

> For God speaks in one way, and in two, though man does not perceive it. In a dream, in a vision of the night, when deep sleep falls on men, while they slumber on their beds (...)
> – JOB 33:14-15

"He is just a dreamer!" "You wish, in your dreams, man!" Our culture teaches us that we should not take dreams too seriously. But the culture of the Kingdom of God is different. From the very beginning God spoke through dreams. In the Bible there are at least twenty-two encounters in the night between people and God. They were not always people of importance, but often regular people like you and me.

As we have seen, on average you sleep one-third of your life. Can you imagine how much you can receive from God in that time? Probably there have already been moments that God spoke to you in the night, but perhaps you have not noticed it yet.

So how does that work? The Bible verse above calls us to awaken. The Hebrew word used here for sleep is *katheudo*. That means being dead, running from salvation, or continuing to live in sin. The Bible does not speak about physical sleep at night here, but of spiritual sleep. While we spend years sleeping physically, we can consciously choose to be spiritually asleep or awake for God's intentions for the night.

Come Closer

> But now in Christ Jesus you who once were far off have been brought near by the blood of Christ. For he himself is our peace, who has made us both one and has broken down in his flesh the dividing wall of hostility ...
> – EPHESIANS 2:13-14

Do you find it hard to believe that God wants to communicate with you in the night? Do you wonder if He doesn't just want to point out your stupid choices or hidden sin? Are you already feeling ashamed, or are you afraid of an angry Father in heaven? Or are you already familiar with dreams from God but has it been silent for a while now? Then it is essential to keep in mind who God is and why He does what He does.

God loves us, His children, passionately. He could not bear that He and humankind were separated in the Garden of Eden. A future without His children close to His heart is not what He had intended. There was only one solution: He came to earth Himself as a human, and showed who He is, what His will is and what He desires for His children. Jesus took everything upon Himself that stood in our way and may still be standing in our way: guilt, shame, sin, sorrow, sickness, loneliness, confusion, panic, ailments, rejection, anger and fear. Jesus died so that all of that would die off. The veil was torn, the separation was no longer and the way was open to us. We can go to God and know Him as He truly is.

But something else happened in that moment: Jesus went to the realm of the dead to take back the power of death and the keys to Hades from satan's hands. He took back all authority, and defeated the enemy once and for all. Then He showed who rules over heaven and earth: God's breath of life filled Jesus' lungs and His body came back to life. He arose victoriously as the King of kings.

Jesus left His throne to be born in a dirty stable, so that we do not need to remain in the mud any longer, but can become a child of the King. What a glorious plan! There, before God's throne we meet God. We stand before Him clothed in white, forgiven, redeemed and restored by Jesus' blood. The separation that we may now still experience is an illusion. You are seated with Christ on the throne. You cannot get any higher than you already are. You can only lower yourself by not accepting your true identity. Based on our faith in Jesus and God's Word, we are adopted children of the Father, hidden with Christ in God.

> Awake, O sleeper, and arise from the dead, and Christ will shine on you.
> – EPHESIANS 5:14

Thank You, Jesus, that You have removed the barrier between me and God. Forgive me for my doubts about You and Your desire to speak to me during the day and the night. I no longer want to be afraid to meet You, I want to get to know You better. Thank You, God, that You have never changed. You want to speak to me in dreams just as You spoke to Daniel and Joseph and so many others. I no longer want to miss anything that You have for me. Help me to receive Your gifts and use them. Holy Spirit, will You fill me and my nights? Will You give me dreams and help me to remember them? I trust You and I cannot wait to meet You tonight!
Amen

Do I Dream Too?

> Jesus Christ is the same yesterday and today and forever.
> – HEBREWS 13:8

Scientists have done their research and decided: all people dream, whether or not they are aware of it. Of every eight hours we sleep, we spend an average of two hours dreaming, mostly during the REM sleep. During this phase of sleep there is a great deal of activity in our brain. Our muscles are pretty much paralyzed, which keeps us in bed instead of acting out what we are dreaming. That is a reassuring thought!

The REM sleep phase lasts longer as the morning approaches, which causes us to dream more and longer in the early morning and we are more capable of remembering our dreams. We can also dream during our deep sleep, but we often forget these dreams, unless we awaken during such a dream.

The length of our dreams varies from a few minutes to an hour. All kinds of things can occur in that time, as we are not bound to a time or place in a dream. Research shows that we can remember a dream in the first five minutes after we awaken, but after ten minutes more than 90 percent of our dreams have dissipated.

Researchers have suggested that our brains process our "emotions and information" during our dreams, or that our "deepest desires" are mirrored in our dreams. But dreams are also called "foolish activities". In spite of extensive scientific research there are still many questions about dreams that remain unanswered. There is still no real scientific answer to the question as to why we dream. That is understandable, as the research does not take the Creator of humankind, the Inventor of sleep and the Giver of dreams into account.

God has created humankind as a trinity. He has created us in a magnificent way and everything expresses His love for us. Would He withhold his goodness from us for eight hours every day? No, He wants to make Himself known during the day and the night. If God has not changed since the time of Daniel and Joseph, then we can count on Him still giving dreams today.

Moreover, in the time of Daniel and Joseph the Old Covenant still applied. In the Old Testament the Holy Spirit often came "over" someone and only a few were "filled". But since Jesus' ascension and the outpouring of the Holy Spirit, the Holy Spirit lives *in* us when we accept Jesus:

> In him you also, when you heard the word of truth, the gospel of your salvation, and believed in him, were sealed with the promised Holy Spirit, who is the guarantee of our inheritance until we acquire possession of it, to the praise of his glory.
> – EPHESIANS 1:13-14

That makes the chance of dreaming even bigger, and that is good news! Many people say that they never dream, or that they do not remember their dreams. I believe that that will change from this moment forward!

Turning Your Thinking Upside Down

> Do not be conformed to this world, but be transformed by the renewal of your mind, that by testing you may discern what is the will of God, what is good and acceptable and perfect.
> – ROMANS 12:2

The Bible says that our way of thinking should be turned completely upside down if we want to discover what God's will is for us. That means that we accept God's thoughts as the truth, instead of our own. That can be a real struggle for us. Often we have formed our opinions over a number of years based on what we have learned and experienced. They are colored by our collected knowledge, our experiences and pain, the things we have enjoyed and that which makes us feel safe. We have to let go of many so-called securities if we want to surrender ourselves to God's truth. Thankfully we do not need to meet a deadline, as it is a lifelong journey, in which we stumble and fall and get back up again as He lifts us up.

God invites us to learn how to understand the way He speaks. Throughout the Bible God speaks through symbols and parables. There is a powerful meaning to colors and names in the Bible. And items and materials are not just functional, they also portray something. That was part of the Jewish culture. And God communicates in the same way: He uses more than just words.

Jesus often spoke in parables and used a lot of imagery when He spoke. People needed to think about what He had said; they often did not understand immediately. But couldn't He have just said what He meant? I believe that Jesus chose the "longer road" on purpose so that His words would have a much greater impact when the people thought for themselves. That way, His words would have time to really enter their hearts. And that was what it was all about for Him – their hearts.

This method of teaching led to resistance. The scribes and scholars had a very different way of thinking. They thought the law was the most important thing, and believed that knowledge equaled power. They wanted to prove they were right. That became evident when they brought a woman to Jesus who had been caught in the act of adultery. The scribes wanted to teach Jesus a lesson. Full of self-righteousness, they threw the woman at Jesus' feet. But Jesus did not even respond to their accusations. He saw her heart that was broken and ashamed. He saw the proud and cold hearts of the scribes. And He said: "Let him who is without sin among you be the first to throw a stone at her" (John 8:7). Jesus knew that if He could reach their hearts, they would be changed forever.

This was not just a clash of thoughts in how the scribes saw God, but a confrontation between two trains of thought. One was aimed at rigidly obeying the rules and at attaining as much knowledge as possible, and the other was primarily interested in their hearts. The first reminds me of Western society of our time. We have learned that money, honor and power are the highest goals. We attain those through knowledge and "doing good" in the eyes of the world. We need to be fast, be seen and we cannot make any mistakes. Just keep an eye on the competition and compare yourself to them, and make sure you do it more beautifully, better and faster. Then you will earn big bucks, then you will be seen, noticed and heard. This manner of thinking has a downside. It causes stress and burnout.

This problem in our society was exposed years ago by Roger Sperry, an American neuropsychologist.[7] He described how both sides of our brains function (the left hemisphere is used for knowledge and analytical thinking, the right hemisphere for creativity and emotions) and he won a Nobel Prize in 1981 for this. One of the results of his research showed that both hemispheres of the brain need to be used in order for us to function well and be healthy. Sperry saw that this was not the case in the Western world. According to him this was greatly due to our education system, that is mostly set up to develop and reward the left hemisphere, the knowledge side. His conclusion was as follows: The Western education system destroys creativity and emotional abilities and is solely focused on making children understand the scientific side of life. After seven years in our school system, 10 percent of the children are still creative. After ten years only 2 percent of the children are still creative. Moreover, children are taught at a young age that using the right hemisphere (creativity and feelings) is not rewarded and is even considered useless. A scientific education is valued much more than the art school, because you cannot earn any money with this sort of degree. This takes the heart out of things, and the brain, the left hemisphere, actually, is placed under a disproportionate amount of pressure, with all of the ensuing consequences.

We can learn a lot from this research. It shows that all of us are creative, made in the image of God, the Creator. It will also help us as we take a closer look at dreams and how God speaks to us. Just take a look at the various functions of our brains.

Left hemisphere: Physical functions of the right side of the body
language • verbal skills • arithmetic • writing • reading • logical reasoning • analysis • scientific thinking

Right hemisphere: Physical functions of the left side of the body
feeling • music consciousness • artistry • imagination • intuition • dreaming • awareness of things outside yourself • sensing the atmosphere and thus sensing God

We need the right hemisphere to hear what God says. The Holy Spirit speaks to our spirit, and our brains form the image or word that we have received. That is how we can recognize God's message and translate it to words, images or movements. In short, there is a creative interaction between God's words and our spirit and our body. That makes it possible to translate what God is saying into prophecy, flags, painting, dancing and music. The possibilities to express what God is saying are endless!

If we use both hemispheres, then we can hear more of God. Not only that, but images are retained up to 40 percent more than words. That is the reason why dreams can stay with us; we have seen them! Dreams are often processed in the right hemisphere and are therefore hard to explain rationally with our left hemisphere. Many people probably forget their dreams because they are so used to functioning from their left hemisphere, that when they wake up that part is wide awake and says: "I do not understand this, therefore it does not exist."

In order to understand what God is saying, we need to let go of some of our frameworks. Perhaps you have heard this before – we need to learn how to think in Hebrew (biblically) instead of in Greek. The Greek way of thought, focused on the left hemisphere, leaves very little room for God to communicate with us in any other way than through knowledge and understanding. And though knowledge is good, it only stimulates our left hemisphere, not our fruitful, creative side. Additionally, our left hemisphere has no clue what to do with the Holy Spirit's expressions. This is how we miss an important part of who God is and what He wants to do. We have learned that it is not profitable to entertain dreams, intuition or creativity – we must limit ourselves to rules and attaining knowledge. It is something that is deeply ingrained in our Western society and is strengthened even more by Calvinism. This has caused the Church in the West to sway from God's original plan. Our culture is based on values such as serving God in humility. No dancing in church. No waving flags, no prophetic images or speaking in tongues. But God says: "I have created you in My image as a creative being, and I want to communicate with you. I have created your body as a temple for My Spirit." Shall we give God the room again that we pretend to give Him now? If we want to attain knowledge, then let us read what the Bible really says. It is time for the Church to repent of the rigid Greek mindset and to surrender itself to the many forms through which God wants to show Himself.

> (...) God, who has made us sufficient to be ministers of a new covenant, not of the letter but of the Spirit. For the letter kills, but the Spirit gives life.
> – 2 CORINTHIANS 3:5b-6

Renewing our mind requires training. We need a relationship with God's Word and Spirit in order to make our brains function in a new way and to see things differently. We need to move from Greek thinking to Hebrew thinking. Because this is so important, we will stay on this subject just a little longer.

Greek thinking is linear. Our path with God goes in a straight line from A to B, and then the route is completed. Hebrew thinking is relational. It is not about a one-time journey with a point of destination. The question we need to continually be asking God is: "What is Your will for me?" Greek thinking says: 'I first need to get to B, before I can be a blessing to others.' With Hebrew thinking we will know that we have been found sufficient by God to bless others, while God is changing us in the meantime 'from one degree of glory to another' (2 Cor. 3:18). You can imagine that due to Greek thinking, many people are on the sidelines, waiting until it is "their turn", until they are suitable enough. At the same time there are people who limit God's work in their lives because they think they have already arrived at their destination. That is a pity, because it is in our personal relationship with God that we are changed. There is so much more! And what we have received, we can share with others!

Greek thinking
It is about me • I need to be seen • I need to grab every opportunity • A driving pace • I need to be fast • Ruling • I need to be the best • Perfectionism • I cannot make any mistakes • Setbacks are for losers • Competition • Comparison • Never rest • I am what I do

Hebrew thinking
It is about God • I am an instrument • I am part of a greater whole • God opens doors for me • God determines the tempo • Relax • Celebrate • Enjoy • Excellence • Making mistakes is essential • Authentic, without comparison

Now that we know more about the left and right hemisphere, questions about how to actively implement this may arise. There is good news! Our brains are a muscle, and we can train them. There are various activities that stimulate our right hemisphere. It is always good to activate our right hemisphere, but even more so if we are feeling overstimulated or overwhelmed. The chance is great that this signal is being sent by our left hemisphere. It is important that our left hemisphere can rest and that we focus on our right hemisphere. This does not mean we should just lay on the sofa doing nothing. We can listen to music or make it ourselves. We can sing, draw, take a walk or dance in our living room. We can play a game, exercise or engage in sports. This is how our right hemisphere is activated. This will help us to relax, and an added bonus is that it is then easier to hear God's voice.

Dreaming Dreams

> And it shall come to pass afterward, that I will pour out my Spirit on all flesh; your sons and your daughters shall prophesy, your old men shall dream dreams, and your young men shall see visions.
> — JOEL 2:28

I am writing this book in the middle of the coronavirus pandemic. All over the world people are locked in their homes. Suddenly our agendas are empty, all kinds of securities have disappeared and the whole earth is shaking. It is a difficult and unique time. And in this time there are many people who are dreaming dreams. Could it be due to this crisis that many people are more rested than usual, and many of the impulses for our left hemisphere have fallen away? At any rate, I am convinced that God wants to reveal Himself through dreams. The prophet Joel describes how at the end of the ages God will pour out his Spirit on all flesh, those who are Christians and those who are not (yet). That means that people will not be able to remain standing in the greatness of God's presence, and every tongue will confess that Jesus Christ is Lord (Rom. 14:11). We will experience that time. Everyone will dream dreams and see visions. We are living in a special and amazing era; the great harvest has started and the best is yet to come!

In order to understand what God has said, we need to take a look at the original text. Let us take a look at the Hebrew text of Joel 2:28. What does it really say if we read it word for word?

"And afterward [*achar:* the hind or following part] I will pour out [*shaphak:* to spill forth, to expend, to sprawl out] My Spirit [*ruwach:* wind, breath, exhalation, life, thoughts from heaven, spirit] on all people [*basar:* flesh, body, person, the pudenda of a man]. Your sons [*ben:* a son] and daughters [*bath:* a daughter] will prophesy, [*naba:* to prophesy, speak, by inspiration] your old [*zaqen:* old] men will dream dreams [*chalown:* a dream], your young men [*bachuwr:* selected, a youth] will see [*ra áh:* to see] visions [*chizzayown:* a revelation, a dream]."

What can we expect according to this prophecy given nearly 3,000 years ago? This prophetic promise is on the heels of another verse, that tells us what God will do when we give our hearts to Him once again and repent:

> "Yet even now," declares the LORD, "return to me with all your heart, with fasting, with weeping, and with mourning; and rend your hearts and not your garments." Return to the LORD your God, for he is gracious and merciful, slow to anger, and abounding in steadfast love; and he relents over disaster.
> – JOEL 2:12-13

When that has happened, God will pour out His Spirit and with that, His heart and thoughts. He will pour them out like breath on all that is living: man and woman, young and old, great and small, believer and unbeliever. The more room that person gives to God's Spirit, the more they will receive. At the same time unbelievers will dream dreams. They will not have consciously made room for the God they do not know, but they will be hungry for the Truth, yearn for the Life and will ask about the Way to get there (John 14:6).

In the original Hebrew of Joel's prophecy, it says the following: Dreams will be prophetic and inspired by the Holy Spirit. Dreams will bring restoration, health and strength in and through the dreamer. God will give dreams to every old person, to everyone who grows in maturity and authority. Children of God have been given authority over the earth and will therefore dream dreams and see visions. They will have heavenly encounters in which God will provide their needs and will speak about His will. The people will pay attention to these dreams and visions. They will see and understand what God is saying and this will transform the world through them.

The Dew of the Night

> I slept, but my heart was awake. A sound! My beloved is knocking. "Open to me, my sister, my love, my dove, my perfect one, for my head is wet with dew, my locks with the drops of the night."
> – SONG OF SOLOMON 5:2

As God never sleeps, and His Spirit is one with our spirit (1 Cor. 6:17), that means that our spirit is wide awake while we are sleeping. The Holy Spirit continually glorifies the Father and Son, and is always revealing His will to us. He searched the depths of God and knows them, the Word says (1 Cor. 2:10). The Holy Spirit invites us to follow Him in these things. When we sleep, the boundaries of our rational thinking fall away, and God has room to reveal Himself to us in new ways.

Isn't the verse above from Song of Solomon beautiful? Our beloved comes to meet us in the night. He knocks on the door of our heart. Our heart is awake while our body sleeps. He calls our name and He does not show up empty-handed. He comes with dew. Dew is formed in the early morning. Exactly during the time when we dream the most!

The word used for "dew" in the original text in the Bible is *tal*, which means mist in the night, and from the word *talal*, which means to cover. The word "dew" is used many times in the Bible. For example:

> May my teaching drop as the rain, my speech distill as the dew, like gentle rain upon the tender grass, and like showers upon the herb.
> — DEUTERONOMY 32:2

> A king's wrath is like the growling of a lion, but his favor is like dew on the grass.
> — PROVERBS 19:12

> It is like the dew of Hermon, which falls on the mountains of Zion! For there the LORD has commanded the blessing, life forevermore.
> — PSALM 133:3[8]

All of these verses are connected to God's blessing and presence that wants to cover us. Or better yet: rest on us like dew. God wants to give, give, give. It is His character and His being; He cannot do otherwise! This verse from Song of Solomon is a direct invitation by God to meet Him in the night, so that He can cover us during our sleep with His blessing and glory like a pleasant blanket. Let's read it again, and now with God's invitation in mind:

> I slept, but my heart was awake. A sound! My beloved is knocking. "Open to me, my sister, my love, my dove, my perfect one, for my head is wet with dew, my locks with the drops of the night."
> — SONG OF SOLOMON 5:2

Receive Your Gift

> Every good gift and every perfect gift is from above, coming down from the Father of lights, with whom there is no variation or shadow due to change.
> — JAMES 1:17

God is the Giver of good gifts. What He gives, He does not take back. You do not need to do anything to earn this from God, but in order to receive what He gives, you do need to "do" something. I want to talk about this in more detail in the following chapters. Because we need to change the way we think for this; we can learn to receive His gifts and get to know God as an incredibly good Father who gives.

> Or which one of you, if his son asks him for bread, will give him a stone? Or if he asks for a fish, will give him a serpent? If you then, who are evil, know how to give good gifts to your children, how much more will your Father who is in heaven give good things to those who ask him!
> – MATTHEW 7:9-11

Perhaps you started reading this book because you are interested in dreams. Or maybe you struggle with how to interpret your dreams. It is possible that you desire to dream more and sleep better. Just know that you can boldly ask God the Father for this. Many people have a hard time asking God for something that is for their own pleasure. But we should not worry about that, for the fact that we want more dreams and encounters with God, shows our hunger for more of Him – and that is exactly in line with His desires for you.

The following verse precedes the promise about prayer:

> Ask, and it will be given to you; seek, and you will find; knock, and it will be opened to you. For everyone who asks receives, and the one who seeks finds, and to the one who knocks it will be opened.
> – MATTHEW 7:7-8

Are you prepared to seek? Or would you rather have it the moment you ask for it? Our society is set up in such a way that we can directly access what we want. We order our favorite meal and can have it delivered to our home fifteen minutes later.

We order nice clothing online and have it in our home the next day. And if we want to go on vacation, we can leave immediately. Within moments we can be in contact with everyone and everything all over the world! But if we seek God, then we need to step out of the busy world and into the silence. The more often we do this, the easier it gets and the more we will love God's quiet presence. Our focus is the key. Then we will experience God's presence, even in the midst of great unrest.

And are you prepared to receive? Just as asking and seeking may be a struggle for some; there are people who have a hard time receiving the gift that God gives. You are not alone, there are many who struggle with this.

The way I see "receiving" is holding out both hands and joyfully grabbing hold of a gift. Holding it tight. From now on it is yours! God is the Giver of all good gifts, and He expects that the receiver of the gift grabs ahold of it and starts to happily use it. So why are we often so slow to accept His gifts? He has carefully chosen these gifts for us, and they are to be appreciated and shared. They provide solutions for the needs in our life and the needs of the world. God's gifts show His love; they are meant to bless the receiver and to strengthen them to bless others.

God does not take back what He has given you. It is time to unwrap your gifts and enjoy them.

Awakening in God's Safety

> "Awake, O sleeper (...)"
> – EPHESIANS 5:14

In the previous chapters I mentioned many things that will either help you grow, or actually prevent you from sleeping well and dreaming. Sometimes, however, there is something else going on preventing you from receiving what God wants to give you in your sleep. As I was teaching the classes for our *School of Night & Dreams* – a conference I give about God's plan with the night – I discovered how many people did not feel safe, and that this can block them from receiving the heavenly abundance in the night. Not feeling safe is a big part of many people's lives and whether this is due to something in their childhood or it developed later, it is something serious that needs to be dealt with and transformed by God's Spirit. During the course we saw that time and again people received a breakthrough in the night as they entered deeper into God's safety. One of the ladies who attended the course experienced a big transformation. This is her story:

Christy's story

I went through serious ritual abuse in the past. This trauma caused me to close myself off from my body and what I was feeling. The past few years I have been through an intense course of pastoral counseling and Sozo[9], in order to find healing and freedom. Jesus faithfully helped me through all the pain and has shown me that He really is always by my side. In the meantime I am doing very well and I receive abundant life from Jesus every day. There is now a unity between my spirit, soul and body and I dare to feel again. I did sleep well, but my nights were bland. I barely dreamed, but I sure did want to! I decided to attend the School of Night & Dreams and to find out what God wanted to give me in my sleep. During the course I was frustrated: I seriously tried to apply all the different tips and tricks, but there was no breakthrough. During the last evening session I asked for and received prayer for my frustration. After receiving insight from the Holy Spirit, I received prayer for dissociation[10] during my sleep. This seemed to have been formed a long time ago as a protective measure, a mechanism so I would feel safe during the night. But this also prevented me from receiving from God as I slept.

The Holy Spirit showed me a vision of myself sleeping and I was wrapped in cloths as if I was dead. I cried because I had slept like this for so long and I asked God to remove the cloths so that I would no longer be "offline" as I slept. In the vision I saw that Jesus took the cloths off of me. I felt so happy! That was the last part of my healing of my past. Thank You, Jesus, nothing can remain hidden from You.

Even though I slept well, the fact that I was unable to receive from God in the night was something that I missed. I really want to receive everything God has for me with open arms!

This has been life-altering for me. My nights have been transformed, I dream and enjoy sleeping and awakening in God's presence. The night is no longer a basic reoccurring moment, but a wonderful time to meet God.

What a powerful testimony! I believe there are many people who sleep in such a state. Whatever the reason may be, they have been dissociating during the night. Often this would happen due to lack of safety and the urge to escape reality. Perhaps it was because of something that happened in your bedroom or something you heard or experienced while you were in bed. Examples could be marital fighting and domestic violence. The dissociating may have helped you to feel safe in the past, but it never stopped, so that today it is still an automatic function as you sleep. No matter the cause, Jesus can stop it and He can teach you that He is your safety as you sleep. He can awaken you from a state of sleep in which you are "offline" for encounters with God. He says to you: "Awake,

O sleeper." If you feel like this applies to you, then I want to encourage you to ask God to align your sleep with His order and plan. The exercise in the chapter *Fantasies* can help you do this (visualizing a safe place). Is this hard to do or do you need more help? Then find someone who can help you with this! You do not need to do this alone![11]

Remembering Dreams

> He will fly away like a dream and not be found ...
> – JOB 20:8a

Based on this verse it would seem that forgetting your dreams is a well-known problem. In this chapter I will share three keys to remembering your dreams.

First of all: Your relationship with Jesus. When Job's friend Zophar said the following thing in the verse above, the Old Covenant still applied. We are now living in the New Covenant era, so that we now have unlimited access to God's presence. Jesus says in John 10:7: "I am the door of the sheep." He is the door to God's presence and all of His heavenly mysteries. Every time you believe that there is a separation between you and God, this will prevent you from receiving from Him. It may seem as though God is not giving you anything, but God is always giving. You are just not able to receive it if you believe that you are out of the reach of God's presence. Focus your thoughts on Jesus and you will see that it will flow again and you will be better able to remember what God gives you in the night.

Secondly: Your relationship with the Holy Spirit. You do not need to remember every dream, but you do not want to miss the dreams that God gives you and through which He speaks. Now, there are many people who struggle to remember their dreams, and that is why they decide that their dreams are meaningless. They shrug their shoulders and carry on with their daily affairs. Before you do this, ask the Holy Spirit first. He can help you to remember your dreams when you are awake. Trust that He knows precisely which dreams are from God. The Bible says:

> For who knows a person's thoughts except the spirit of that person, which is in him? So also no one comprehends the thoughts of God except the Spirit of God. Now we have received not the spirit of the world, but the Spirit who is from God, that we might understand the things freely given us by God.
> — 1 CORINTHIANS 2:11-12

Finally, it is essential that you know that God is good. It is God's joy to make you aware of your dreams and to allow you to discover how He wants to speak to you through them. He yearns to help you discern and remember your encounters with Him in the night. But God does want our attention, so that we see and notice what He is doing. While we spend years of our life sleeping, we can choose to spend that time rejoicing in his presence. Psalm 37:4 says: "Delight yourself in the LORD, and he will give you the desires of your heart." So what does it look like to delight ourselves in God's presence? The essence is knowing God's character: knowing that He is good and only has plans to prosper us. We can expect Him to come and we can expect Him to do things in our lives, whether or not we see it in the present. You could compare it to the expectation of looking forward to a lovely vacation or a day out. You can already enjoy what He is going to give you, because He always brings something good. If your heart's desire is to receive dreams from God, then delighting in God and His presence is a key to receiving and remembering dreams.

Stewardship as a Key

> While I was with them, I kept them in your name, which you have given me. I have guarded them, and not one of them has been lost except the son of destruction, that the Scripture might be fulfilled.
> – JOHN 17:12

God loves to take care of what is precious to Him: He takes care of our life for all eternity. God also stores our tears in his bottle (Ps. 56:8). They are very valuable to Him; He collects them carefully so they are not shed and then disappear.

We can follow God's example and take great care of those things which He gives us. An important key in remembering your dreams is stewardship. That means that you take care of that which God gives you, and you take it seriously. Even if you are not sure or you do not (fully) understand it, write it down and talk to God about it. It is like a costly jewel; you don't leave it laying around but put it away somewhere safe. God promises that which you take care of, will always be expanded. The Bible says:

> One who is faithful in a very little is also faithful in much, and one who is dishonest in a very little is also dishonest in much.
> – LUKE 16:10

Just the very fact that you take your nightly hours seriously as a moment to hear from God, is valuable to Him. The Holy Spirit will respond and, perhaps even more importantly, you will become aware of God's plan for your nights.

The dreams that God gives you are worth writing down. People often say that they do not have the time for that. Do you really not have the time, or is it just not a priority? Here is a tip: record your dreams. You can do that anywhere, anytime, even if you awaken in the middle of the night.

Pick up your phone and record your dream. It will still be fresh in your memory and you can do something with it later. Or write a short note about that one moment with God. You can always add to it later on with more details.

Sometimes you dream of something small or insignificant; sometimes your dreams are majestic and impressive. No matter what your dream was like, after some time you can forget them. Busyness, worries and the daily grind of life can cause those heavenly encounters to fade. Then it is nice to re-read or listen to your dreams. It is great to be able to look back at what God has done. That will give you hope, and faith for a new encounter.

Ask yourself as soon as you awaken if you have dreamt. Scour your memory for your dream or dreams before you allow other thoughts in. Give your spirit the time to bring back the images of your dreams and then write them down or record them. Just start, even if you cannot remember the whole dream. You will notice that as you start to write it down more and more will come to you.

In order to be a steward, you need to focus. If we focus on God, then we will always see more of Him. If we delight ourselves in the Father and His plans, then we will see an increase of His presence in our lives. This is so true: everything you focus on, grows! So if you delight in the dreams that God will give you and the encounters that you will have with Him, then God promises that He will give you the desires of your heart!

The Bible encourages us:

> But seek first the kingdom of God and his righteousness, and all these things will be added to you.
> – MATTHEW 6:33

And that is so true! Even if you have never asked for dreams or supernatural encounters, God can give them to you just like that. It is enough for your heart to be focused on getting to know Jesus. He wants to be known, also in the night.

If we want to discover what God has in store for us, then we need to know that He is close to us. We are in Christ (Col. 3:3). We do not need to travel many light years from earth to reach Him in heaven. We are *in* Him, and that requires a new way of thinking. What can we discover in Him?

The first time I received a dream from God, I had only known Him for a few weeks. When I awoke from this dream, I heard the words *"Deo volente"*. These were totally new words for me. I woke my husband in the middle of the night and asked him if he knew what those words meant. He was wide awake right away and told me it was Latin for "If God so desires". He immediately wanted to know what I had dreamt. This confirmed my suspicion: God had given me a dream. The funny thing about this story is that many of my friends have a bitter taste in their mouth when they hear those words. They associate it with their own religious upbringing in which there was a fear of dying and doubt about the will of God for their life. I did not have that association; instead those words caught my attention because I did not know them. I did not understand the dream right away, but because of those words I was intrigued and I knew that God was present during my sleep and that He wanted to speak to me.

Now perhaps you are thinking: 'That is nice for you, but I don't hear God say things to me.' That may be, but God knows exactly how to reach you in a way that you will understand. Sometimes God does not give a clear message right away, but first just a signal to get your attention. This will awaken you to the truth that God wants to speak to you. Later in this book we will look at how you can learn to hear God's voice.

Slumbering

> At this I awoke and looked, and my sleep was pleasant to me.
> — JEREMIAH 31:26

A vague beam of sunlight appears behind the curtain and announces a new day, just a little before your alarm goes off. As you slowly awaken, you feel your body resting on the mattrass and your eyelids are still heavy. The first thoughts fill your mind: 'Today I need to take the car to the garage. I am supposed to start an hour later, aren't I, or was that tomorrow? Oh, I mustn't forget my neighbor's birthday.' You slowly awaken more and you grab your phone to check the time. You open your WhatsApp to read those seven unread messages and then you take a quick look at Facebook and Instagram. Before you know it, your brain is running a mile a minute and you haven't even been awake ten minutes. Does that sound familiar?

Yet it is in the phase of awakening that something interesting happens. You awaken from your REM sleep, in which your right hemisphere is fully active and your left hemisphere is not yet. The boundaries of your rational thought are not yet erected; what you see behind closed lids does not have to be logical. Now, what if you do not stimulate your left hemisphere right away with your thoughts and your phone, but remain in that moment of awakening? Just for a few minutes. This is called slumbering, and it is a wonderful moment to hear from God.

In the quote from Jeremiah at the top of this chapter, we can see an example of how God speaks during a time of slumbering. After Jeremiah has awoken, God continues speaking (Jer. 31:27). Jeremiah had slept really well and heard from God; and as he woke up, God was still with him and their conversation continued.

If you want to experience this too, then all you need to do is go to Jesus as you are slumbering, and that you open your heart for the Holy Spirit. This is not a matter of words; it takes place in your heart. You attention turns to Him:

> As for me, I shall behold your face in righteousness; when I awake,
> I shall be satisfied with your likeness.
> – PSALM 17:15

If you focus on God, you can receive what He wants to give: peace, love, warmth or an answer to a burning question. Perhaps a song will pop into your mind or you will think of a Bible verse. Maybe you will see an image or you will think of a person you know. Or there will be a smile on your face because God is smiling over you and loves you.

This is what David says:

> How precious to me are your thoughts, O God! How vast is the sum of them! If I would count them, they are more than the sand. I awake, and I am still with you.
> – PSALM 139:17-18

What a lovely thought! When I awaken, I am still with Him. God's thoughts about a person's life are endless and only good. It is no wonder that God wants to use the day *and* the night to make his thoughts known to us.

PART | 4

Dreams in the Bible

> Jesus Christ is the same yesterday and today and forever.
> — HEBREWS 13:8

Daniel the dream interpreter, Joseph, the king of dreams and Paul who used his visions as a GPS. Are these exceptional circumstances in history or are they the life stories of people that we can learn from? The Bible is our indispensable manual when we start to work with our dreams, a guide that makes sure that we do not get bogged down in half-truths or our own interpretation.

The dreams that are described in the Bible were given with different goals in mind and had various characteristics. We can see a clear distinction between literal dreams and symbolic dreams. In this part we will discover why God uses symbolic speech. We will learn about the characteristics of various kinds of dreams. We will answer the following questions: When is a dream a predictive dream? Or is every dream perhaps a taste of the future to come? And does God still warn us? The Bible deals with these subjects and has answers for us that will bring great clarity.

The Bible describes dreams that are given to those who serve God, but also to those who are wandering, living in doubt or those who do not yet believe. Today it is still the same; God gives to who He wants, however He wants. We cannot earn dreams by our good behavior, but we can anticipate them and receive them in every phase in our life.

Dreams of Direction

> I bless the LORD who gives me counsel; in the night also my heart instructs me.
> — PSALM 16:7

Jesus is the Way. He carries the compass for our life and wants to take us in the direction that the Father has for us. That is why He speaks to us at night with dreams of direction and visions that guide us, just as He did for Paul.

> And a vision appeared to Paul in the night: a man of Macedonia was standing there, urging him and saying, "Come over to Macedonia and help us." And when Paul had seen the vision, immediately we sought to go on into Macedonia, concluding that God had called us to preach the gospel to them.
> — ACTS 16:9-10

This vision in the night had the direction Paul needed from God in order to continue on his journey of spreading the gospel. Paul was expecting guidance from God; he had learned to listen to the voice of the Holy Spirit and to obey Him. Earlier in that chapter Paul had discovered it was not God's intention for him to travel to Bithynia or to bring the Word of God to Asia. As Paul was on the move and was seeking God's will, he let the Holy Spirit determine the direction.

Have you ever realized that this was how the gospel came to Europe? How Paul responded to this vision has impacted all of us!

It can be quite scary to hand over the control of our life to God. But if we do it, step by step, then God can become the driving force in our life. His plan for our life can then become a reality. He does not want us to be wandering around aimlessly, but gives us direction, during the day and in the night.

The characteristic of dreams of direction is that they can often be quite literal, as we have read in the example above. The Bible talks about more of such dreams with a literal command. Often we read that the dreamer of such a dream acts immediately and takes the dream seriously. God confirms it in our hearts so that we not only see the direction, but also receive courage to respond to what the Holy Spirit is speaking about.

The following testimony is about a dream of direction.

Frank and Gerdien's story

My husband and I are street evangelists and we travel around Europe bringing the gospel everywhere. In 2017, there had been a terrorist attack in Manchester. On that day, we felt we should go to Manchester. When we got there a while later, we saw billboards everywhere with: "Pray for Manchester." It was an intense time for the city and an opportunity for us to make Jesus known. We started looking for a suitable and affordable place to stay. We found a hotel and booked a room. Then my husband started searching for other street evangelists on the internet. He came across YouTube videos of a street preacher that included contact information. He contacted this man. There was an immediate spiritual click and he invited us to stay with him. He had been living in the home of an elderly woman for some time. We thought this was quite a big step. We had a seven-month-old son and we did not know these people. We prayed for wisdom. Should we spend the night at the booked hotel or with this unknown man? That night I had a dream. In that dream, I was in a hotel. Somewhere in the floor was a hole and you had to go through it to get into the room. It was very cramped and we felt trapped.

This hotel was in Manchester. When I woke up, I knew immediately that this was a dream from God in answer to our prayer about the direction we should take for our stay in Manchester. We cancelled the hotel and went to the house we were offered. We had a special time there and developed a close relationship with those people. We remain in contact with them to this day. The street preacher no longer lives in this house … but the elderly woman still welcomes us warmly. And so we have a wonderful base from which we can reach Manchester with the Good News. How good God is! He promises to provide everything we need and says: "Trust in the LORD with all your heart, and do not lean on your own understanding. In all your ways acknowledge him, and he will make straight your paths" (Prov. 3:5-6).

Dreams of Prediction

> And beware lest you raise your eyes to heaven, and when you see the sun and the moon and the stars, all the host of heaven, you be drawn away and bow down to them and serve them, things that the LORD your God has allotted to all the peoples under the whole heaven.
> – DEUTERONOMY 4:19

People are fascinated by predictions of the future; they want to know what is going to happen. Nearly every magazine has a horoscope section with a prediction about the future. There are those who do card-reading to see when they will marry and how many children they will have. The moon is made a god and the universe is seen as a guide. The enemy is working hard to bind souls to himself by copying that which is of God. People have been created with curiosity, and that points to the endless supernatural possibilities that are available when we return to the Father.

Before I became a believer, I was curious too and started looking for supernatural things. So I really do understand that desire. One of the first verses I learned about in the Bible was John 17:16, that I am in the world but "not of the world". Those words touched me deeply. I knew that this was the reason why I had never felt truly at home here on earth. For me, this was the proof that there was more than meets the eye, more than the natural world. I did not need to ignore my supernatural experiences. I just needed to find the right Source!

God exists outside of time and space. There is no limitation for his Spirit, who can reveal to us things of the past, present and future. Predictive dreams give us a glimpse of the future. This is a special gift from God: He gives us faith and prepares us for what lies ahead. An example of a dream of prediction can be found in Daniel 4:1-28. King Nebuchadnezzar had two dreams. This is what it says about the second dream:

> I saw a dream that made me afraid. As I lay in bed the fancies and the visions of my head alarmed me.
> – DANIEL 4:5

Nebuchadnezzar told Daniel what happened in his dream. An enormous tree filled with fruit was chopped down. Only the stump remained, held together by a band of iron and bronze. This predictive dream was a message to him. The king was rich and powerful, but also full of pride and arrogance. This eventually would knock him off his throne and turn him into a beastlike being, chained up.

God gave Daniel the interpretation and through this gave the king the opportunity to change his ways. But Nebuchadnezzar did not intend to do that, at least not yet! What must he have thought when he was eventually chained like a beast and eating grass? It was exactly as he had dreamed and what Daniel explained to him. It was not the first time that he had seen God's mighty power, either. Do you remember the story of Daniel's three friends? They were thrown into the furnace, bound, yet they were seen walking around in the blazing hot oven and were not hurt in any way. As if that was not amazing enough, Nebuchadnezzar saw a fourth Man in the midst of the flames! God still showed Nebuchadnezzar mercy in spite of his stubbornness and his future happened exactly as the dream predicted:

> At the end of the days I, Nebuchadnezzar, lifted my eyes to heaven, and my reason returned to me, and I blessed the Most High, and praised and honored him who lives forever, for his dominion is an everlasting dominion, and his kingdom endures from generation to generation (...)
> — DANIEL 4:34

Based on the examples of predictive dreams in the Bible, we can conclude that biblical dreamers had received a prophetic ministry or were in leadership, given by God. But since Pentecost God has poured out His Spirit on all who believe in Him and we are all kings and priests in Christ (Rev. 1:6). And right now something special is happening. More and more people are embracing and using the gifts that God gives through His Spirit. The gifts of revelation and the prophetic ministry are being restored and returned to the body of Christ at an incredible pace. And dreams are part of all this. Now, it is not the case that every dream from God is a dream of prediction. God can do so much more than see the future! However, you can receive dreams of predication from God if He so desires.

Dreams of prediction require a certain measure of insight from the one who receives it. It is important that we have an intimate relationship with the Holy Spirit, and that we ask Him for insight for such dreams. This will prevent us from just using our own interpretation. Predictive dreams cannot be tested until they have come to pass. It will not scare us or surprise us when a dream like that happens in real life, because we will have already seen, felt and tasted it.

We can receive a predictive dream for ourselves, for someone else or for a church, business or another group of people. God can also show us in a dream what He is going to do in a region, nation, or the body of Christ worldwide. Do you have a prophetic ministry, are you in a leadership role or are part of or lead a ministry of intercession? Then this will happen more frequently and you will learn to understand what God wants to say to you in such dreams. There are more examples of predictive dreams later in this book.

Dreams that Provide Insight

> I have counsel and sound wisdom; I have insight; I have strength.
> – PROVERBS 8:14

Jesus is the Truth. We know this. Yet it is not always easy to find the truth about a certain subject. It is as if we are looking through a veil that sometimes hides the truth or twists it. We need insight from heaven in order to see things for how they really are. God wants to give that to us, through dreams as well as in other ways.

A dream that gives insight can show us the truth about a situation, ourselves or who God is. We are given a view of the bigger picture and discover how everything is connected. The veil is lifted and the truth has been exposed. Not through knowledge of the mind, but through an encounter with God, who is Insight personified. An example of a dream that provides insight can be read in the Bible:

> Besides, while he was sitting on the judgment seat, his wife sent word to him, "Have nothing to do with that righteous man, for I have suffered much because of him today in a dream."
> – MATTHEW 27:19

In the middle of Jesus' trial, God gave Pilate's wife a dream. We do not know what God's intention was with this dream, but we do know that He was the Director in those hours. Pilate's wife really suffered from the dream. It is not said what occurred in the dream, but it had become clear to her that Jesus was innocent. The dream awakened her to the truth and she understood the urgency of that message. While her husband was already on the judgement seat and was at the point of condemning Jesus, she sent him a message about her dream. Pilate heard her insight and washed his hands in innocence. "I am innocent of this Man's blood," he said and handed Jesus over to the people (Matt. 27:24).

Did you notice that Pilate's wife was not a follower of Jesus? Perhaps she was not even aware of a God who wanted to speak to her through dreams. This is a beautiful example of how God reveals Himself through a dream to an unbeliever.

Maybe you met Jesus like this, or you may have heard of people who have found Jesus in this way. Many non-Christians receive insight about who Jesus is like this: Muslims see Jesus in their dreams, Buddhists dream about a Man in white. All over the world there are testimonies of people who were of a different religion and who had a dream about Jesus.[12]

Dreams of Warning

> (...) for I did not come to judge the world but to save the world.
> – JOHN 12:47b

Many people are afraid of warnings from God. Maybe this is due to our deep roots of our old nature, that expects punishment when we do something wrong. Even though we know the Bible tells us that Jesus has borne the punishment for us!

If we look at dreams of warning, then it is important to first deal with this lie. We are not being punished; Jesus took all of our punishment so that we could be free. That is the beauty of the gospel! But why, then, would we still receive warnings from God? Because He knows what the consequences are of certain choices we may make. Just look at the example of Abimelech:

> And Abraham said of Sarah his wife, "She is my sister." And Abimelech king of Gerar sent and took Sarah. But God came to Abimelech in a dream by night and said to him, "Behold, you are a dead man because of the woman whom you have taken, for she is a man's wife." Now Abimelech had not approached her. So he said, "Lord, will you kill an innocent people? Did he not himself say to me, 'She is my sister'? And she herself said, 'He is my brother.' In the integrity of my heart and the innocence of my hands I have done this." Then God said to him in the dream, "Yes, I know that you have done this in the integrity of your heart, and it was I who kept you from sinning against me. Therefore I did not let you touch her.
> — GENESIS 20:2-6

God did not condemn Abimelech, but showed him the truth, so that he could make a different choice. God immediately restores his honor by saying that He has seen the integrity of his heart. That is amazing and beautiful! That is what God's heart is like. He restores our dignity and value.

Mary's husband Joseph also received a dream of warning. God made sure that he, Mary and Jesus could escape the wrath of king Herod.

> Now when they had departed, behold, an angel of the Lord appeared to Joseph in a dream and said, "Rise, take the child and his mother, and flee to Egypt, and remain there until I tell you, for Herod is about to search for the child, to destroy him." And he rose and took the child and his mother by night and departed to Egypt (...)
> — MATTHEW 2:13-14

This dream was very clear. God spoke to Joseph Himself. There is no doubt about what he needed to do. Joseph acted immediately and brought his wife and child to safety. Joseph lived with God, he knew he could trust Him and he sought God's direction in his life. He had had an encounter with God in a dream before this, when he heard that Mary was pregnant by the Holy Spirit, and that she would have a son. They were to give Him the name "Jesus" and He would bring redemption to all people. That was incredible information for Joseph! How did he respond to this? He did not hesitate for a moment and called Mary the moment he woke up.

Dreams of warning are often literal and clear. The emotion that the dream brings does not have to be fear, it can also be determination and thankfulness. When God warns, it is always to protect us from the consequences of a choice. He is a good Father. If you doubt whether or not you have received a dream of warning, then ask God. Ask Him what He wants you to know about that dream. God does not bring torment and confusion and loves to help you if you ask Him, when He is actually warning you.

Encouraging Dreams

> Have I not commanded you? Be strong and courageous. Do not be frightened, and do not be dismayed, for the LORD your God is with you wherever you go.
> – JOSHUA 1:9

William, Tammy and Irma: hurricanes and tornados are often given a name. In Bible times storms were given names as well. The big storm that Paul and his travel companions went through was called 'Euroklydon'. In their panic they tried to save the ship and their lives, but it seemed hopeless in the face of such violence of nature. That night God appeared to

Paul and encouraged him to stay the course on the path they had taken. This is what he said about it:

> Yet now I urge you to take heart, for there will be no loss of life among you, but only of the ship. For this very night there stood before me an angel of the God to whom I belong and whom I worship, and he said, "Do not be afraid, Paul; you must stand before Caesar. And behold, God has granted you all those who sail with you.' So take heart, men, for I have faith in God that it will be exactly as I have been told.
> – ACTS 27:22-25

Sometimes the road that you are on with God seems difficult and exhausting. You do not know how to carry on. Your heart is overwhelmed with doubt and your thoughts with hopelessness. Was this really the right choice? If it is so difficult, is it really from God? But God never said the road would be smooth. He promised never to leave you and always wants to help by giving you new strength. God is an encourager, that is His character. He wants to use dreams to encourage you, give you affirmation and new strength to continue. As soon as you wake up, the sky will have cleared and the doubt has made way for assurance and perseverance: God sees me and is always with me!

I will give you an example of an encouraging dream that God gave me, as well as the interpretation I received afterward. Then I will share a few things that may not be clear yet, but will become clearer later on in the book.

DREAM
Love Drives Out All Fear

The luxurious upholstery of the house is colorful, beautiful lamps illuminate the long hallway. The rich fabrics in warm colors are familiar and make me feel safe: this is my home. As I walk down the hallway, I notice turmoil in one of the rooms. I approach it, feeling calm because it is my home and I do not tolerate unrest in my home.

I open the door to the room and there is a large man; he is disproportionately large. His bald head is wet with sweat and his black eyes look at me with fury. With one movement he picks me up and spins me around and around. I look at him. That seems to make him even angrier. He opens his ugly mouth and starts screaming incessantly.

In this strange situation, I know not to be afraid. I am stronger than him, even though I seem completely powerless. Quickly I grab my taser from my pocket and aim it at his head. The taser does not emit pain or violence, but thick divine love. It comes over him like a cloud.

I watch as the love intoxicates him. His eyes roll back and the strength with which he held me captive earlier, weakens. Like a drunken sailor, he falls to the ground, limp and powerless. I stand beside his huge body as love swallows him until he is completely dissolved.

Well, that was that! I turn and walk back into the hallway. To my surprise, another huge man comes storming down the stairs towards me. This time he is not alone, but in the company of a second ugly man. Roaring with rage, they run toward me.

Without hesitation, I point my taser at the first man and as he spins drunkenly on his feet. I take a step forward so that I also have the second man under fire. Both men dissolve into the cloud of love and disappear. The turmoil is gone. My house is safe again, as it should be.

Interpretation

Type of dream: dream of encouragement and insight, symbolic
Main character: me
Main emotions: peace and fortitude
Context: I had just stepped into a new season with new possibilities. At the same time, doubt and fear also came up.

The house I was in in my dream, is an image of my life (Matt. 7:24). God has built it and filled it with beautiful things: His favor, gifts and talents, dreams and desires. Just as Proverbs says: "In the house of the righteous there is much treasure, but trouble befalls the income of the wicked" (Prov. 15:6). I did not recognize the house, yet knew it was my house and that I had authority over the house.

The man in the dream represented the fear in me, fear which had been sown by the enemy through lies. Fear can sometimes pop up in a new situation, such as this new season in my life. Fear causes a feeling of unrest and can be very distracting, just like the man in the dream kept spinning me around and around. Fear can cause chaos in our mind and influence how we see things.

The man was screaming at me. Fear intimidates and wants you to believe that that which you fear is bigger than everything else, even bigger than God. Fear brings doubt about who God is and who you are. It paralyzes us, so that we no longer do what God has called us to do.

The taser would not seem to be effective against such a large, angry man, but because it was filled with the love of God, it was a powerful weapon; the only weapon that could take out that man! I have never used a taser, but in my dream I felt totally capable and not at all surprised that I had one on me. A taser is a protective weapon that you can carry in your pocket. In the same way we always carry the Holy Spirit in us. He is love and truth, the most powerful weapon there is.

The emotion in the dream is very important. I was determined to clean up the unrest in my home. In everyday life there are many times when I do not respond to fear with a sense of peace, but God showed me this is totally possible with my dream. And even better, He has given us the authority over our own life and He will always help us to eliminate fear.

The dream showed me the reality and it taught me that there is no fear I cannot conquer through the love of God. He encouraged me, affirmed me and made me hungry for more of God's love.

> There is no fear in love, but perfect love casts out fear.
> — 1 JOHN 4:18a

God showed me what the solution was for fear. That is important; it shows that it is not a dream from my soul or a dream from the enemy, but a dream from God. These are not my thoughts or expectations, but God's truth that gave the dream meaning. The main emotion was peace and steadfastness, even though this was a pretty frightening dream. If this had been a soul dream, then the main emotion would have been fear. In this you can also see the difference between a soul dream and a dream from God. Later in this book I will take you on a journey of discerning the source of your dream, discovering the main character in your dream and the importance of your emotions during your dream.

Dream Interpretation

> As for these four youths, God gave them learning and skill in all literature and wisdom, and Daniel had understanding in all visions and dreams.
> — DANIEL 1:17

God wants to give everyone dreams, but understanding the dreams can often be difficult. This was no different in the time of the Bible. God gave the interpretation of a dream to only a few. What did God intend with this gift? The story of Daniel gives us a lot of insight.

Let's take a closer look at his life. As a young man he was taken from conquered Jerusalem to Babylon. He was probably no older than eighteen when he was brought to the king's court to serve him. Daniel means "God is my judge", but his name was changed to Belteshazzar, which means "Bel protects his life". Bel was one of the gods of Nebuchadnezzar (Dan. 4:8). This immediately tells you what kind of place Daniel ended up in. Babylon was a place of confusion and idolatry, where Daniel's faith was tested. Daniel was given a high position in the court of the king and that is how he had a position of influence. God gave him a special gift:

> (...) because an excellent spirit, knowledge, and understanding to interpret dreams, explain riddles, and solve problems were found in this Daniel, whom the king named Belteshazzar. Now let Daniel be called, and he will show the interpretation.
> — DANIEL 5:12

The gift that we read about here is not listed in 1 Corinthians 12, where the various gifts of the Holy Spirit are mentioned. It is probably a combination of revelatory gifts: wisdom, knowledge, prophecy and discernment. But the Bible also speaks clearly about a gift to interpret dreams. This probably is closely linked to the time in which Daniel lived. He still lived in the Old Covenant era; Jesus had not yet come and the way to God was not yet open to all people. The Holy Spirit was *with* certain people that God had chosen, so that they could serve the people and bring them into contact with Him. Through the dreams that Daniel could interpret, the king had a change of heart! We also see something extraordinary about the gift that God gave Daniel: He had knowledge and understanding about all kinds of writing, and he had received wisdom. In those days it was special if you could read and write, and even more so if you had insight and wisdom about what you read. Daniel was a very gifted man; God gave him great wisdom. Now God does give these gifts for free, but the maturity to walk in those gifts comes at a price: "The fear of the LORD is the beginning of wisdom, and the knowledge of the Holy One is insight" (Prov. 9:10).

There is never a lack of wisdom from God and we can always ask Him for wisdom. But we must first acknowledge that we need God's wisdom. It requires a humble heart to draw from the Well of wisdom.

God knew that Daniel had a deep respect for Him and was humble of heart. Daniel's life shows that he was focused on serving the king, he was not focused on power or riches and was not seeking fame. He acted from a culture of honor, and he knew how to conduct himself within the palace walls. At the same time he knew what his identity was in God and he was brave enough to follow God and not bow to the lies, in spite of the laws and rules at the time. He prayed to God while the government had forbidden this and he paid a price—the lions' den. Through this he showed incredible character and that was not formed overnight. Daniel needed that character as a strong foundation for the ministry that God gave him.

The king for whom Daniel worked had a disturbing dream, and he called on all kinds of magicians and fortune tellers. They need to tell him not only the dream but the interpretation as well, he said. They were unable to do this. The king decided: "If my dream is not explained, then all of the wise men in my palace must be killed." This is the moment that Daniel jumped into action with God's gift:

> Then Daniel replied with prudence and discretion to Arioch, the captain of the king's guard, who had gone out to kill the wise men of Babylon. He declared to Arioch, the king's captain, "Why is the decree of the king so urgent?" Then Arioch made the matter known to Daniel.
> – DANIEL 2:14-15

His life is at stake, but Daniel remained calm and figured out what was going on. Then he asked the king for more time, so that he could hear from God. That is actually quite bizarre when you read how the preparations for the executions were already in full swing! Daniel asked his friends to pray with him that the dream and the interpretation would be revealed. He went to his room and prayed. This is what happened:

> Then the mystery was revealed to Daniel in a vision of the night. Then Daniel blessed the God of heaven. Daniel answered and said: "Blessed be the name of God forever and ever, to whom belong wisdom and might (...) he reveals deep and hidden things; he knows what is in the darkness, and the light dwells with him.
> – DANIEL 2:19-20,22

Daniel did not doubt for a moment about what he had received, and he went straight to the king. But before he gave the interpretation of the dream, he set things straight:

> Daniel answered the king and said, "No wise men, enchanters, magicians, or astrologers can show to the king the mystery that the king has asked, but there is a God in heaven who reveals mysteries, and he has made known to King Nebuchadnezzar what will be in the latter days. Your dream and the visions of your head as you lay in bed are these (...)
> – DANIEL 2:27-28

Here we see once again that Daniel was not afraid. He first dealt with all of the idolatry in the king's household. Then he shared exactly what the king did in his bedroom:

> To you, O king, as you lay in bed came thoughts of what would be after this, and he who reveals mysteries made known to you what is to be.
> — DANIEL 2:29

He then shared the dream and the interpretation with the king without any hesitation, in which he repeats that the interpretation did not come from himself but from God:

> But as for me, this mystery has been revealed to me, not because of any wisdom that I have more than all the living, but in order that the interpretation may be made known to the king, and that you may know the thoughts of your mind.
> — DANIEL 2:30

Nebuchadnezzar was overwhelmed; he knelt down and bowed deep in front of Daniel as he recognized God as the Lord. He promoted Daniel and made him ruler over the province of Babylon. What a twist of events!

> The king answered and said to Daniel, "Truly, your God is God of gods and Lord of kings, and a revealer of mysteries, for you have been able to reveal this mystery."
> — DANIEL 2:47

By interpreting one dream, Daniel went from "death row" to being the ruler over a large territory within twenty-four hours. Only God can do such a thing!

Daniel received the gift of interpretation of dreams. This gift from God was not for him to keep to himself, but to serve others with. The Bible says that we can chase after and hunger for the gifts of the Holy Spirit, which includes this gift. And yet, God wants to speak to us personally all the time and give us wisdom and insight into the dreams that He gives us.

Visions

> The hand of the LORD was upon me, and he brought me out in the Spirit of the LORD and set me down in the middle of the valley; it was full of bones.
> – EZEKIEL 37:1

The Bible says that God speaks through dreams and visions. Daniel, Ezekiel and John were familiar with visions of God. They saw things from heaven as if projected on a screen, such as the valley of dry bones. These were not static images, but complete movies that God's Spirit showed them.

God speaks to us visually in different ways. For example, He can give us a picture, a dream or a vision. But what is the difference between these?

I will show you the difference with an exercise. Close your eyes and think of an orange. Do you see it? Close your eyes again and see that there is a twig with a green leaf at the top of the orange, as if it had just been picked from the tree. Do you see the leaf?

Your thoughts are inspired by the words you read and you picture them with your eyes closed. God can use our thoughts as a blank sheet on which He projects images. Then they are not shaped by our own thoughts, but inspired by the Holy Spirit.

Another way that God speaks to us visually, is through a vision. A characteristic is that it is realistic; it is as if you are in the middle of a movie, just like Ezekiel when he saw the dry bones. You can feel, smell and hear what is going on. That is why a vision has such a deep impact. There is also an experience called an open vision. A vision like that is seen with your eyes open. This can occur at night, but also during the day.

The following is an example of a vision that God gave me.

VISION
Strong Cords of Love

It was a rainy Sunday evening and we had gone to bed early so we could read a book. It was not yet completely dark outside and the lights on our nightstands bathed the room in a warm glow. I was reading an amazing book about supernatural encounters with God; it made me hungry for more and I was enthusiastic. I put the book down for a moment so I could ponder on what I had just read. In my heart I said to God: "I am so hungry for more encounters with You!" This was in a period in which I would often burst into tears just because I was so hungry for more of Jesus. This may sound strange, but the more you get to taste of God, the hungrier you become. At least, that was the case for me! As I was telling God about how much I wanted to be with Him and wanted to hear from Him, it was as if I was pulled upward and out of my body. For a moment gravity was lost as the cords of God's love were pulling me closer. I felt the wind blow past me because of the speed that God was taking me. The next moment I went straight through a large cloud. There was such an enormous amount of power and energy in the cloud that my body shook from the electrical current. I heard thousands and thousands of people, all at the same time. They were calling out and praying and were very happy and excited. In that moment I knew that I had gone straight through the cloud of witnesses in Hebrews 12. I heard, saw and felt it. That was so overwhelming, it was indescribable. The next moment I was back in my bed, still overwhelmed by what had just happened. I had never had an encounter with this part of God's family and it was very encouraging to know that these people, who have gone ahead on the path of our faith, encourage us and call us to persevere (Heb. 12:1).

We can see another example of a vision in the life of Jacob:

> And God spoke to Israel in visions of the night and said, "Jacob, Jacob." And he said, "Here I am." Then he said, "I am God, the God of your father. Do not be afraid to go down to Egypt, for there I will make you into a great nation.
> — GENESIS 46:2-3

Jacob often received visions from God, but what he described here is a vision in which God called him by name. The word that is used in the original Hebrew text is *ma'rah*. That means vision or looking glass. It should not be confused with *mara*, which means bitter (Ex. 15:22). In another place in the Bible the word *ma'rah* is used as mirror:

> He made the basin of bronze and its stand of bronze, from the mirrors of the ministering women who ministered in the entrance of the tent of meeting.
> — EXODUS 38:8

The answer to the question, "How do I receive visions from God?" is hidden in this verse. The mirrors mentioned were not just for any women, but for the ministers at the entrance to the tent of meeting. They were servants. I can imagine that the mirrors were broken into pieces and were attached as a mosaic to the washbasin. When you were standing in front of it, you would see yourself from many angles. There at the washbasin people cleansed themselves so that they could enter the tent of meeting, where God's presence was. This verse points to the Servant Jesus, who washes us so that we can approach God. When we allow ourselves to be washed by Jesus, then we gain entrance to the tent of meeting; the place where God gives us eyes to see. We cannot earn visions, only receive them.

Characteristics of Biblical Dreams

> He reveals deep and hidden things; he knows what is in the darkness, and the light dwells with him.
> — DANIEL 2:22

What can we learn from the dreams in the Bible? First of all: Encounters with God in the Bible are unexpected and unearned; this applies to us as well. There are twenty-two biblical stories of people who met God in the night. Of these, only four of them received a message that was meant for someone other than themselves. It is possible to receive a message for someone else, but in most cases the dreams God gives are for you.

There is a misconception that dreams from God are always full of singing angels and peaceful emotions. God does not give fear, but He can help you to realize how serious a situation may be. That happened to the wife of Pilate, who said she "suffered much" (Matt. 27:19) during a dream. Nebuchadnezzar also was "troubled" (Dan. 2:1) when he awoke from the dream that God gave him. Again, God gives clarity and hope, but sometimes we need to be alerted to a certain situation. When we wake up and are deeply impressed by a dream, then that can motivate us to first go to God instead of quickly moving on to the daily grind and forgetting the dream.

What is interesting is that many of the dreams in the Bible are symbolic. The message that God gives is wrapped in a riddle. An example of this can be found in Genesis 40, where two men dream on the same night. The cupbearer dreamt about a vine with grapes and the baker about baskets with bread that was being eaten by birds. The meaning has little connection to the vine or baskets, and yet God chose this way to tell these men what was about to happen to them. Sometimes God speaks literally in a dream and He says exactly what He means, but usually He speaks through symbols.

Another interesting fact is that the people who received dreams from God were not always seeking to dream. For example, the Pharaoh of Egypt, the wife of Pontius Pilate, King Nebuchadnezzar and the baker and the cupbearer. These people did not even believe in the God of Abraham, Isaac and Jacob.

So it is not a crazy idea to ask God for dreams when you are praying for someone. It does not matter whether that person knows God or not, that does not prevent the Holy Spirit from giving dreams! When the dreamer does not yet know the God of the Bible, you can see that the interpretation is given by people who are inspired by the Holy Spirit. In all other cases, God Himself gives the interpretation to the one who received the dream. Some people have a lot of experience with dreams and can help others discover the interpretation, but you do not always need an interpreter of dreams to find out what the meaning of your dream is. The Holy Spirit lives inside of you, and He wants to help you understand your dreams. We will take a look at that in the next part!

PART 5

Getting to Work With Your Dreams

> They said to him, "We have had dreams, and there is no one to interpret them." And Joseph said to them, "Do not interpretations belong to God?"
> – GENESIS 40:8a

When God speaks through a dream, it is not always immediately clear what He wants to say. That was the case in the time of the Bible and it is still the same today. Everyone has experienced this at some point – in your dream everything seemed logical, but once you awoke, nothing seemed to make sense anymore. Have you ever considered the fact that God may do this so that we will seek Him? After all, Proverbs says the following:

> It is the glory of God to conceal things, but the glory of kings is to search things out.
> – PROVERBS 25:2

God is looking for stewards, people who will join Him in stewarding and sharing things of value. According to the Bible (Rev. 5:10), you and I are kings; it has been given to us to figure out these things. It is still possible to interpret dreams. Just as Daniel was given the gift to understand dreams,

God still gives this gift to whoever He chooses. But even without this supernatural gift we can interpret dreams through the Holy Spirit. He gives knowledge and revelation. We can ask for gifts, and we can grow in knowledge and understanding. But the interpretation of a dream comes from God. I will say it again, just so it is clear:

> Joseph answered Pharaoh, "It is not in me; God will give Pharaoh a favorable answer."
> – GENESIS 41:16

What do you do if you receive a dream through which God wants to speak to you? What do certain symbols mean and how do you discern the source of your dream? And perhaps the most frequently asked question: How do you recognize a dream from God? In the next part I will take you on a journey of interpreting dreams. I want to prepare you ahead of time. It is a lot of information to take in in one go. Perhaps you can see it as a toolbox that you can take from when you need it. Do not do this alone, but always with your Helper, the Holy Spirit.

> Trust in the LORD with all your heart, and do not lean on your own understanding.
> – PROVERBS 3:5

God's Voice as a Compass

> When he has brought out all his own, he goes before them, and the sheep follow him, for they know his voice. A stranger they will not follow, but they will flee from him, for they do not know the voice of strangers.
> – JOHN 10:4-5

One of the most important reasons that people do not hear God's voice is because they do not believe that this is possible for them. They think this is only reserved for the pastor and some other "super-holy Christians", that it is unattainable for "normal folk". This thought is based on a lie that has been around for centuries: God is far away. Yet Jesus Himself said that we would all know his voice (John 10:4). God does not say: "Here is my book, the Bible. Now I am going back to heaven and I will watch and see if you do what it says and understand what I mean." That would be weird, wouldn't it? Yet this is how many think God is, distant and cold; all contact is one-way traffic. Perhaps you recognize this feeling. If so, then you are in a for a wonderful new phase!

Let us start at the beginning. God wants to speak and has made it possible for us to hear and understand Him. I shared previously that right after I had gotten saved I received dreams from God and heard His voice. I was a new-born baby in the faith and my knowledge of the Bible, but I got to know God as a Father who speaks. This may be very different for you and you may struggle to hear God's voice. That is why I want to show you this amazing truth.

During the Old Covenant God only spoke to a few select people. But that is now a thing of the past. Through Jesus' sacrifice the veil was torn (Matt. 27:51) and God's deepest wish was fulfilled. The way is open for His children to approach Him. The relationship that He had in mind when He created us has been restored. We are now no longer slaves of the law and sin (Rom. 6:16-17), but adopted children (Rom. 8:15) and citizens of heaven (Phil. 3:20). The truth is, God is always nearby.

Communication is important in a relationship and helps you get to know each other. Because you exchange information, thoughts and emotions, you will understand each other better; it draws you closer to each other. Communication helps you to not only hear what the other is saying, but allows you to get to know their heart. This determines *how* you hear the words the other person is saying. It is foundational in a relationship.

The measure in which we know God's heart determines how we hear His words. He is love, truth and goodness; every word that He speaks is drenched in these things.

So let go of your doubts. Doubting is an enormous blockade in hearing God's voice. Many people do not dare to take God's words in faith, and keep on doubting. Their doubt grows bigger than their faith and it tells them over and over again that it was not God who they were hearing. Doubt has become a close companion who not only makes them feel safe, but also gives them an excuse to not have to mature in this area. Let go of the doubt, it is your enemy. Faith is your faithful friend in hearing God's voice.

There are many people who also want to hear God's voice audibly, just like He did with Saul on the Road to Damascus. The truth is that God usually whispers. You only shout when you are competing with other voices. God's voice is above all other voices. He does not shout but speaks softly and waits patiently until you draw closer to hear Him.

God the Father is interested in us, He wants to know what we are thinking about and loves to hear our voice, whether it is as we hum as we look in the mirror, or share about our desires for the future, or cry out in the middle of life's struggles. Even when we grumble or are angry, He still wants to listen to us! And He doesn't want to just listen, but make His thoughts known to us. God wants to let us know what He is doing in our life and where He is taking us. God wants to be known and He does this through speaking. And He does even more!

> "For who has understood the mind of the Lord so as to instruct him?" But we have the mind of Christ.
> – 1 CORINTHIANS 2:16

The word used here for "mind" is the Greek word *nous*. That means more than just the mind, it is the God-given capacity of each person to *think* (reason); the *mind*; mental capacity to exercise reflective thinking. For the believer *nous* is the organ of *receiving God's thoughts*, through *faith*. That is a lot more than just your intellectual capacities. Jesus wants you to feel with his heart and see through his eyes. He wants to show you who the Father is and help, encourage, guide and reassure you. But He also wants to share His wisdom with you. Why does God share His thoughts with us? So that we can be His hands, feet and mouth on this earth.

God speaks in all kinds of ways to you personally. You are unique and He knows exactly how you can hear Him and what works for you. God not only speaks your mother tongue, but He also speaks the specific language you speak. His creative options to reach us are limitless. He can reach us through nature, music or the arts. Or He can give us thoughts that we may hardly notice as they are similar to our own; thoughts like a gentle whisper. He can suddenly highlight a Bible verse which really speaks to us, or He can place an image in our mind or a tingling sensation in our stomach. God can use all of our senses to make something clear to us.

You can ask the Holy Spirit to help you understand God. He really wants to help and is always available. Just start practicing. For example, when you pray, take the time to listen quietly to Him. God does not shout but waits until you listen. Quietly listening is not the same as not talking. When you say nothing, there can still be thoughts racing through your mind, making it difficult to listen. Listening quietly to God is as if you are taking a step back into an alcove, stepping out of the busy stream of thoughts. Many people like to pray in tongues (the heavenly language Paul talks about in 1 Corinthians 12-14) in such a moment, because that can help them to focus on God and to subject their thoughts to God's thoughts. Take a deep breath and rest before God's throne before you start rattling off your list or wants. In that moment you give the Holy Spirit room to speak to you the way

He wants to. Perhaps He first wants to tell you that He loves you, before He says anything else. Asking is an important part of receiving, as the following verse shows us:

> For everyone who asks receives, and the one who seeks finds, and to the one who knocks it will be opened.
> — LUKE 11:10

This verse gives us such wonderful assurance. Ask God for a Bible verse or His thoughts for the day. Ask for a person to give something to today, a compliment or a helping hand. Ask Him what He wants you to focus on today. Do not be afraid, take your time and take notes, even if it seems simple or unimportant. You will notice that after some time it will be easier and easier to discern His voice from your own thoughts. God is Father and Friend and He wants to be involved in everything. We often think that God only wants to be a part of big life decisions, but He also wants to talk about that nagging thought in the back of your mind that has been robbing your peace for several days, or about the small desire which you think it is unimportant. Remember that we often make things overly complicated in our minds, while God just likes to talk to us where we are. So just relax and don't forget to enjoy your private conversations with Him.

Recognizing God's Voice

> My sheep hear my voice, and I know them, and they follow me.
> — JOHN 10:27

As you are learning to hear and understand God's voice, you will sometimes make mistakes. That is not a problem. The prophet Samuel didn't understand at first that it was God who was speaking to him in the night. As time passes you will understand God better and hear Him more clearly. And most of all, you will get to know Him more intimately.

There is no reason to worry; the only thing you need is faith the size of a mustard seed (Matt. 17:20) and an open heart.

How do you recognize God's voice? First of all: God always speaks in line with His Word and character. He does not contradict His Word and you will often find Bible verses that confirm and expand on what you have heard from Him.

Secondly, his voice is that of a loving Father. He encourages and affirms. This does not mean that God cannot correct you, but His tone is never condemning or punishing. After all, He has already washed away all your sins; He no longer sees your shortcomings. The things that you so dislike about yourself, He has already removed. In Jesus Christ you are perfect, cleansed, holy, forgiven, accepted and a beloved child of God.

Satan's voice is radically different than God's voice:

God's voice:
soothing • reassuring • convincing • encouraging • clarifying • guiding • assuring • warming

Satan's voice:
judgmental • discouraging • rushing • confusing • frightening • pushing • stressing • worrying

Do You See God?

> But blessed are your eyes, for they see, and your ears, for they hear.
> – MATTHEW 13:16

You can find God in everything, but also miss God in everything. We need eyes to see and ears to hear. When we receive those heavenly senses, we can discover God anywhere and everywhere. Simply because He promises that He is always with us.

When we pray, we may think that we should do so piously and reverently. It doesn't feel very spiritual to come to Jesus with everything we are feeling and experiencing at the time. But the whole point is to be ourselves! Let's take a deep breath and then breathe out all doubt. That will help us to listen, relax and enjoy our time together with God. Prayer is really nothing but a conversation between Father and child, a conversation between two close friends. So simple and so powerful at the same time, because these conversations can move mountains.

God's heart goes out to us in such a way that there is nothing in our lives that He does not want to talk about. God wants to be involved even when we are making our morning coffee. So choose a daily activity and invite God into it. Ask Him to open your eyes to see how He is involved in what you are doing. What He wants to say to you right now. Thank God for His love and for Him being near in your life and take note of the things He speaks to your heart. Do this for as long as you want, and learn to experience God's involvement and be attuned to what He is saying. When your attention is focused on Him, God is hard to miss.

> O LORD, in the morning you hear my voice; in the morning I prepare a sacrifice for you and watch.
> — PSALM 5:3

There are two common misconceptions about dreams. First, that every dream comes from God; second, that no dream comes from God. As people get better and better at understanding God's voice, it is often thought that every dream comes from heaven. Therefore, it is important to first determine the source of your dream. A reminder I use is this—not every dream comes from God, but there is no dream in which He is not present. We may have peace of mind knowing that nothing happens out of the Father's sight; He is always there and always wants to speak.

Various Kinds of Dreams

> For when dreams increase and words grow many, there is vanity; but God is the one you must fear.
> – ECCLESIASTES 5:7

Dreams can be divided into several categories. For example, there are dreams inspired by the Spirit of God, and dreams inspired by another spirit. The Bible gives an example of the latter:

> If a prophet or a dreamer of dreams arises among you and gives you a sign or a wonder, and the sign or wonder that he tells you comes to pass, and if he says, "Let us go after other gods," which you have not known, "and let us serve them," you shall not listen to the words of that prophet or that dreamer of dreams. For the LORD your God is testing you, to know whether you love the LORD your God with all your heart and with all your soul.
> – DEUTERONOMY 13:1-3

That dreams can come from a spirit other than the Holy Spirit is not something you need to worry about. Your heart yearns for Jesus; He answers when you ask.

So what types of dreams are there?

Dreams from the Soul

Our soul encompasses our will, emotions and thoughts. There are those who imply that we should ignore our soul and should not let it speak. The truth is that our soul has very useful information for our general health. God created us with a spirit, soul and body, as a perfect triune whole. As soon as we ignore one of these three, this has huge consequences and disrupts the balance that God has in mind. A dirty or wounded soul is like having a pair of glasses with smudges on them. How we then see ourselves, others and God can be tremendously influenced by what we have been through. So it is of vital importance to listen to what our soul is saying so that it can be comforted, healed and warmed by the Holy Spirit. Our soul can speak. Information that may be hidden during the day can come up during the night in a dream. Dreams from the soul can be about things that we do during the day, but they sometimes also contain deeper messages about what is happening in our soul, such as memories, suppressed emotions and our deepest motives. Our soul is the source of these dreams, but God also wants to use these dreams to speak to us. He wants to make our soul whole and let his living water flow through it, so that all of the dirt will wash away and we will be clean, refreshed and healthy.

God's Spirit can bring things up in our soul that need our attention. He can do this in all kinds of ways, including our dreams. Dreams from our soul can be uncomfortable and not feel nice, but God only wants the best for his children. We can view this as a loving invitation. If we bring our suppressed emotions, hidden lies or trauma to Him, we can be healthy and free. Dreams from our soul invite us to be honest, so that God can work through them with power.

Dreams from God

Because the Holy Spirit lives in us, God is always with us. As we sleep, we are not limited by our thoughts or boundaries and there is a lot more room to receive what God wants to give to us. He can speak about our life in a dream, or give us new insights and heavenly ideas. Or He can let you know how much He loves you and how He sees you. Dreams from God are limitless, everything is possible! Dreams from God can be literal and symbolic and we will often remember them after we wake up. It may happen that we can still remember those dreams years later. Dreams from God can have unknown colors and images that we have never seen before and evoke emotions that we have never felt so deeply. In a dream from God, we can go to places where we have never been and they can contain sounds that we have never heard. A dream from God changes you. What He says will give you new insight and bring you closer to the Father.

Revelation about Spiritual Warfare

These dreams have the same source: They are dreams from God. Yet it is good to focus on these dreams separately because there is a lot of misunderstanding about them. God can give us insight in the enemy's plans through a dream. He can alert us and encourage us to pray. The Bible says the following about satan:

> For we are not unaware of his schemes.
> – 2 CORINTHIANS 2:11 (NIV)

We have the opportunity through the Holy Spirit to unmask and dismantle the plans and schemes of the enemy. If God allows us to see the hidden strategies of the enemy, then He will often give us peace and steadfastness in the dream.

These dreams can be very clear, but they can also be as misty as a cold fall morning. Mist is like a veil that wants to hide what the enemy is scheming, but nothing remains hidden from the eyes of God. If you have such a dream, it can be quite frightening, but God will give you insight, the solution and a way out. In contrast to a nightmare, these dreams are from God and not from the enemy.

Physical Dreams

> Or do you not know that your body is a temple of the Holy Spirit within you, whom you have from God? You are not your own (...)
> – 1 CORINTHIANS 6:19

Our body also belongs to the triune God who created us with a spirit, soul and body. It has been given to us as a temporary outfit that is to serve us during our time here on earth. It has not been carelessly chosen as a shell. No, God knit each of us together in our mother's womb, as we read in Psalm 139, and He made us wonderfully intricate. Our body is a part of God's unique plan for our life, which is meant to represent Him. We can take good care of it and use it to express ourselves and Him. Many people actually hate their bodies; it does not work the way they want or does not look the way they want it to. That is why they choose to punish their bodies, by filling them with the wrong things or denying them good things. It is as if they drag their bodies around with them and kick them when they do not function properly; they treat their body as some kind of useless evil thing, as an enemy. How healing would it be if we were to embrace our bodies as the temple that they are? Then every part of our body would be freed from rejection and given the love it deserves. It would cause it to grow healthy and increase in strength.

When we sleep our muscles are fully relaxed and when we dream they are even slightly paralyzed. However, our bodies can still receive and emit various signals. It is possible for us to dream that we have lost an arm when we are lying on our arm causing it to feel numb. Or we dream that we cannot breathe, because there is a blanket on our face. Our bodies can tell us that we are exhausted and have a hard time keeping up with the pace we are forcing on it. It can even show us in a dream where there is discomfort or illness. Let's not underestimate our bodies, they have been created by the mastermind of God, and for Him there are no boundaries between the natural and the supernatural! The Spirit of God is in us, He can warn us in a dream so that we can respond quickly to what our bodies need. Imagine how much suffering could be alleviated if we were to have more of such dreams!

Nightmares

We can have nightmares that are inspired by the enemy. The book of Job speaks about nightmares and Isaiah speaks about fearful dreams. But we need to remember one thing—the enemy cannot create anything; he can only use the doors that we have left open and then project images. He can only have power in our lives when we give him access. His plan is to frighten us, to rob us of our faith and trust in God and to steal our God-given identity. Often our nightmares are related to losing something or someone: our life, our voice, our freedom, our strength, a loved one. We can see a nightmare like an antenna on a radio. Have you ever had a nightmare out of the blue? Then you can ask the Holy Spirit to help you adjust your antenna to God's frequency. Do not pay any attention to the enemy, he feeds off our attention. Many people will easily ascribe dreams to "the enemy" when they do not understand them or experience unrest. More often than not, however, these are dreams from the soul realm.

When we continually struggle with nightmares, there is a big chance that a door has been opened through which the enemy has access to us. We then need to think carefully about what we have been filling ourselves with; which thoughts are running through our mind? Horror movies, violent games and occult activities are also invitations for the enemy to enter our life. We need to stop doing these things and close the door. Do the nightmares continue or are you struggling to close the door? Then you need to ask your local church, Christian family members or Christian friends to help you. Another person can help you with this, so that your nights are pleasant again and filled with God.

Recognizing God's Dreams

> Incline your ear, and come to me; hear, that your soul may live (...)
> – ISAIAH 55:3a

I give prophetic training to help people hear and understand God's voice. One question that is asked frequently is this: 'How do I know it is God's voice I am hearing and not my own thoughts?' Your own relationship with the Father is always the answer. He teaches you and gives you discernment and wisdom, He points you to His Word and takes you on a journey of discovering the various ways of hearing Him. But above all, He lets Himself be known by you. We can teach and testify as people, we can lay hands on people and pass on anointing, but we will also need to go to God ourselves with all that we have learned.

Many people want a quick answer to the meaning of their dream, without having a connection with the Giver of that dream. But that was never what God intended. God does not give a formula for the understanding of your dreams. He wants to walk alongside you and share the secrets of His heart with you. You will grow in your understanding of God the longer you spend time with Him.

There are several things to recognize a dream from God by.

First of all: Do you feel like your interest has been piqued? That you need to act on the dream and record it? If God wants to speak to you through a dream, He will draw your attention. Sometimes He will use bizarre dreams to do this.

God speaks in the context of a conversation and the relationship you have together. He can show you things about your future that are not meant for the here and now. You can cling to those things and keep the dream in your heart. But usually the dream will be in line with your life in the here and now and about the things that you discuss with Him.

Dreams from God can often be recognized by color and light. Because these are characteristics of God Himself. The Bible says the following about Jesus:

> In him was life, and the life was the light of men. The light shines in the darkness, and the darkness has not overcome it.
> – JOHN 1:4-5

Dreams from God are often full of light, life and color. As if the sun is shining brightly in your dream. The enemy is darkness and will come with dark colors like black and gray, or with muted colors. Now, there are variations to this; God can give a dream that may not be full of color, but it is full of light and vibrant. At any rate, you will feel the life! You can even have a dream from God in black and white, but it will be vibrant black and bright white.

Another important characteristic: God's presence. Did you feel like God was present? This is difficult, because it is not measurable. Even if you cannot readily answer this, or you find it difficult to determine, it can still be a dream from God.

And another thing: Does the dream align with God's character and His Word? If you speak to the Holy Spirit about the dream, He will give you insight through God's Word and will always point to the character of a good God.

As soon as you have determined the source of your dream, you can start to seek the meaning of it. Many people often just guess at something that they think may be important, without really feeling a connection, nor hearing the message that God wants to give them. In order to prevent you from throwing your dream into the trash, it is good to work with a step-by-step plan if you are seeking the meaning of it.

Interpreting Dreams

> You know when I sit down and when I rise up; you discern my thoughts from afar. You search out my path and my lying down and are acquainted with all my ways. Even before a word is on my tongue, behold, O LORD, you know it altogether.
> — PSALM 139:2-4

God speaks in the context of the relationship that you have with Him. God does not give a formula for understanding your dreams. And no matter how much we would like to put our dreams into a prefabricated mold, He does not work like that. God the Father wants a relationship with us and He wants to reveal more and more of Himself to us. There are guidelines for understanding dreams. Perhaps you have previous experiences that can help you, but do not hang on to them; give God room to do what He wants to do now.

There is one main rule for the interpretation of dreams —always return to God with everything He has given you. He is the only one who can interpret dreams, through His Spirit. He knows how we think, see things and talk. He knows what we did yesterday and what we are thinking about. Even the things that we missed, He saw. That is what makes Him the perfect helper for the interpretation of our dreams.

It is a good idea to write down your dreams. Here are a few guidelines to get you started:

What kind of dream is it?
What is the source of your dream? Is it a soul dream, a dream from God, or a dream from the enemy? It can be a problem if we incorrectly interpret the source of our dream, or switch halfway to another source. Later on I will tell you more about how you can recognize a dream from your soul. Ask God for the gift of discernment (1 Cor. 12:10). This gift is meant to help us know if something is from God, from the enemy, or from ourselves. We can also practice recognizing the source. Are you in doubt? Then first take a look at the following steps. Perhaps you will then be able to distinguish the source.

Is the dream literal or symbolic?
Ask yourself the question: Does this dream have a literal message or is it symbolic? Most of the dreams in the Bible are symbolic, and today most dreams are still symbolic. That is why many dreams are so strange. Jesus often spoke to His

disciples in parables and they learned to listen to what He had to say. We can also learn to listen to the symbolic language of our dreams.

What is the context of the dream?
This is very important. What is going on in your life, what are you thinking about and how do you feel? What have you been talking to God about lately? What have you been asking Him for insight on, direction, healing or freedom? In the examples later on you will see that I also share the context. Try to be honest about your context, then you can be honest with God and recognize what He is saying.

Who is the main person in the dream?
If you move, talk and act in the dream, then you are the main person. In other words, the message of the dream is for you. That is also the case when there are other people in your dream. Most of the dreams in the Bible are about the person who is dreaming; there are only four dreams that are about someone other than the dreamer. So most of your dreams will be about you and that should always be your starting point. So ask yourself the question: If I were removed from the dream, would the story keep on going? If the answer is "no", then you are the main person. If God speaks to you about another person, then He will make this clear to you. Always ask Him if He wants you to share the dream, or if you should not but instead pray and intercede for this person. I will talk about this more later on.

Which emotions do you experience during the dream?
The emotion that you experience during the dream is important in order to understand the dream. Besides the images in the dream, it is the emotions that determine the explanation. After all, everything is possible in a dream; flying on a golden

bike can feel very normal, yet it can feel very strange to be chopping broccoli. Sometimes you will experience multiple emotions, but in most dreams you will only recognize one emotion. You may feel peaceful, even if the dream is filled with scary or confronting events. And the opposite can also be true, you can feel deep fear or terror during a dream that in and of itself is not even strange. These emotions will tell you a lot, and will help you to understand what God wants to say. So do not try to explain them, just write down what your main emotion was.

What kind of activities are taking place in the dream?

Which events or activities are taking place in your dream? On average there are about four to seven activities in a dream. It could also be just one thing. Write down every activity separately. Not every detail is important; first look at the main "storyline" of the dream. Which things determine the "story" of your dream?

Which symbols are in the dream?

A place, an object, color or animal, clothing or a name—all of these things can be symbolic. You will recognize them by the fact that you notice them in your dream. Which symbols were in your dream? What do these symbols mean to you? Ask the Holy Spirit to help you discover what these symbols mean and open God's Word as your guide. There will be a lot more on symbols later on in the book too!

Is the dream for now or later?

God can show you things for the future that are not meant for now. You can hang on to these things; you can keep them in your heart. But often your dream will be about your life in the here and now.

What do you want to call your dream?
Give your dream a title. This is how you will summarize the core message of your dream, often unwittingly. You will discover what was the most important. If you want to read about the dream again, you will often see what the dream was about by the title.

Dreams to Process Things, or an Invitation?

> Beloved, I pray that all may go well with you and that you may be in good health, as it goes well with your soul.
> – 3 JOHN 1:2

God lives in us and wants to be the King of our heart. He wants all of us – spirit, soul and body! That is why He also speaks to us through dreams from our soul – or dreams through which we process things. He wants to help you clean up everything that gets in the way between you and Him. God can point to blockades and reveal hidden things through dreams. Dreams of the soul are often loving invitations from God to find our freedom.

I have also experienced how dreams to process things can bring us closer to God. I had many blockades and was damaged in my soul when I came to know Jesus. I was not aware of this, but I did notice that I struggled to connect with my feelings. My emotions and my will were locked away. For years I had numbed myself by working hard, exercising a lot and exhausting myself. You could say that I was afraid of feelings, I didn't know what to do with my emotions. I was convinced that my life was normal, until God started to speak to me through dreams and other ways. Hidden memories were revealed by Him and He touched my suppressed emotions. Initially I did not understand this; I hoped it was temporary. It rattled my self-defense mechanism. But my carefully constructed walls could not remain standing in the face of Jesus' love.

I was about to learn how Jesus wanted to bring restoration at a deep level. He determined the order, the speed and the manner in which it happened, and that was really good. God lovingly led me out of my emotional prison through all kinds of dreams, and reconnected my heart to my head. I learned to no longer fear my emotions and was better able to express them. This also prevented me from getting tangled in my feelings and thoughts, and the flow of living water could wash through my soul without getting stopped by all the blockades. I became a lot more sensitive to the Holy Spirit. I discovered this truth: "where the Spirit of the Lord is, there is freedom" (2 Cor. 3:17). Freedom in every part, every thought, memory and emotion.

Many people will recognize my story as their own. God wants to take you on a journey to health and connection with your soul. Then He can pour out abundant life in that part of you too. Start at the beginning. Give yourself permission to feel. You can do this in a practical sense by saying it out loud and asking God to help you. God is in our hearts and knows what is in there. Nothing is hidden for Him, not the beautiful things nor the ugly things. It really is safe with Him. He wants to lead you to more freedom, even while you are sleeping: "You have tried my heart, you have visited me by night" (Ps. 17:3a). The word "heart" has been used to replace the word "kidneys" in several places in the Bible. Yet it is the word for kidneys (*kilyah*) that has a beautiful meaning in the original text—the seat of emotion and passion. Our old nature wants to be independent; the world even promotes and celebrates independence. But God made us as emotional creatures who can live in dependance on Him.

Even medical science has evidence that the kidneys and adrenal glands are the place where memories, trauma, frustration, pain and stress are stored. This is the place God wants to search, sanctify and cleanse. The Bible says:

> I bless the LORD who gives me counsel; in the night also my heart instructs me.
> — PSALM 16:7

Most dreams are ignored because they are "only" dreams for processing emotions and thoughts, a dream in which your brain processes the impressions of the day. Some dreams are so strange and illusive that initially they may seem meaningless. But if you know that God will never leave you, that His hand is resting on you, and His Spirit lives inside of you, don't you think that He is involved in every little detail of your life? He is a good Father who is passionate about His children, and His heart goes out to you. He is the defender of your heart and the lover of your soul. What is important to you is important to Him.

Throughout the day we experience things that do something to us on the inside. We can see it as a seed that is sown in our lives. It can be from God, which is a blessing. It will sow truth and love, it will revive us, comfort us, affirm us and encourage us. Perhaps we didn't notice it, but God wants to bring it to our attention once again so that this good seed will grow roots in the soil of our hearts. This is how we learn to pay attention to what He is doing in our lives and so that we can hear His voice, see His goodness and receive His love.

The seed can also come from the enemy through a bad experience or nasty words that were spoken. Then the seed will bring fear, lies, discouragement, confusion, stress, division and doubt. We may not have even noticed that it happened, but God did and He does not want that dark seed to find a place to shoot root into our hearts. He wants to help us to be free and remain free from these things.

Now, perhaps you dream about something that you have experienced, or an event that took place. Imagine that you were to stop for a moment and ask: "What do You want to tell me about this?" Sometimes things that may seem irrelevant will have a big influence on our hearts. God says: "Keep your heart with all vigilance, for from it flow the springs of life" (Prov. 4:23). In other words, what we think, feel and do flows from our heart.

Maybe you had a bad dream in which a memory from the past came floating up. The seed that was sown into your life at the time is something you want to forget, but God wants to remove it. These dreams can bring up all kinds of things. It is often easy for us to remember the details when we talk about the dream afterward. When we awaken the dream is still pounding through our mind: "That was an awful dream! It must have been from the enemy!" I want to reassure you; the enemy cannot just walk in and out of our dreams whenever he feels like it. God watches over us in the night. He does not "slumber nor sleep" (Ps. 121:4) and He does not nod off for a moment, either. If we have closed the doors to the realm of darkness, then they remain closed at night as well. The enemy must stay out. So what do we do with a weird dream like that? It is much more likely that God's Spirit wants to make us aware of something that is in our heart. Something that is preventing us from living in the freedom that God has given us. Fear, worries, trauma, pain and shame—our heart and kidneys can be full of these things that will rob us of our peace.

Certain situations can bring up old pain and unhealed emotions. We instinctively shove those feelings into a dark corner of our soul. If those feelings are "pushed", then all the alarms go off: *Danger! Lock all the doors!* Because we often do not know how to access those painful places, the Holy Spirit will help us. Now, this may not be nice, but it is needed in order to be free and healthy. We should not worry, though; God knows what He is doing and when we are ready to take the next step in our healing. We don't need to dig around in our soul; instead we can trust God the Father and follow His lead to healing.

Does God give us fear-filled dreams? No, but we do allow fear into our life. We do that through thoughts, experiences and by believing lies about ourselves, others and God. That fear can surface in a dream. God's Spirit can show these things in a dream as an invitation to come to Him, so that He can free us from the baggage.

God has one great passion: He wants His children, the crown of His creation, to live a life of abundance so that the full sacrifice of Jesus will be at work in us. He wants us to accept His deliverance and redemption in every part of our heart, thoughts, and life. Because "you were called to freedom" (Gal. 5:13a)

The next time you have a strange or even nasty dream, or a dream that makes things come up, ask God: "Are You showing me a wound, pain or worries that are tucked away in me?" Ask the Holy Spirit to lead you and don't just ignore the pain that you find, but bring it to Jesus in prayer. Receive His cleansing for your thoughts and your soul. And if it really is "nothing but nonsense", then the Holy Spirit will tell you that too so you can shake it off.

> *Thank You, Father, that You know me inside out. Thank You for your passion to see me free. My heart and my kidneys are yours. I bring this memory / pain / fear / loneliness to You. Heal my heart and cleanse my thoughts from the memory. Will You comfort me?*
>
> *Thank You that You want to give me a new truth to replace the old lie. Will You show me what that is? Holy Spirit, help me to guard my heart and not just ignore this. Amen*

Take the time to receive the love and comfort that God gives and write down the new truth, so that you won't forget it.

Tip: If you struggle to hear God's voice clearly, then you can ask the following: "If You want me to do something with this, will You then bring it to my attention again and again? If You want me to leave it be, will You then remove it from my thoughts?"

I will share an example of a dream that I had that came from the soul. First the context of the dream and what happened prior to it. It had been a nice but busy festival; there were various game activities, bouncy castles and a party tent, my nieces were running around, friends had been over to visit and hundreds of other people had been there for the festivities. My husband and I arrived home around eight that evening. The next day I was to speak at a church and I wanted to prepare for that. I had been mulling it over all day, but due to all the activities in the past week I had not had the time to prepare in the way I wanted.

Once I was home, my head was filled with thoughts of the past day's festivities and I could not concentrate. I decided to go to bed and set the alarm for early the next morning, so that I could take the time to listen to the message that God had for this church. That night I had a dream.

DREAM
Poorly Prepared

I was in the church to speak. When I went to the front, I realized that I had forgotten my Bible. I excused myself and went in search of my Bible. I had to take a flight of stairs, and then another one and I felt extremely embarrassed that all those people had to wait for me. When I had returned, I saw that there was a screen between myself and the people. I could not see them and they could not see me. I also noticed to my horror that I was only wearing a thin, white, sheer undershirt and had forgotten my top. How was that possible?!

When I looked up again, people had stood up from their chairs. They said: "I don't believe in God." One by one they left the church hall. I looked around and thought: I will speak for a smaller group then. But then everyone stood up to leave. It was a disaster!

I awoke feeling angry and sad. I was filled with discouragement and was all tense. When I shared the dream with my husband, his first response was: "That is the enemy being nasty! He wants to discourage you before you even speak." Maybe more people would arrive at the same conclusion when they have a similar dream. But this is a typical example of a dream from the soul.

Interpretation

The dream came from my soul and showed fear that was in me. Subconsciously I was insecure about my preparation and afraid I would forget something – the Bible, the words of God. I felt like I had not done my best to seek God; the two flights of stairs that I had to run up meant that I thought I had to work to get to God. I was insecure about being able to convey the message properly, hence the screen between me and the people. And I would be ashamed of that, and that is why I had only a thin, white, sheer undershirt on, making me feel uncomfortable and embarrassed. I was afraid that I would not draw the people closer to God, but instead repulse them, hence the people leaving and saying that they did not believe in Him.

When God asked me to speak several years ago, I was very scared! I needed to break free from fear of failure and shame. Because these are old weak spots, they came back up when I was in a new situation.

In short, this dream was not a torment from the enemy, but a root of fear in me. If I had gone to the Lord the evening before, He would have removed my fear and there would have been no room for unrest.

That morning I brought my fear about not being well-prepared to God, I repented of my need to be in control, and I asked the Holy Spirit to fill me and help me to trust God. He would place the words in my mouth when I spoke. It was a perfect preparation! My speaking engagement went well that morning and many people were touched powerfully by the Holy Spirit.

If I had seen this dream as a dream from the enemy, I would not have dealt with the core issue – my own fear. Whoever is fearful believes the enemy's lies. God wants to set us free from this. The biggest battlefield in spiritual warfare is our own minds. It is of vital importance that our minds are renewed and aligned with God's truth – free from every fear, no matter how small or how great; free from insecurity, guilt and shame; free from inferiority, pride and self-righteousness; free from worries and unbelief. We have been born for this freedom, made for it, it is in our DNA. The world does not know it and is fretfully seeking this freedom. It is what was on Jesus' mind when He died for us. It is the Father's heart's desire—no longer slaves but sons. Freedom is within our reach!

How God Reveals Himself

> And the four living creatures, each of them with six wings, are full of eyes all around and within, and day and night they never cease to say, "Holy, holy, holy, is the Lord God Almighty, who was and is and is to come!"
> – REVELATION 4:8

God reveals Himself in all manner of ways. The Word says that He is both Father and Mother at the same time (Gen. 1:27). He was born as a baby and is the Ruler of heaven and earth.

His Spirit is wind, oil and fire, but also water and a dove. He is in the storm, but also in the silence and in the rushing of the wind in the tops of the trees. God cannot be captured in one image. The beings around God's throne all have eyes that see something new in Him, and they bow down again and again and cry: "Holy, holy, holy are You."

No one has ever seen God, and yet the Bible says that when we see the Son, we see the Father. Most of the time both of them are invisible. That is why it sometimes may seem that God is elusive and unknowable. But everyone has the option of knowing Him and becoming familiar with a least a part of who He is.

In our relationship with God we go through various phases. When we first become believers we probably had a different view of Him than after we have spent many years with Him. That is not a bad thing. The Holy Spirit takes us on an ever-deepening journey of knowing who God is.

A relationship with God cannot be compared to a relationship with a person. People disappoint, they are not perfect and everyone struggles with their own "beams and splinters". But God knows our deepest thoughts, intentions and feelings. Our intense desires and dreams that we probably don't dare to say out loud. He knows what we struggle with in ourselves and in the things and people around us. He knows about our unbelief and difficulties in trusting Him. He knows where we have come from and where we are going. He knows our deepest valleys and our bitter tears. He sees our joy and how we struggle with the distractions that try to draw us away from Him again and again. He knows our "if only I had ..." and our "what if?", our doubts and our pride. Our insecurities about what the future holds and the security that we try to find in all kinds of things that can never really give us security deep down inside. There is nothing that God does not know about us and yet His love for us never changes.

If we meet God in a dream, then He can show Himself in a way that will fit for us at the time. But sometimes He will also invite us to adjust our view of Him. Perhaps you struggle with seeing God as a Father because your memory of your own father wasn't very nice and you cannot imagine what a good father looks like. God may then show Himself in a different way, so that it fits with your relationship with Him at this point.

When my husband, Joost, had just become a believer and had a new relationship with God, he was serving in the army. He viewed God as the leader of the world. In a dream God showed Himself to him as President Trump. Now that would not seem like the most logical image, but it fit for Joost at the time. Because they knew each other in the dream, and how the president responded and spoke to Joost, it was clear that the dream was not about the president of America, but about God Himself.

God is Immanuel, God with us, close by and trusted. Like a Father. It is His wish that we get to know Him like that. Jesus even calls us his friends:

> No longer do I call you servants, for the servant does not know what his master is doing; but I have called you friends, for all that I have heard from my Father I have made known to you.
> – JOHN 15:15

Jesus not only calls us friends, He also tells us what God tells Him! I remember meeting Jesus in a vision in which He called me His friend. I was touched so deeply that all I could do was cry. *You call me your friend.* When I tried to tell Joost that evening, I wasn't even able to speak because of complete awe. This friendship is not cheap; it is not permission to treat Jesus as our equal. No, it actually gave me a deep awe for who He is.

Since then I often see Jesus in my dreams as my best Friend. I feel very close to Him and know that He is always near me. Often I can ask Jesus questions in the dream or talk to Him about what is happening in the dream. This is amazing and at the same time a logical result of the day-to-day relationship that I have with Him. Why wouldn't He be with us and talk to us in our dreams?

Think of all the characteristics of God that can be found in the Bible. We can also see these characteristics in a dream. A lion, king or eagle, for example. Or Jesus as a fisherman, carpenter or shepherd, as a judge or lawyer. The Holy Spirit as wind, fire, oil and water. Besides the many biblical examples there are also extra-biblical examples such as a superhero or a person of authority, the ruler of a nation. We could see Him as a doctor who is performing surgery on our soul or body.

An encounter with God in a dream can literally change you so that you awake as a different person. You could fall madly in love with a person in the dream who symbolizes God, and awaken literally drunk with love. If so, there is a big chance that you had a wonderful encounter with God.

So if you have a dream about a person that you do not know personally, but who felt very familiar in the dream, and you experienced other feelings as well in the dream ... then chances are you dreamt about God. Imagine how you see Him right now. Maybe your image of God in your dream is also in the Bible. If so, you can look it up and learn more about Him. Because your dream is an invitation to get to know God better!

Symbolic Dreams

> Behold, we were binding sheaves in the field, and behold, my sheaf arose and stood upright. And behold, your sheaves gathered around it and bowed down to my sheaf.
> – GENESIS 37:7

Anyone who reads the Bible will know that some words have more than one meaning. There is bread that we eat as a sandwich, and the Bread of Life (Jesus). The entire Bible is full of symbols and metaphors. The Old Testament was written in Hebrew, a language that is full of symbolism. Every letter has a name and a numerical value. That is so very different from our alphabet. God uses these symbols as an invitation to come to Him and to understand Him in new ways.

Most of the dreams in the Bible are symbolic. As soon as you become more aware of your dreams, you will notice that most of your dreams are symbolic too. We are easily inclined to see those dreams as "weird", but often it is the symbolism in the dream that makes them seem weird and illogical. Because we do not always understand what the dream means right away, we would rather just ignore it. Yet there is a hidden message in them. Symbols are often recognizable or evoke a certain feeling. This is what makes dreams so personal. Symbols that are in dreams are frequently objects, colors, numbers, people and animals. The surroundings in which a dream takes place can also be symbolic. Symbols often represent a part of ourselves, our life or our surroundings.

We can see an example of this in the symbolic dreams that Joseph had. The dream was about a field and about sheaves of grain (grain on the stalk that was bound together in a bundle). This was the language that Joseph spoke. He was out in the field every day; binding sheaves of grain together was a job he did on a daily basis. But he had never seen sheaves that were alive. There was a message in this symbolic dream. The sheaves symbolized himself and his brothers. It does not say if Joseph understood the dream right away, but he did take it seriously.

And God confirmed the message of Joseph's future rule in a following dream. That dream too had a lot of symbolism; Joseph often slept under the stars with his flocks.

> Then he dreamed another dream and told it to his brothers and said, "Behold, I have dreamed another dream. Behold, the sun, the moon, and eleven stars were bowing down to me."
> – GENESIS 37:9

Different symbols, same message. The eleven stars in Joseph's dream are symbolic for his eleven brothers. This brings us to the first type of symbol.

Numbers

Numbers are important in the Bible. God counts the stars (Ps. 147:4) and even weighs the water in His hand (Isa. 40:12). Every hair on our head is counted (Matt. 10:30) and God's thoughts about us are more than the grains of sand on the seashore (Ps. 139:18). The foundational languages of the Bible are full of number symbolism. That makes numbers important and significant symbols.

There was a period when I woke up every night and didn't know why. I resolved myself to check the time I woke up. This was always at 3:33 a.m. I still did not understand what this meant, but every time I lay awake, God spoke of new things that I had not heard before. I wrote them down and much of it ended up in this book. Why did I always have these nightly encounters at the same time? It was a mystery to me. Until my eye fell on the following Bible passage:

> Call to me and I will answer you, and will tell you great and hidden things that you have not known.
> – JEREMIAH 33:3

Do you see the number of this Bible verse? It was exactly the time when I woke up and God revealed things to me that I didn't yet know!

In the Bible there are several dreams with numbers. In Genesis 40, the baker and the cupbearer both had the number three in their dream, and in Genesis 41, Pharaoh had a dream about seven cows.

A number can have both a literal and a symbolic meaning, adding another layer to the message. We see an example of this in the Bible verses regarding Jesus' death and resurrection. In these we see the number three over and over again. This is no coincidence. Three means divine perfection or fullness. By repeating the number three again and again here, God shows us that Jesus is the perfect sacrifice for all humanity. Here are a few examples. Jesus was betrayed three times by Peter and died at the third hour. There were three crosses on Golgotha and after Jesus' death it became dark for three hours. He rose from the dead on the third day and Jesus' last words were three words: "It is finished" (John 19:30).

The explanation of numbers is mostly found in the Bible. That makes it a good symbol to explore. A number can have multiple meanings. The message of your dream will determine the exact meaning of the number.

You can find a podcast about numbers and their symbolic meaning on my website, ditecoumou.com.

People

People in your dreams often represent a particular character trait, talent or ministry. When you dream of someone you recognize, ask yourself these questions: What word first comes to mind when I think of that person? What do I admire about them, or what do I find unpleasant? Are there character traits in that person that I also recognize in myself? Perhaps it is a person you do not recognize but who clearly conveys a particular profession, such as a police officer or nurse. If so, it may symbolize a part of you, such as your controlling or nurturing side, in this case. What is the person in your dream doing or saying and how do you feel about it? Note that if your dream is symbolic and you are the main character, the dream is for you, even if another person appears in it. A common mistake is to project a dream onto another person, even though the message is for you and the person you are dreaming about is symbolically portraying something in the dream. Further on you will read an example of this. What can also happen is that God wants to invite you to deal with something in your heart regarding the person you are dreaming about.

Animals

Our emotions, strength or characteristics can be depicted by an animal. This makes it a common symbol in dreams. Does the animal appear in the Bible, and if so, what does it depict there? If not, how did God make this animal? What are the characteristics of this animal? Remember that God is the Creator of all animals; they are made for His glory. All of them have unique characteristics. Consider a dog, which represents loyalty and friendship, and a cat, which has an independent nature. What emotion does the animal evoke? You can also look up an animal's characteristics. For example, a wolf is a pack animal and an ant is a strong, hard worker. An animal can symbolize positive and negative messages. For example, the faithful dog is at the same time a territorial animal, which can symbolize a dark power over a certain area. What is the animal doing in your dream and what is the context of the dream? Below you can read an example of a symbolic dream about an animal.

DREAM
White Crocodile

I was with some people I could see from behind. These people felt like friends, but I didn't recognize them right away. I tried to stay with them while they kept walking away from me. In the dream, we went into the water. They sat in a boat with each other. I was alone on a surfboard. Then I saw a huge white crocodile. It appeared under the group's boat and swam in my direction. Strangely enough, I was calm as I watched the crocodile. I had seen him. As I floated away from the little boat, I suddenly saw another crocodile approaching from another side. Its mouth surfaced and bit my leg. He was holding onto my skin. I hit his nose as hard as I could, but he wouldn't let go of me. I wasn't really scared but became very worried.

Interpretation

Immediately when I woke up I knew the dream meant something and asked the Holy Spirit for the explanation. A crocodile is a predator that suddenly appears from beneath the surface of the water. It has a large mouth and a long tail that it swishes back and forth with force when it has a hold on to its prey. God showed me that the words we speak produce death or life. Then the Holy Spirit showed me that the crocodile is a picture of gossip. It is a predator and its nature is to kill, its big mouth brings death and its long strong tail spreads it.

The color of the crocodile was white, which makes you think it is clean and pure, but nothing could be further from the truth. Underneath that "pure" layer is simply a proud heart that speaks evil. Sometimes people gossip with a Christian "sauce", they portray it as a "prayer request" and they want to "not speak evil" about another person. But they are still words of death.

The crocodile had grabbed me. He could have killed me at once, but only grabbed the skin on my leg. Still, that left me unable to move. The crocodile had me in its grip. I was created to surf the waves of the movement of God's Spirit, but now I couldn't move. The setting in this case was also symbolic.

We were in the water, a spiritual environment. Think of the water flowing out of God's throne; of Jesus, the Source and of the Holy Spirit as the living water.

Through this dream, God made me aware of the influence of the gossip being spread about me by people in my spiritual environment. The enemy's purpose was to silence me so that I would stop moving with God.

I brought the dream to the Father and expressed forgiveness. I felt sad. Still, forgiveness is the key to break free from such influences. Then, in Jesus' name, I broke the spiritual powers of gossip about my life and continued doing the things God called me to do. It was like surfing!

This was a dream in which God showed His goodness. He revealed what was going on in the spiritual world. You might be mistaken and think that this dream came from the enemy. But God revealed what was hidden from me. In addition to the message, He also gave me the means to deal with it. Of course, you could get very angry at the people who gossiped or worse, start doing the same thing they did. But Jesus says, "Bless those who curse you" (Luke 6:28). I am grateful to God for showing me this and for helping me break free from the "grip" of gossip. Through this dream, I saw the impact of gossip; it was clear how violently it affects the life of that other person. Gossip seems harmless, but you give legal ground to the enemy to work through your words that bring not life but death. Do not cooperate with the devil, rather cooperate with God and speak words of life!

Suppose you dream about a pet crocodile that you cuddle and it sits on the couch. Then this has a very different meaning. You are literally sharing your home, your life, with gossip. You have become friends with gossip. Then the message could be that you need to become aware of that so that you kick your "pet" out of the house and ask God to cleanse your heart and your lips. It's another example, with the same symbolic animal.

So, like other symbols, animals can have positive as well as negative meanings in dreams. The latter does not mean that these animals are made for Satan's work. There are all sorts of wild ideas about that. Black cats are said to bring the devil into your home and owls are said to attract demons. That is nonsense, superstition and lies! God is the Creator of all animals; Satan is incapable of creating even a mosquito. Yes, the devil uses animals, and other things that belong to God, to do His work, but that is another story. He steals them. God did not make any animal to be in the service of Satan. Just as no one was made to be in the service of Satan. The fear people have about such things is a magnet for lies from the enemy. Let's repent of it and enjoy God's creation, made to show His majesty and exalt Him.

> And I heard every creature in heaven and on earth and under the earth and in the sea, and all that is in them, saying, "To him who sits on the throne and to the Lamb be blessing and honor and glory and might forever and ever!"
> – REVELATION 5:13

Objects

An object in a dream may suddenly become magnified or have a distinct color. Such an object attracts your attention and plays a role in your dream. Let's get started with these questions: What is this object used for? What does it stand for? What was I doing with this object in the dream? Was there anything abnormal about it? For example, the color or the size? What does this object say to me personally? What does it evoke in me? Is the object in the Bible, and if so, in what context? These questions can help you figure out the meaning. If you don't know, it may help to look up the object online. The meaning of your dream cannot be found on the internet, but facts can easily be found there. The Holy Spirit does not leave you as soon as you turn on the computer.

Names

Names are an interesting symbol. As with other symbols, the question is: Is this name literal or symbolic? Do you know someone with that name? Who is that to you? Is it a place name? Write the name down and see if it has meaning or a deeper layer. God once gave me a dream with a place name: Nieuwland (Dutch for Newland). Now look at this name differently – new land. The name suddenly takes on a very different meaning than a place of residence. Does the name appear in the Bible? If so, what does this biblical person or place stand for? Below you will read an example of a dream with a name in it.

DREAM
Gold Found

I had a short dream in which I was in the place where I used to live. There I saw a girl with who was a classmate of mine as a child, her name was Leora. She pointed to my house and said, "Here!" It was as if she wanted to show me something.

Interpretation

I was on vacation in France at the time I had the dream. I was writing this book and God talked a lot about the "gold" He put in me, encouraging me. He wanted it to work with me in this book. Some of the gold He was talking about I recognized, but some of it I didn't. I asked Him where I had lost gold. This was the context of the dream.

I didn't understand why that girl was in my dream, I hadn't seen her in twenty-five years and had never thought about her. After many questions and especially sitting in silence with God, suddenly the penny dropped—her name! Leora... if you take that name apart you get Le or a. In French it says *l'or a*, which means *to have the gold*. She pointed to the house where I used to live. The meaning of the dream was the answer to my question to God—where is the gold? Here, this place has the gold! During the time I lived in that house I had a traumatic experience, which caused me to partially lose sight of the gold within myself. But God did not lose it, He showed me where it lay. He wanted to heal me in a deeper way from what had happened there. When I had the dream, I was surrounded by French-speaking people. God took me into another way of understanding Him—in French. He knew that if I discovered the meaning, my trust in Him and in myself would immediately increase!

Environment

The environment in which your dream takes place often tells you a lot and can be symbolic. Let's take a house as an example; a common symbol in dreams. A house can stand for your life. This is how Jesus says:

> And the rain fell, and the floods came, and the winds blew and beat on that house, but it did not fall, because it had been founded on the rock.
> — MATTHEW 7:25

This parable is a literal example with a symbolic layer. Who is the rock? Jesus Christ. And what is the house? Our life. A literal house of stone is not of eternal value, but our life is. Jesus makes us aware in this verse that we may build our lives on Him, the only solid ground.

When a house appears in your dream, ask yourself these things: Is it a recognizable house? What does it look like? Where are you in the house? What is happening in the house? How do you feel? The room in the house can be symbolic. Think of the bathroom, where you can wash yourself. The kitchen, where (spiritual) food is prepared. The bedroom, a private place where there is peace and intimacy. The attic, where you'd rather not go because all the junk is stored there. You can read an example of a dream about a house in the chapter 'Encouraging Dreams' (page 97).

There are also other symbolic environments that are common. For example, an airport, which can indicate a transition—after all, you are flying to another place in a short period of time. A jungle in which a way has to be found through the thick growth. A pool, sea or water, which represents the spiritual environment.

The environment in a dream can also be literal—your former elementary school that brings back certain memories, or your grandparents' garden. Ask yourself, what does this environment do in me? What emotion does it evoke?

Below is another example of a dream of God containing a symbolic environment and a person with symbolic meaning.

DREAM
Transition Through Intimacy

I am in an airport and have a task there: I have to look for the rooms where speeds and directions are determined. The person who helps me and shows me the way is evangelist and author Michael Koulianos. He works at the airport and knows every place like the back of his hand. I walk around the airport with him. I go up flights of stairs and take elevators. Sometimes I lose him and start running; I get rushed and therefore uncertain and confused. I see myself running faster and faster across the airport, in all directions, looking for stairs going up.

The stairs disappear before my eyes and I can't find the rooms.

Then I find Michael again. I stop running and walk quietly but determinedly and we find the next room. This occurs a few times; I walk away from Michael and start running, all the stairs going up disappear, then I find him again and we walk calmly but quickly to the next room.

Then Michael takes me to a place with a large open body of water. In the water there are some huge sharks. He says, "Now swim!" And I enter the water, and with my eyes raised I swim on my back to the other side.

That was the end of the dream.

Interpretation

This is an insightful dream from God. It is symbolic and I am the main character. The airport represents the transition period I was in when I had this dream (context).

I had first seen the man in my dream, Michael Koulianos, at a conference several weeks before the dream. This man has a wonderful global ministry. I was deeply impressed by the intimacy he has with Jesus and how he spoke about it. It changed my life and I experienced how Jesus invited me to experience deeper intimacy with Him from that moment on.

In the dream, Michael Koulianos represents my intimacy with Jesus. The rooms where speed and direction are determined represent the effect of that intimacy. By walking with Jesus, I will see that my direction and speed are determined by Him. He is the driving force in my life.

Every time I walk away from Jesus and try to manage things myself—changes, speed or direction—progress stops. The steps disappear, and as a result I remain stuck at the same point. I run but don't make progress. I get confused and start doubting.

Fortunately, I quickly return to "Michael", to intimacy with Jesus, and so I learn more and more not to lean on my own mind but on Jesus alone. To not run and rush, but to stay with Him.

The sharks and the water represent my greatest fear. All my life I have been afraid of swimming in open water, but in the dream I do. I enter the water and I surrender more deeply to Jesus. On my back I don't see the sharks, but I look up, to the sky. Through this period of transition, I get to continue to deal with fear together with Jesus. Even my very greatest fears go away! A time of transition can feel very strange and even unpleasant. How loving of the Father that He gave me clarity in this time through this dream. Through it I knew what Jesus was doing in me and what my focus in it should be—staying close to Him and not running and flying by myself. Trusting God above every fear and surrendering myself more deeply to Him.

Colors

God loves colors. The first sign He gave us after the flood was the rainbow. He could have given a sign in so many other ways, but chose an exuberant show of color. Seven beautiful colors as a sign of His endless faithfulness. It is no accident that there are seven; seven is the number of perfection. There is a reason why we cannot find the beginning and end of a rainbow, God's faithfulness is eternally and endlessly perfect.

Have you ever paid attention to what colors you dream? Whether your dreams are in color or not is very personal. One person always dreams in color or just in shades of gray. It doesn't necessarily say anything about the source of your dream. When you dream in color, the colors can be like in everyday life, but they can also be faint or just tremendously bright and even unrecognizable. I have even heard an example of someone who is completely colorblind, dreaming in color!

When you dream in color, but nothing stands out to you, then that is not a symbol through which God wants to speak. Does a certain color become clearly visible, or do you notice something else about the colors? Then there is a good chance that God wants to say something with it. So a color in your dream can have a symbolic meaning. The meaning of the color can be either positive or negative, as you saw in the dream about the white crocodile. Always keep consulting the Holy Spirit on this and don't rely on your own understanding more than on the wisdom of God.

There is much to say about symbols in your dreams. Ideally, we would like to find a list of absolute meanings. Even though there are some general symbols with corresponding meanings, we can never establish them as facts. Just look at the Bible. In Luke 13 a seed stands for faith, but in 2 Corinthians 9 seed stands for giving and in Matthew 13 for spiritual nourishment. If the Bible gives multiple meanings to one symbol, we cannot stick to just one meaning. So always consult the Holy Spirit; interpretation flows from relationship with Him.

On my website ditecoumou.com you will find a podcast on colors and their symbolic meaning and a series on symbols in dreams and visions.

Missing the Mark With an Interpretation

> For we are his workmanship, created in Christ Jesus for good works, which God prepared beforehand, that we should walk in them.
> — EPHESIANS 2:10

We can learn from mistakes. That is why I want to share with you how I have missed the mark with an interpretation. We should not be afraid to make mistakes. That fear paralyzes and prevents us from moving forward, yet it is in the movement that we are affirmed and grow. God says in His Word that we can walk in the works that He has prepared for us ahead of time. I like the way the word "walk" symbolizes movement; you cannot walk without it. Moving into that which God has planned for you and prepared for you. That does not rule out making mistakes, because He knows that we will learn from them and become more bold and not worry about losing face as we advance God's Kingdom.

The main person determines the meaning of the dream. Are you the one doing things and interacting with your surroundings? Then you are the main person and the message of the dream is for you. This is where most of the mistakes are made with dream interpretation, so we need to keep this in mind. In the following dream you can read how I was the main character; I got into the helicopter, felt the speed and was in contact with the people in the dream. I was given the gifts and felt the excitement about receiving them. That meant that the message of the dream was for me. When another person is in dreams like this, they are often symbolic for a characteristic. In the following dream the other person symbolized worship.

DREAM
A Helicopter Flight

I dreamt that I got into a helicopter with a young man I know. I will call him Tim. He got into the pilot's seat and started the helicopter. We took off and accelerated at a tremendous speed, flying up so fast that I squeezed my eyes shut and held on to Tim. When I opened my eyes again, I saw that Jesus was holdimg the control stick. He was taking the helicopter to different places. I had never been there before, and every time we landed in a new place, I got out to explore. I came across the most beautiful things, and Jesus said, "Take it!" I was tremendously surprised and delighted by the gifts and felt intensely happy to be able to take them home and share them with others.

When I woke up, I wrote the dream in my phone. When I met Tim that same day, I shared the dream with him and I said, "I believe that God is going to take you on a journey and is going to teach you to fly." It was a nice message for him, but I was totally wrong! The dream was not meant for Tim, but for me. Later that day I heard the soft voice of the Holy Spirit: "The dream was for you." I answered: "What did I miss, Lord?" God said, "How did I create Tim?" I started to think about him. He is a true worshiper, so that is something of God that Tim carries inside of him. Immediately the Holy Spirit confirmed my thoughts and said, "While you are in worship, I take you to new places where you have not yet been. Your worship opens doors to heavenly storehouses, where gifts are waiting that I want to give to people on earth." Wow, that was a totally different meaning than what I first thought! So you see, I made a mistake but that was not a bad thing. I learned from this and other mistakes. Our relationship with God is always the first goal. Whether or not we interpret a dream correctly is less important than our relationship with Him.

Common Dreams

> Oh, that I had wings like a dove! I would fly away and be at rest (...)
> – PSALM 55:6

I will share some common symbolic dreams as I am sure there will be some that everyone will recognize, and perhaps you have dreamed these as well. I will help you a little with the interpretation, but keep in mind that the meaning of your dream may be more extensive or very different.

Flying

The dreams in which we can fly are amazing! It is something that we cannot do in day-to-day life, but in our dreams it is possible. If you have had a dream in which you can fly, you can ask the following questions: What am I flying in or on? Where am I flying to? What is happening around me and how does it make me feel? Perhaps you feel as though you are rising above yourself in a certain area in your life. You were created to live by God's Spirit. His Spirit is not bound to a location and is not oppressed by heaviness. God can show you that in a dream.

> If we live by the Spirit, let us also keep in step with the Spirit.
> – GALATIANS 5:25

Falling

The opposite of flying is falling. Dreams in which you are falling occur often and are often not pleasant. You can ask the following questions if this occurs: Where are you falling off of? Where are falling into or onto? What is the landing like? What do you feel during the dream? Could it be that you feel like you are not able to hang on in real life? Are you afraid of losing control? Perhaps you land softly or you are caught halfway and you do not need to remain in control.

Being pursued

Many people have dreams in which they are being pursued. You run away quickly because you do not want to be caught. Ask yourself: Who or what is pursuing you? Many people struggle with pressure at work, or stress. You could be pursued by your boss, or a clock, or even by your agenda. Or what about being pursued by money, or your wallet? You could be pursued by something or someone that you are afraid of. Ask yourself: What am I trying to suppress in my emotions? Is there something that I would rather not deal with?

Unable to move forward

This is something that many people recognize—they want to run and cannot seem to move forward, or only very slowly. It often is an unpleasant feeling. You could ask yourself: Can it be that you are doing too much and have lost yourself in the process? Do you feel worn out and exhausted? Many people feel overwhelmed by life and the pressures of society. Make sure you rest enough. Fill yourself with the Word of God and ask God if He will lift you up above all of this. He promises:

> (...) but they who wait for the LORD shall renew their strength; they shall mount up with wings like eagles; they shall run and not be weary; they shall walk and not faint.
> — ISAIAH 40:31

Arriving late

Everything is fast-paced nowadays and we always have to be on time. The clock is like a referee running our day. It is not strange that many people dream about arriving late at a meeting, bus or train station, or an airport. You could ask yourself: In which area do I feel like I cannot keep up or am unable to fully function? Take a moment with the Prince of Peace (Isa. 9:6); He can give you the much-needed rest for the day that lies ahead. You can also dream that you have taken the wrong taxi, turnoff or airplane, or that you have forgotten your train ticket, wallet or passport. Ask yourself: Are there situations in my life in which I am afraid of making the wrong decision? Is there something that I am missing that I need in order to reach my destination? What am I missing on my way to the destination? Destination is often an image of our calling.

Connection
We are no longer able to function without them and they connect us to the entire world—a smartphone and a laptop. Ask yourself: What is happening in the dream with the laptop or smartphone? Who are you trying to connect to? Does the phone no longer work, or have you lost it? It could be that you miss connection in your life or you struggle to connect. Do you feel out of reach for other people? A dream like this is something that we need to pay attention to.

Water
Dreams about water, drowning, floating or breathing under water are quite common. Ask yourself: Do you feel like you are being thrown into the deep end? Or that the water is up to your mouth? Are you perhaps performing an exceptional feat at this time, like breathing underwater? Dreams that say something about a new season in your life often involve crossing a river or sea, as Moses crossed the parted sea with the Israelites. Water can also be a picture of your spiritual environment.

Testing
Dreams about taking a test or passing an exam can make you feel uncomfortable. Ask yourself: Are you prepared for the test in the dream? Do you feel you have to show what you have to offer? Do you feel you have to perform? Perhaps you expect this of yourself. Or are you ready to be "tested" because you have grown recently?

Teeth

Another subject that is familiar to many people—teeth that fall out, are just growing or rotting away. These dreams can really scare you for a while. Your teeth are for chewing; in this case, think of the spiritual food you chew. Do you need wisdom? Then you may dream that you are missing a tooth. Or, on the contrary, do you receive wisdom from God in the form of a golden tooth? It also relates to your appearance, your smile and your personality. Do you worry about how you come across and what others think about you? Ask God for wisdom or ask Him to help you grow in identity and self-esteem.

Cars

Many people dream about a car over which they have lost control or the brakes don't work. Perhaps you are not behind the wheel yourself and that worries you. Ask yourself: Who is behind the wheel? Is it Jesus, who you have asked to lead your life? Is the car moving forward or backward or in danger? Is there enough gas in it? Or, are there no brakes? Can you see what the car looks like? A car often speaks of your life's journey, including your ministry. You may feel that God is increasing your speed or you may be afraid of losing control or direction. You may also receive another car from God in a dream. Take note the details, such as the color, model and size.

The following is an example of a dream with a car:

DREAM
The Car Switch

I was riding in a car on a dark road. It felt safe, like being in a protective bubble. An oncoming car approached, then stopped in front of me. I stopped too, and while there was no one in sight, the other car's door swung open. I was surprised and my interest was piqued. I turned off my engine, took off my seat belt and opened my door. I knew there was going to be a car swap and that the intention was to leave my car behind. I got out of my car and took a seat in the new car. It was a large, strikingly tall pickup truck with large all-terrain tires in a shiny black color.

God had called me to go into new areas as a prophetic forerunner and discover mysteries of God to pass on again to others. The color of the car was black, the color of mystery. The tires could reach difficult terrain. The car was high; this gave a better view and the ability to see beyond other cars. It was a three-seater, showing that I would not be going with many people, but that I could take a lot back in the trunk to hand out again. A prophetic image hidden in a car. That's what makes a car an interesting symbol!

The Click

> When the Spirit of truth comes, he will guide you into all the truth, for he will not speak on his own authority, but whatever he hears he will speak, and he will declare to you the things that are to come.
> – JOHN 16:13

You walk through your dream holding the Spirit's hand. You write down what you see and describe what you feel. The Holy Spirit shows you what needs your attention and what is not important. His light shines on the highlights and peels back the deeper layers. When the complete picture is visible, there it is—the "click". Your spirit says, "Yes, this is it!" You experience God's peace and presence. There is such a confirmation! He speaks to you and is involved in your life.

This click is your goal when interpreting your dream. The Holy Spirit points you to that which your spirit already knew. It feels like a key fitting in a keyhole; it clicks into place!

If you do not (yet) have this click, but you cannot get the dream out of your mind, then take a step back and look again. Sometimes you need to look at it with a little more intention, or from a fresh perspective. You could ask someone to pray with you about your dream. Daniel also asked his friends to pray with him about the dream that God had given Nebuchadnezzar (Dan. 2:17-18). Keep in mind that the interpretation comes from God and not from people. He speaks through His Spirit to you and to others. You could see it like a flashlight; we all have one and together we have more light, and therefore we see more. Some people are given the gift of dream interpretation by God, others can help because they dream often themselves. Keep in mind that the Holy Spirit spoke to you personally through a dream, focused on your emotions and experiences. Do not let someone talk you into an interpretation that you do not feel a "click" with.

Again, the context is important, even when someone is helping you with the interpretation of your dream. Some people think that Daniel was a dream interpreter who could just interpret people's dreams without any additional information, but that was not the case. Keep in mind that King Nebuchadnezzar did not know God at the time he had his dream. He needed a mediator in order to reach the Giver of his dream. Besides that, Daniel worked for the king, he knew him and knew about his daily affairs. So he understood the context of the dream. He also knew that the king lived in a palace where there was a lot of silver and gold—symbols that were present in his dream and of which Daniel knew what they represented. The king had also indicated that his "spirit was troubled" (Dan. 2:1), which told Daniel something about the king's emotions in the dream. God then gave Daniel the interpretation:

> Then the mystery was revealed to Daniel in a vision of the night. Then Daniel blessed the God of heaven.
> – DANIEL 2:19

We read the same about Joseph and Pharaoh's dream. Joseph knew God and knew that only He could interpret the dream. So Joseph was the mediator between God and the unbelieving Pharaoh. He was focused on serving Pharoah with the interpretation of his dream.

> And Pharaoh said to Joseph, "I have had a dream, and there is no one who can interpret it. I have heard it said of you that when you hear a dream you can interpret it." Joseph answered Pharaoh, "It is not in me; God will give Pharaoh a favorable answer."
> – GENESIS 41:15-16

You can ask the Holy Spirit for confirmation if you are in doubt. If it is urgent, then He will give you the same dream again, in the same or varying form so that you will understand. He does not abandon His children when they do not understand Him right away. Pharaoh had two dreams with the same message:

> And the doubling of Pharaoh's dream means that the thing is fixed by God, and God will shortly bring it about.
> – GENESIS 41:32

Maybe you want to help someone with their dream. Then keep in mind that the Holy Spirit speaks to you, but also to the person in question. The Holy Spirit convinces the dreamer of the truth and will give the click. You can serve the other and walk with them, holding God's hand.

Clean Glasses

> [God gives] to another the working of miracles, to another prophecy, to another the ability to distinguish between spirits (...) All these are empowered by one and the same Spirit, who apportions to each one individually as he wills.
> — 1 CORINTHIANS 12:10-11

If you are going to interpret your own dreams or the dreams of someone else, it is important to have "clean glasses". In other words, a clear view based on God's Word and through His Spirit, not clouded by pain or wounds in the soul. The danger of these wounds is that your pain or experiences can cloud your vision, like a milky filter. The dream will look very different to you and you will have a clouded interpretation. No one is perfect, and that has never been an obstacle for God to work through people. But be aware of your responsibility for the condition of your glasses when you start to interpret dreams.

We can hear what God says, or we can listen selectively. That means, hearing what we think we should or want to hear. I will give an example. The weather report says that tomorrow will be a bright sunny day with a chance of thunderstorms in the evening. Selective hearing is that we hear that tomorrow will be a bright, sunny day, because we have plans to go out for the day. Listening with dirty glasses means hearing mostly or only that there will be thunderstorms, and listening through glasses clouded with fear and pain is hearing that the thunderstorms will ruin the bright and sunny day. All three conclusions are partially true, but what do we emphasize? It is important to have the Holy Spirit clean and polish our glasses. The fact that we have provided a good interpretation one or more times does not mean that our glasses have been cleaned once and for all. We must keep returning to the Source of living water.

God wants to give us another gift besides cleansing our glasses. Perhaps one of the greatest gifts of this time—the gift of discernment. This gift makes it possible for us to discern the source. Does this originate from God's Spirit, from our flesh or from the devil? This is vital to hearing from God and interpreting our dreams. It is the gift of the Holy Spirit.

We can ask for this gift. Just as with every other gift of the Holy Spirit we are given this gift to use. That sounds like a given, but for many people a gift is still a kind of medal that they hang in a showcase, only to be worn for special occasions. But a gift from God is for every day and for every situation. It is likely that you will notice that you have received a gift when you start to operate in it. He will make you more sensitive to the things that He speaks. When you speak to another person, you will notice more readily if someone says something that is inspired by God, even if that person does not know this themselves. You will also know when something is inspired by the enemy and that it is meant to twist the truth, to discourage and to cause division. If you want to find out what the source of your dream is, you will find that the line between a dream from your soul and through which God is speaking, and a dream from God, is very thin. In that case it is not so much important to discern the correct source; it is more important to find the message hidden in the dream. The gift of discernment will help you with that and will teach you to recognize what God wants to say and what your soul is trying to tell you. In the following chapter you will read several examples of dreams that may have a very different message than you initially may think.

Difficult Dreams

> But he said to me, "My grace is sufficient for you, for my power is made perfect in weakness."
> – 2 CORINTHIANS 12:9

There are certain subjects that people would rather not dream about. They are uncomfortable or raise a lot of questions. Remember that 'God is love' (1 John 4:8), there is no trace of darkness in Him (1 John 1:5). He does not want us to be fearful or confused when we wake up. At the same time the Holy Spirit may want to get our attention with a dream that awakens us to reality, so that we do not miss it and can no longer suppress it. The key is being honest with ourselves and with God.

What kind of subjects make us uncomfortable?

First of all: **war**. These can be very intense dreams. Have you been through a war and are the images of this surfacing? This can be very intense. You would rather never think of it again, but God wants you to be free. He wants to remove those images from your mind's eye and heal your heart from those traumatic experiences. Dreams about war can also be symbolic and may be from an internal struggle. The question is: What is happening in your dream and what is your emotion? Is this fear, or anger, or something else? Ask yourself what you are in conflict with. Something, someone or a part of yourself? God wants to bring you back to a healthy connection with yourself or the other person.

Imprisonment is another difficult dream subject. Dreams in which you are imprisoned or bound to something can really upset you. Ask yourself the following questions: Which part of you is not free? Who or what makes you feel bound or trapped? What are you keeping yourself imprisoned in? What do you not dare to make public? God wants to help you break free from these things.

There are few subjects that make us more uncomfortable as **intimacy** in dreams. Especially if it is about us hugging, kissing or having sex with someone other than our partner. Usually these dreams indicate a connection with someone, or a desire for relationship. Who do you want to have a stronger bond with, more openness or connection? Or do you want to be more in contact with yourself? Perhaps there are parts of yourself that you are not in contact with right now? These dreams are not to be confused with dreams that have been inspired by an unclean spirit. These unclean spirits can be present in your life through things like looking at pornographic material in your past or present. If that is the case, then make sure you get rid of it. You can ask for help with this, you do not need to do this alone.

Dreams about **dying** are often unpleasant, because they bring confusion or fear. Usually such dreams are about something dying on the inside of you. That could be pride, self-righteousness or control. The Bible speaks extensively about laying down our life in order to receive Jesus' life:

> Truly, truly, I say to you, unless a grain of wheat falls into the earth and dies, it remains alone; but if it dies, it bears much fruit.
> – JOHN 12:24

Maybe you have asked God to remove something from you. If another person is in the dream, then the question is: What does this person represent, what characterizes that person? Are you afraid of death? God wants to remove that fear.

Nakedness is a familiar theme in dreams. Ask yourself if you feel unprepared or vulnerable. On the contrary, have you consciously begun to show more of yourself recently? If so, this may reveal fear or shame. Ask God for help in this situation. It is in our vulnerability that His power becomes most apparent. You may not experience the nakedness as vulnerable at all in the dream and have become increasingly comfortable with showing your vulnerability.

Pregnancy or **childbirth** is also a topic with a guaranteed shock effect, especially when men dream about it! Suddenly you find yourself in the middle of childbirth or find that you have been pregnant for months. It can leave you unsettled, confused and anxious, even though it is often a beautiful thing. Just as Mary became pregnant when the Holy Spirit came upon her, we too can become "pregnant" after being touched by the Holy Spirit. God has put something new in you, a gift, desire or plan, something He wants to do through you. He has chosen you for it and knows you can carry it. What do you feel in the dream? Do you perhaps doubt your own ability to carry or raise this "child"? Or are you afraid that your surroundings will react strangely to your "baby"? Ask the Holy Spirit for insight, He wants to help you.

These are some examples of dreams from your soul that God wants to speak through. There is no need to be alarmed; He wants to lead you to freedom and a deeper connection with Him, yourself and others. If you have received a similar dream, first assess what the source of your dream is. Is the dream coming from your soul and is the Holy Spirit shining His light on something? Or is the dream coming from the enemy? Usually it will be the former, and you can work through it with God.

A Dream With Impact

> As I was considering, behold, a male goat came from the west across the face of the whole earth, without touching the ground. And the goat had a conspicuous horn between his eyes.
> — DANIEL 8:5

Some dreams in the Bible are so strange that it upsets the dreamer. Daniel had a dream about the end of time. This dream was full of monstrous figures, an army of stars and a place he called "the glorious land". The Bible passage above is part of that dream.

Just imagine—a goat is in reality 80 centimeters tall at most, but here it suddenly travels over the whole earth and does not touch the ground. Isn't that strange? God could have just told Daniel the whole message. But He chose to do it this way—a symbolic vision to one person about something that affects the whole earth. It gets even stranger when Daniel tries to understand what he sees:

> When I, Daniel, had seen the vision, I sought to understand it. And behold, there stood before me one having the appearance of a man. And I heard a man's voice between the banks of the Ulai, and it called, "Gabriel, make this man understand the vision."
> – DANIEL 8:15-16

Imagine this: Jesus (for we now know this is Jesus) tells the angel Gabriel to explain the vision to Daniel. When Gabriel stands beside Daniel and begins to speak, Daniel falls down as if he was dead (Dan. 8:17)! The whole experience must have had a tremendous impact on him. In fact, it is so overwhelming for Daniel that he is sick with bewilderment for several days after seeing this heavenly image (Dan. 8:27). No one knows what he has seen and he probably cannot put it into words. Daniel is unable to process this quickly. But God chooses him to serve all generations after him.

Keeping your feelings

Daniel is not the only one who was so overwhelmed. The apostle Paul was not approachable after his encounter with Jesus on the road to Damascus, and John, in Revelation must have been equally awestruck. What they saw and experienced was incomprehensible, just as it was with Daniel. The message they received had impact, but probably the feeling they had while receiving it was at least as overwhelming. But even if you don't see images about the end of the world, you can be quite overcome when you meet God. Take your time to process this.

Daniel wrote down his encounter with God, and that must have helped him. We can follow his example. A dream or vision is partly about the images we see, and partly about what we feel about those images. These feelings shape the dream. For example, you see a beautiful field of flowers with all kinds of colors. That is beautiful but not life-changing. However, the freedom you experience in that field of flowers may be greater than you have ever known! That is what characterizes the dream and what you want to remember about it. Besides "seeing", other senses may prevail in your dream. One person feels what God wants to speak and another just knows. Yet another hears tones or smells odors. God can use all of our senses to express His heart, and it is the same with dreams. You can describe these things, but you can also paint, sing or express everything through dance. In this way you can recall the dream and experience it again. You keep the feelings in your heart, so to speak. You want to preserve God's gift in a way that best expresses what it is. Be yourself and be creative, even if you normally never are. Take time to capture the essence of the precious encounter. It doesn't have to meet worldly standards of beautiful or good. After all, your dream doesn't fit within those standards, either. Just start and let God's Spirit guide you. As time passes, it can be so good to be able to look at something tangible that takes you back to that one special encounter.

How Do You Write Down a Dream?

> And the LORD answered me: "Write the vision; make it plain on tablets, so he may run who reads it.
> — HABAKKUK 2:2

Dreams are outside time and place. They go beyond our logical frameworks. You can dream that you are a child again, or dream about something that is yet to take place.

You can dream about a 5-meter object in a room with a 2-meter ceiling, and it still fits. During the dream, everything seems completely normal, but when you wake up, you realize how strange that was. When we tell or write down our dreams, we imperceptibly try to place them within a framework of time, place and logic. As a result, we bend the dream so that we somewhat understand it. As a result, we may miss the message of the dream.

All kinds of things can help us keep our dreams without changing them. I have mentioned this tip before—when you wake up, grab your phone and record your dream. That way you have the dream recorded immediately, before your head starts telling you what is not possible.

You can write down your dream in a circle instead of between the lines. This sounds a little crazy, but it helps to not look at your dream directly from your rationale. The circle takes you out of your logical thinking.

It's a good idea to make drawings of your dream. Sketch the pictures you saw and write down words that describe the feeling you had during the dream.

You can also write out your dream in mind map form. The main character is placed in the center of your paper and each aspect of the dream is placed in a cloud around it.

As I mentioned earlier, the feeling you had during the dream and the atmosphere of the dream is important. Your feeling often tells part of message already. Suppose you dream that you can fly. You enjoy it and don't think it is strange at all. This tells you that you were made to move in the Spirit and not in the flesh. You were made to do impossible things with God. The fact that you don't think it is strange to fly in your dream tells you the truth ... even if it is miles away from what is happening in your life right now.

Here is another example, but the other way around. You dream that you are at work. You are sitting at your desk and your boss walks in. You give your pen to your boss. On that pen is the word "future". After you do this, you feel sad and angry. What happens in your dream is not really something to be very angry and sad about. Yet your feelings are telling the truth. As you surrender your pen to your boss, this is a symbolic image of the authority you give to your boss to write your future. In other words, how your future turns out has a very large part to do with your job and depends on your boss. It is quite logical that this makes you sad and angry; that pen should not be owned by your boss, it belongs in the hands of God. He is writing your future together with you!

Do you see that your feelings during your dream are very decisive? Try to capture the dream as much as possible as it was. You don't want to reduce that special, wild, wonderful encounter to some words on paper. Find a way that suits you and write or draw out the dream. Just like that, you can break open the meaning of the dream.

I Am Doing Something New

> He did not speak to them without a parable, but privately to his own disciples he explained everything.
> — MARK 4:34

Do you recognize this? Suddenly you don't have clear dreams, or you don't hear God's voice like you did before. And just when things seemed to be going so well! Or you get overwhelmed by all the things you experience in the spiritual world and can't see clearly anymore. Negative thoughts swarm around your head and whisper, "I must be doing something wrong," or "God is not speaking to me at all." Yet these thoughts are all lies! Laugh loudly in the face of them.

God is inviting you to hear His voice in other ways and is taking you into something new. Follow Jesus into a new way of listening. There is so much more and He wants to speak in and through your life. This is just the beginning!

No matter how experienced or inexperienced you are in hearing God's voice, His desire remains the same—a relationship with you, close, honest and open. If you are struggling to understand God well, you need to take time to sit at His feet. For a moment, shut out all noise and become still. Let your heart be filled anew with peace and faith, and realize: God has never been gone.

What an incredible promise—when we are alone with Jesus, He wants to explain to us what we do not yet understand. Walk with Jesus, watch Him and learn from Him. We will never finish discovering in Him. There is always something new.

PART | 6

There is Always More With God

> (…) for he gives to his beloved sleep.
> — PSALM 127:2b

You are God's darling, and He wants to give you what you need in your sleep—rest and restoration, dreams from His heart and much more. You may find the following chapters challenging—you may have never heard about certain opportunities to receive from heaven before. Angels, divine "downloads" and sacred encounters—God gives special and challenging invitations to partner with Him. This is accessible to everyone. Moreover, we cannot adapt the good news of the gospel to our standards and limited way of understanding. Jesus is the standard and He walked in these things. Open your heart so that your faith can grow. Faith is the hope for the things you don't yet see (Heb. 11:1). If you are hungry for more of God in your nights, and you want to *see* it, faith is the key that opens new doors. Let's dive deeper into the heavenly encounters we can have in the night.

You Are New

> Therefore, if anyone is in Christ, he is a new creation. The old has passed away; behold, the new has come.
> — 2 CORINTHIANS 5:17

When I think of the opportunities in our sleep, my head spins. But since there are no limitations in God, we too should not limit our thinking. So my daily prayer is, "Father, I give You permission to take away the limitations I have placed on You. I want to know You as You really are." I don't think we have any idea how often we still put God in a box so that He fits in our heads. For example, how often do we think God speaks only in "Christian ways" such as through Christian music, the Bible and the like? The first time I found out that this is not so went like this: I was exercising and having a hard time. My body was telling me it couldn't last much longer. Then the sports instructor spoke these words, "Don't give up, you don't know your own strength and can handle much more than you think!" Suddenly my thoughts became crystal clear. God spoke to me and encouraged me through a sweaty sports instructor. Not primarily to finish my workout, but in other areas where I needed encouragement in that moment. I laughed to myself about God's creative way of speaking and about my own small-mindedness. How could I have ever imagined that God would be limited by anything! God made, saved and conquered the world; would anything stop Him from speaking?

Perhaps you are reading this and think it is funny, and it is! Think about how often you still make such boxes for God. What do the boxes you have formed for Him look like? What do you really believe about Him? The conclusion: God is simply incomprehensible and His ways are unfathomable. There is only one thing to do—we should not try to make God fit into us; rather, we fit into Him. We dwell in a new world; our lives are "hidden with Christ in God" (Col. 3:3).

From the moment your mouth said "yes" to Jesus, you were transferred in an instant from the kingdom of darkness to the Kingdom of His light. You were torn loose from the bonds of the world and placed in Christ, who sits at the right hand of God. The charges against you were erased and your name was written down in the Book of Life. Your heart of stone was taken out of you and you were given back a heart of flesh (Eze. 36:26). In that one moment, God made you a new creation. Not cleaned up or refurbished, but completely new!

When God makes something, it is not subject to the laws of the world. It is not constrained by human ability and cannot be described in a scientific framework. It is a heavenly design! As a new creation, we are not to be caught by darkness, not to be snared by the world and not to be stopped by death. We are detached from all these things and reunited with Christ.

> But he who is joined to the Lord becomes one spirit with him.
> – 1 CORINTHIANS 6:17

Separation from God is an illusion and distance is a lie. God is closer than your own breath. There is no such thing as going in and out of His presence. You are in it; that is your home, or as it says in Luke's Gospel:

> (...) nor will they say, "Look, here it is!" or "There!" for behold, the kingdom of God is in the midst of you.
> – LUKE 17:21

To learn to see what God's Spirit wants to do, we need ears to hear and eyes to see. These are not natural but spiritual senses, attuned to the Father's heart. We may come to know Him and learn to walk in the "new normal".

I used to think that everything God did or wanted to do had to be useful. God's Spirit taught me that this is not true at all. He wants to teach us to enjoy the life Jesus gives us. As a result, we may experience joy and wonder at Him and at ourselves. He has an abundant life in store for us, that is really not just filled with serious talk and serious business! Heaven celebrates over "one sinner who repents" (Luke 15:7).

I don't know how you picture that, but I believe that it's a little more lavish than a cup of coffee and a slice of cake!

We get to marvel anew at the mighty God who is our Father. Through the torn veil, we have gained sight of eternity and access to the throne of grace. Let us not remain waiting on this side of the veil. Can you remember what I wrote earlier? A sweet encounter; we are one with God, a merging that gives unlimited possibilities. As we look further into what God wants to give us in the night, we need to look at this truth with new eyes. Perhaps you have never looked at yourself this way before, but you are a walking miracle, placed on the earth for a reason and able to do all things through Him who empowers you.

We have looked at dreams in the Bible before, but as always with God, there is more! God can touch us in a radical way in the night. He already did that in Bible times and still wants to do it.

Creative Dreams

> He said, "To you it has been given to know the secrets of the kingdom of God (...)
> — LUKE 8:10a

In heaven there is provision for every shortage and a solution to every problem. There is an unstoppable flow of music, art and creations. God has in His heart the blueprint for a heavenly Kingdom on earth. He wants to give us these plans so that we can carry them out. Then we can work and protect the earth with God. Is there a problem that affects you—famine, war refugees, injustice? God wants to give you a strategy to deal with this problem! He can do this through a dream, for example.

Imagine this. You go to sleep at night just like any other night, but the next morning you get up and are capable of whole new things! Solomon experienced it: "At Gibeon the LORD appeared to Solomon in a dream by night, and God said, "Ask what I shall give you." (1 Kings 3:5).

Solomon asked for wisdom and this is how God responded:

> Because you have asked this, and have not asked for yourself long life or riches or the life of your enemies, but have asked for yourself understanding to discern what is right, behold, I now do according to your word. Behold, I give you a wise and discerning mind, so that none like you has been before you and none like you shall arise after you. I give you also what you have not asked, both riches and honor, so that no other king shall compare with you, all your days. And if you will walk in my ways, keeping my statutes and my commandments, as your father David walked, then I will lengthen your days."
> — 1 KINGS 3:11-14

What a fantastic story! Solomon becomes the wisest and richest man in the world because of that one dream, that encounter with God. His response changed his history and that of his people. A completely different way of life came to Israel—everyone was full of joy and peace, there was enough for everyone. There were so many people and yet all were free, each under his own fig tree (1 Kings 4:25). We need a government like that too!

But there are more Biblical examples. Jacob had a dream with an idea about expanding his livestock (Gen. 31:10-12). Joseph was able to help Pharaoh save the people from the famine that Pharaoh had seen in his dream (Gen. 41).

There are endless opportunities available for us to receive ideas, strategies, solutions and plans and thereby make heaven visible on earth. You don't have to be a prophet to receive a heavenly plan! Imagine restaurants with a menu full of heavenly recipes, museums with divine art and CDs with music straight from the Holy Spirit. But there is so much more—structures for businesses and insights for politics to run a country through heavenly principles, medicine that eradicate diseases for good, educational systems inspired by the best Father there is. Anything is possible!

God wanting to give people ideas like this is not new; important figures in history testify to this. Einstein was given a dream that gave him the idea for the theory of relativity, and the idea for search engine Google was given to Larry Page in a dream. The design for the needle of the sewing machine was given to Elias Howe in a dream, and that is only a small sample of the creative ideas that have been received in a dream. God is making His will known and shaping a new world according to His plan—including through dreams.

If you want to make a difference, to be a transformer, don't conform to what is already there. Go to Jesus. He is the access to all knowledge and all that is beautiful, good and righteous. All that is new is at your fingertips right now.

> *Father, thank You that I get to enjoy the gifts You gave thousands of years ago and continue to give. How wonderful to know that You want to share the treasures of hidden places with me (Isa. 45:3). I am thankful for the Holy Spirit dwelling in me and the access I have to heaven through the sacrifice of Jesus. I believe You want to give me new ideas, solutions and strategies and am ready to receive them this night. I long for You to speak to me as You spoke to Solomon. Help me to listen, understand You and walk out what You give, so that Your dream for the world may become visible on earth, through my life. Amen*

Dreams in Business

> Commit your work to the LORD, and your plans will be established.
> — PROVERBS 16:3

Do you know the story of Jacob who had to work seven years for Laban in order to marry his daughter Rachel? He was deceived by him and ended being given Laban's other daughter, Leah. Jacob had to work another seven years for the woman of his dreams. Then Laban promised him all the striped and spotted animals of his flock, and tried to deceive him. But God did not allow Jacob to be wronged again by Laban and performed a business miracle, which He showed Jacob in a dream.

> In the breeding season of the flock I lifted up my eyes and saw in a dream that the goats that mated with the flock were striped, spotted, and mottled. Then the angel of God said to me in the dream, "Jacob," and I said, "Here I am!" And he said, "Lift up your eyes and see, all the goats that mate with the flock are striped, spotted, and mottled, for I have seen all that Laban is doing to you."
> — GENESIS 31:10-12

I love how this Bible story shows that God hates injustice. He straightened out what was crooked and took care of Jacob. Jacob noticed that this was God's doing. That must have given him a huge boost after all those years of deceit and injustice: God is for me! This is what Jacob said to his wives Leah and Rachel:

> You know that I have served your father with all my strength, yet your father has cheated me and changed my wages ten times. But God did not permit him to harm me.
> — GENESIS 31:6-7

Isn't that wonderful? And still God fights for justice for His children's businesses. It is His will that things succeed. This reminds me of the following incident.

For many years I worked as a horse trainer, also riding horses for clients so that they could be sold for a good price. One of those horses had been for sale for some time. It was a beautiful horse, but somehow the sale was not going well. The owner of the horse was in a hurry because there was a baby on the way and the horse had to be sold before then. I received an email from someone who wanted to buy the horse. The horse would be shipped abroad with a special transportation company. They agreed to the asking price. Only part of the shipping had to be paid in advance, and the question was whether the seller wanted to pay a sum of €1,500 in advance to the company that would arrange the crossing. The new owner would refund this once the horse arrived safely. After some emailing back and forth, this buyer indicated that we could be sure that the horse would be fine, and even described their faith in God. It all sounded great, but that night God gave me a dream. In the dream, He showed me that we were being deceived. I saw an image of Eve being deceived by the devil in the Garden of Eden. I knew immediately that something was wrong. The next day we investigated further and found out that the company that would ship the horse did not exist. It was just an account number. After searching some more, we came across more people in the horse industry who had been scammed in this way. We immediately called off the sale. If we had gone into business with these people, we would have lost the horse and €1,500 as well. Moreover, we would never have gotten the sale amount. You see, God hates injustice and does not want you to lose business.

But the opposite also has happened, more than once. This same horse was eventually sold, also as a result of a dream. God showed me that I would meet someone through an acquaintance and even gave her name. In the dream, she bought the horse for a certain amount, and I saw that the sale happened without a hitch. The day after this dream, that acquaintance contacted me and I knew immediately what for! She introduced me to someone with exactly that name. This woman was eager to buy the horse and guess what? Exactly for the amount in the dream.

Below you can read the story of Balt, co-founder of businessasmission.com. God led him in starting a business and convinced him to do it when it seemed impossible.

Balt's story

In 2013, I started a successful business to help charities. In December 2016, I prayed for God's guidance for an opening in Africa and felt the boldness to tell God I would go to Africa the next year. It was miraculously answered, as I participated in a start-up bootcamp to create jobs for African youth. It was June and I sat there in my room in Cameroon after an intensive day on growth strategy. I was impressed by the amazing opportunities for the ICT consulting business I wanted to start. Then it began to dawn on me—who was going to lead this? My wife was fine with me going to Africa for a few weeks a year, but day-to-day management of a new company was quite something else! I broke out in a cold sweat as I realized the huge responsibility.

Prayerfully, I presented my dilemma to God. Often I receive answers through a clear dream. So I prayed for insight through a dream. By now it was well past midnight. The next morning I wanted to go to morning Mass early; the alarm clock was set for six o'clock. At five-thirty I was wide awake; clearly I had not been dreaming. I had rarely experienced that. I was shocked and unpleasantly surprised, for God practically always answered me through dreams. Still lying in my bed I wrestled with this, arguing with God. I was angry and indignant.

Apparently I fell asleep again, because at five to six I woke up after a very clear dream, which showed me that I had received this calling from God. I saw that all kinds of things from my life had prepared me for this situation. The dream was the answer to my question, "Should I set up this business, here in Africa?" God's answer was a clear yes. I had a clear task and assignment. This was a very powerful encouragement!

It has now been four years since we started Africolt.com. Many things turned out differently than planned, as usually happens when you surrender your business to God. Looking back, I am thankful for where we are today, all because of the dream God gave me!

God wants to help us work and prosper in our businesses. What He offers is more than the world can offer. He can help—and warn—us better than anyone else if we trust Him. I know several people who run their businesses in cooperation with the Holy Spirit, and it is amazing to see how God wants to bless. In the midst of society, He is thus establishing His Kingdom with new forms of business management according to His heavenly concept. A beautiful, well-run business in our neighborhood has this on the facade:

> Commit your work to the LORD, and your plans will be established.
> — PROVERBS 16:3

What an incredible testimony for the customers to see!

God's Calling

> But that same night the word of the LORD came to Nathan, "Go and tell my servant David, 'Thus says the LORD: Would you build me a house to dwell in?
> – 2 SAMUEL 7:4-5

It is possible for you to fall asleep one night and when you wake up the next morning everything is different. Your life has taken a different turn. This happened to David. That night God gave Nathan a message for David about his kingship. It is the promise that every king of Israel will come from David's family. That promise of God is completely fulfilled through Jesus, Son of David. Through Nathan's dream, David came to the place God had prepared for him.

God has a unique place for you. He is the one who will take you there if you allow it. The way there is certainly not always easy, but it is an essential part of your destiny. We see an example in Joseph, a young fellow of seventeen. Hated by his brothers, loved by his father and called by God in the night:

> Now Joseph had a dream, and when he told it to his brothers they hated him even more. He said to them, "Hear this dream that I have dreamed: Behold, we were binding sheaves in the field, and behold, my sheaf arose and stood upright. And behold, your sheaves gathered around it and bowed down to my sheaf." His brothers said to him, "Are you indeed to reign over us? Or are you indeed to rule over us?" So they hated him even more for his dreams and for his words. Then he dreamed another dream and told it to his brothers and said, "Behold, I have dreamed another dream. Behold, the sun, the moon, and eleven stars were bowing down to me."
> – GENESIS 37:5-9

Joseph must have felt that this was a special kind of dream and must have wanted to talk about it with his family. They just weren't happy about it. God sees all things and He confirms this to Joseph with another dream and the same message. Years of great difficulty pass, but God does what He promises: Joseph becomes a great ruler.

A Symbol of God's Presence

> Then Jacob awoke from his sleep and said, "Surely the LORD is in this place, and I did not know it."
> — GENESIS 28:16

An indication that God is with you, sees you personally and is involved in your life—don't we all long for that? Don't we all need that? That everything we believe and stand for becomes very real for a moment? I believe that God loves to show Himself to us and in many ways. After all, His name is Immanuel, God with us. Wouldn't He then do what He is?

Jacob was given such a symbol of God's presence:

> And he dreamed, and behold, there was a ladder set up on the earth, and the top of it reached to heaven. And behold, the angels of God were ascending and descending on it! And behold, the LORD stood above it and said, "I am the LORD, the God of Abraham your father and the God of Isaac. The land on which you lie I will give to you and to your offspring. Your offspring shall be like the dust of the earth, and you shall spread abroad to the west and to the east and to the north and to the south, and in you and your offspring shall all the families of the earth be blessed. Behold, I am with you and will keep you wherever you go, and will bring you back to this land. For I will not leave you until I have done what I have promised you."
> — GENESIS 28:12-15

Jacob realized immediately that this was not just an ordinary dream. When he woke up, he said, "the LORD is in this place, and I did not know it" (Gen. 28:16). The encounter in the night had convinced Jacob that God really was with him.

Solomon said, "It was a dream" (1 Kings 3:15), until he saw the promise of God come true. He became the wisest and richest man on earth. Joseph, too, understood that his dream was not just meaningless and told it to his brothers, with dire consequences. But the dream revealed that Joseph would become a great ruler in the future, just as God had shown in the dream. All these dreams are marked by God's power and presence. Such dreams are there for us as well.

God can change your life in one night; you go to bed unsuspecting and wake up as a different person. Then you will be more than willing to go to sleep!

Transforming Word

> For the word of God is living and active, sharper than any two-edged sword, piercing to the division of soul and of spirit, of joints and of marrow, and discerning the thoughts and intentions of the heart.
> — HEBREWS 4:12

There was a period in my life when God spoke to me in my dreams at night in an audible voice. He spoke directly into the core of my person and affirmed me and fired me up. Words do not do justice to what that did to me. He said things like, "Dite, I have chosen you, you can do this." When God speaks, lies must make room for truth and doubt for faith.

What I still experience regularly is God touching me or holding me in a dream. That feeling is absolutely indescribable. You become drunk with His love, so to speak. Often this happens when I am at the end of myself or when I am having a very hard time. They are tremendously powerful experiences, and when you get up you feel like a different person.

There are so many opportunities for us to receive from God's heart! It makes me so happy to know that He wants to give this to you and everyone else. When you think of the endless possibilities in the night, you may not immediately think of something as drastic as a new system of government like Solomon's. So let's make it more personal. God wants to give you something that is just for you and that transforms you. Giovanni (the director of Youth Alive) experienced that as a young man.

Giovanni's story

I was a sixteen-year-old electrical engineering student and had only known Jesus for a short time. My conversion was intellectual and went something like this. The Bible is the truth and therefore I believe in Jesus. Only years later would I give my feelings to God, yet my intellectual way of believing never hindered Him from speaking to me.

Not long after my conversion, I had a dream: I was in the church I was attending at the time. A man I recognized from that congregation was praying for me. He said, "Just wait." I remained silent. Then he said, "Go ahead." I opened my mouth and began speaking in tongues, something I had never done before that time.
When I woke up, I noticed that I could actually speak in tongues. I felt different. I can't explain it very well, but it seemed like I could see differently. I looked at people in a different way and had more insight.

I decided to call the man from my dream, and tell him what I had dreamed. His response was, "Just wait, it's even more beautiful in real life!" Even though this man meant well, and sincerely believed that God wanted to touch me, his reaction made me think that what I had dreamt was not real. I decided not to speak in tongues anymore. Sometimes I even had to hold it back, so strong was the urge to do it. But it couldn't be real, because I had only dreamed it.

Months later I heard a sermon on Psalm 127:2: "... for he gives to his beloved sleep." It resonated with me immediately and I knew it was real. God baptized me in His Spirit during that dream! Since then, I have never doubted that encounter with God and have never held back from speaking in tongues. To this day, I can see the fruit of that touch of the Holy Spirit in my life.

Heavenly Sounds

> By day the LORD commands his steadfast love, and at night his song is with me, a prayer to the God of my life.
> — PSALM 42:8

There are many musicians who draw their inspiration from dreams. It seems miraculous, or is it? Considering that God made humanity as worshipers at heart, He must love music immensely.

The music industry has a huge impact on society. Therefore, it is also one of the areas where you can see the work of satan. He has a clear strategy—*let's make idols that attract thousands of fans. We will make those idols sing songs full of impurity and curses, so that their fans all over the world will imitate these lyrics. That way death can easily spread everywhere and it becomes a legal ground for demons.* Does this sound bizarre? Yes it does, but this is reality. Certain lyrics that are already being sung by young children are downright disgusting. The antithesis to the music that is now everywhere comes from heaven. God wants His music to be heard on earth, from the car radio, in the workplace, in the stores; sounds that bring forth a wave of life and blessing. Are you making music? Or do you have that desire? Ask the Holy Spirit to inspire you in the night.

Choir of angels

A few years ago I was at a large conference in the Netherlands. We had been together from morning to evening for two days, in God's Word and His presence. After dinner, we continued to worship God. The joy of heaven descended and people danced and ran through the hall. Suddenly we heard a sound like a men's large choir. The sound started at one end of the hall and came like a wave toward the other end. Then it rose again on one side of the hall and on it went. At first I thought, "Wow, these people can sing so beautifully!" But it soon became clear that the sound was not coming from humans, but from angels! A continuous singing without a single breath. We heard instruments that were not there at all and the presence of God became so tangible that most people were deep in worship or looked around in amazement. An angelic choir had joined our worship and was singing with us to Jesus. This lasted for at least fifteen minutes. It let a heavenly sound be heard on earth, and that is exactly what God wants to do! It was an amazing and unforgettable glimpse into the supernatural that is always around us.[13]

Heaven is full of music! So why would God not want to give us music in the night? Job's friend Elihu said the following:

> But none says, "Where is God my Maker, who gives songs in the night...
> – JOB 35:10

In their sleep, God gave the psalmists sounds and lyrics to make the most beautiful psalms (Ps. 42:8). This is available to us as well. Think about it—tones, instruments or lyrics straight from heaven. Anyone who hears such music will be immediately taken to its origin: God's heart. God wants to speak not only through words and images, but also through sounds, so that the sound of heaven can be heard everywhere. Tanja (band member of *InSalvation*) also experienced this.

Tanja's story

I regularly dream about things that I am working on at the time. I had this dream when we were scheduling writing sessions for InSalvation's new CD, in August of 2018. I dreamed that I was writing a song on an acoustic guitar with one chord. I already had a melody for the verse, pre-chorus and chorus. I'm not sure if I had also already come up with lyrics for the verse. I did have something for the pre-chorus, the phrase, "Never say never." I kept repeating this phrase. I also had a line for the chorus that was really easy to remember. During the dream, I thought it might be helpful to record it so I wouldn't forget. When I woke up from the dream, I thought again that it might be useful to record it after all, because you never knew what it was good for. That's what I did then. It was around four in the morning and I still have that recording.

During one of the first writing sessions, I showed it to the rest of the band. I happened to hear a worship leader at our church say the phrase "All eyes on You", and I had the idea right away that this might fit that tune. We then proceeded with that idea. And eventually two band members went to England with this, where they continued writing the song. That's how it became what it is today. The tune I had received in the dream remained exactly the same and eventually became the main line of the song[14]

Art

> As for me, I shall behold your face in righteousness; when I awake, I shall be satisfied with your likeness.
> – PSALM 17:15

And it is not just music, but every form of creativity abounds in heaven because the Creator Himself is there. Many artists know dreams as a source of inspiration. Vincent van Gogh said, "I dream my painting and then I paint my dream." One of his most famous works he called *The Starry Night*.

In our house there are several works of art created by God's inspiration. One of them has a very special story.

Annelies' Story

It was during a week when there were 24/7 revival services in my hometown of Dordrecht. I went every night and was touched by God there. That certainly influenced the creation of the image. In the early morning I woke up and the image of a sleeping woman appeared before me, with the hand of God inspiring her, hovering over her. The first thing I saw was her narrow face and her long dark hair. Most striking to me was the deep peace that emanated from her in her sleep. The hand of God above her was very large, larger than I drew.

The woman was in a deep sleep. I felt that that deep sleep was significant. I saw her face clearly before me and I felt that this was someone who really existed. The same evening I went to another revival service and there I made the drawing of the woman. The image became clearer as I was drawing and the colors in the drawing instinctively fit the image, even though I didn't see them very clearly right away. I gave the drawing to Michelle, one of the staff there, and explained that I had seen this woman the same morning. Michelle recognized the woman; she said, "This is Dite, and what you say about the night is true!"

I received a message from my friend Michelle telling me what Annelies had made and that she immediately knew it was about me. I had just started writing this book and was greatly encouraged by the drawing that was made by someone I didn't know and who didn't know me. That evening I was allowed to receive the drawing. Annelies was dumbfounded when I stood before her—the sleeping woman she had seen in an image of God really existed. A funny detail is that she drew me with my head on my hand. That is exactly the position in which I often sleep. It was a wonderful moment in which we were both touched by God's goodness![15]

Spiritual Warfare in a Dream

> (...) all of them wearing swords and expert in war, each with his sword at his thigh, against terror by night.
> – SONG OF SOLOMON 3:8

Have you ever had a dream in which it seemed like you were in a fight? This was probably the case. While you are sleeping, your spirit is wide awake and can experience the battle in the heavenly realms. We cannot ignore it; the spiritual world is real, there is fighting day and night between angels and dark powers for the future of the world. The Bible says we are not fighting against "flesh and blood", but against the governments and powers of hell (Eph. 6:12). But don't worry, that same Bible says we will overcome!

How do you deal with it when you feel like you have to battle through your nights? First of all: I want to say that I understand it is unpleasant and tiring. I pray salvation over your nights and over all those times when you are harassed by the enemy. It is important that you know that you are not the enemy's plaything. You are not his property; you are a child of God. This is not your battle, but God's battle, and He is before you, always! He sends His best fighters to fight for you.

When we talk about spiritual battles, it is good to take a close look at a few things. Let's start by looking at the place where the battle occurs. The Bible speaks of different heavens. First, heaven as God created it (Gen. 1:8), as the division between the ground and the clouds (Matt. 24:30). This is the sky we see when we look upward. The Bible also speaks of the third heaven: paradise and the place where God dwells (2 Cor. 12:2-4). Obviously, then, there is also a second heaven. This is the place where the angel Gabriel fought for twenty-one days with the prince of Persia to answer Daniel's prayers (Dan. 10:13). The second heaven is where the powers reside that the book of Ephesians speaks of:

> For we do not wrestle against flesh and blood, but against the rulers, against the authorities, against the cosmic powers over this present darkness, against the spiritual forces of evil in the heavenly places.
> – EPHESIANS 6:12

This verse is not talking about demons, but about various authorities and powers. God has various tasks and ranks in His angelic army. For example, there are cherubim and seraphim in heaven, and angels who protect people on earth. Since satan cannot create anything, he can only imitate what God does. So he too has an order of precedence among his subjects. So there are the authorities, powers and rulers who reside in the second heaven. Demons, on the other hand, are always here on earth looking for a body to dwell in. They are dark creatures of the lowest order. Therefore, you should not fight demons, you should cast them out, the Bible says (Mark 16:17).

The second heaven is the place where the battle takes place. But what is our position in that battle? The Bible says:

> The heavens are the LORD's heavens, but the earth he has given to the children of man.
> – PSALM 115:16

The earth is the place God has given to us. From the very beginning in Genesis, God says that we rule over the earth, cultivate it and guard it together with Him. The Bible also says:

> [God], even when we were dead in our trespasses, made us alive together with Christ—by grace you have been saved—and raised us up with him and seated us with him in the heavenly places in Christ Jesus (...)
> – EPHESIANS 2:5-6

Now this is the answer. The word translated as "heavenly places" in this text is the Greek word *epouranios*. It means the heaven where God and the angels dwell, the heavenly temple. By Jesus' grace, we have free access to heaven, the third heaven. We are hidden with Christ in the throne of God (Eph. 2:5-6; Rev. 3:21). The second heaven is the battlefield, but not *our* battlefield. Fighting in the second heaven is useless, because it is not the place for us. It will wear us out and it can hurt us and those around us. It doesn't work out the way we had in mind. But when we fight from the throne of victory, it will surely hit the mark! When we pray from our position on God's throne, He sends out His angels with orders to fight the authorities and powers and bring heaven on earth. Everything that stops them in the second heaven must give way because we pray from victory and authority. We don't need to shout, because our calm prayer from the right position sets heaven in motion.

So what can we do when we experience spiritual battles in the night? First of all: Make sure that possible doors are closed to the enemy.[16] When in doubt, ask God to show you if there is another door open.

Second, before you go to sleep, ask God to cover you with the blood of Jesus. You can pray it over yourself and your family, as well as your bedroom and home. The blood of Jesus brings salvation.

> But if we walk in the light, as he is in the light, we have fellowship with one another, and the blood of Jesus his Son cleanses us from all sin.
> – 1 JOHN 1:7

Erica experienced how the blood of Jesus changed everything during her mission trip.

Erica's story

> Several years ago, I went on a mission trip to North Africa with a group. The first night, all five of the women in my group had violent dreams. Mine wasn't too scary. I was attacked by vampires, but knew I had power over them and ran in their direction to deal with them. Probably this was a revelation of the spiritual battle there in that place. But all the other women had really terrible nightmares. The following night we prayed for the blood of Jesus to cover our building. We went to sleep and no one had any more nightmares. The territorial powers wanted to intimidate us, but Jesus paved the way for us to be effective in that area and well rested so we could continue our journey.

The blood of Jesus is the antidote to spiritual battles. It is incredibly powerful as well as wise to cleanse your home and bedroom with the blood of Jesus if you have never done this before. Even when you sleep in another place, this is the first thing you should do. This ensures that any influence from the kingdom of darkness is broken. At the end of this chapter, you will find a prayer you can use for this purpose.

Next, ask God to send His angels to protect you. You may not literally see them, but they are there to protect you when you sleep.

> For it is written, "He will command his angels concerning you, to guard you (...)"
> – LUKE 4:10

Meditate on God's Word as you do this. Especially when you are struggling with fear or unrest, it is important to place God's thoughts over your own thoughts. It is the weapon we have been given by God:

> And take the helmet of salvation, and the sword of the Spirit, which is the word of God (...)
> – EPHESIANS 6:17

And finally, stop glorifying spiritual battles. If this doesn't apply to you, you can skip this bit, but many people have an unhealthy fascination with spiritual battles. It is a popular topic to talk about and keep talking about. It almost seems like a trophy by which to measure how well someone is doing spiritually. Sometimes more consideration is given to what the enemy is going to do to resist them, than to the prosperity and power that God is going to pour out. Remember, satan was thrown out of heaven because he was proud; he wanted the honor that belongs to God (Eze. 28; Rev. 12:7-9). In other words, the enemy enjoys attention. Don't grant him that attention, but glorify God. He will fight for you! The Bible says:

> Do not be overcome by evil, but overcome evil with good.
> – ROMANS 12:21

There is a powerful truth in this Bible verse. By focusing on God, listening to His voice and putting His thoughts above yours, you will overcome evil. Don't keep fighting on the battlefield but shelter in God's safe arms so you can hear His voice. That is what makes the difference when your nights are terrorized by the enemy.

Maybe you have been suffering from spiritual battles for a long time and you think this sounds too easy. Then know that God's Word and the blood of Jesus stands far above the enemy and is towering above your unbelief or hopelessness. The Bible is not a book that is out of date. It is a living Word that continually cuts us loose from lies. Therefore, I want to ask you to open your heart and look at these Bible texts with renewed eyes.

I discovered another weapon, and that is worship. With that you overcome evil with good, as Romans 12 says. Paul and Silas understood this:

> About midnight Paul and Silas were praying and singing hymns to God, and the prisoners were listening to them, and suddenly there was a great earthquake, so that the foundations of the prison were shaken. And immediately all the doors were opened, and everyone's bonds were unfastened.
> – ACTS 16:25-26

What a special deliverance! Paul and Silas were in a literal prison here; you, hopefully, are not. Yet spiritual battles can feel like an oppressive prison cell. It is an attack on the freedom you have been given by God. But in your voice is a sword, and in your song is a stone that overthrows every giant!

> I bless the LORD who gives me counsel; in the night also my heart instructs me.
> – PSALM 16:7

Maybe you cannot imagine yourself singing in the middle of the night. I don't do that, either, when my husband is sleeping next to me. But your heart can silently go out to Jesus and be full of wonder—that too is worship. The most important thing is your undivided attention to Him. Sometimes the turmoil inside or in the atmosphere is very great. This makes it difficult to focus. Then think back to all the good things

God has done for you, starting with your salvation from death and sin. You will then naturally begin to worship Him. Gratitude is the code word for the throne room, where you are constantly in God's presence. You can practice this—the more this is already a habit during the day, the easier it will be in a night of spiritual battles.

I will tell you how I escaped night-time attacks. When God called me to speak, I was confronted with a series of dreams. They were night encounters with darkness. These dreams had one thing in common: I could not speak or say the name of Jesus aloud. Time after time I woke up anxious and unable to move. Then I would fall asleep again and dream that I woke because the bedroom door was opening and a dark presence was coming toward me. This was so real that each time I woke up bathed in sweat and would sit upright in my bed screaming.

During this time, I served on several ministry teams and often prayed for deliverance. I sent demons away in the name of Jesus. I moved in His authority and was not afraid of demons. In these dreams, I wanted to send the darkness away in Jesus' name, but when I opened my mouth no sound came out. It frustrated me greatly that this was happening and I asked God for insight.

He showed me that my fear of speaking was a landing strip for the enemy. Thus He made me believe that I couldn't do it, that I had no voice and no one would hear me. Our thinking is decisive in how we experience battle. The enemy was out to discourage and stop me. But God's plan cannot be stopped by any power or force. I broke with the lies that I would not be fit to speak and that no one would hear me. I asked God for His fatherly love and confirmation about His call on my life.

Maybe you think this is going a bit far, but I also asked Him for a weapon for in my dream. What happened was this. The next time I had this dream, I saw a huge sword in my right hand. I pointed it at the enemy and watched him flee. The sword turned out to be not only the weapon for in my dreams, but also the weapon for the daytime. The sword of God's Word brought down the stronghold of fear in my thinking. The more my thinking came into alignment with God's Word and His thoughts about me, the less I suffered from the battle, until finally it disappeared altogether. That is also exactly what it says in these verses:

> For the weapons of our warfare are not of the flesh but have divine power to destroy strongholds. We destroy arguments and every lofty opinion raised against the knowledge of God, and take every thought captive to obey Christ (...)
> – 2 CORINTHIANS 10:4-5

Finally, I just did what God asked of me: I started speaking. I ignored the fear and opposition. After all, He had said it. No matter how I doubted, what God says is true. The dreams did not stop me from speaking and only increased my trust in God. Asking for a weapon in your dream is not a crazy idea, it is powerful and shows that with God you are unbeatable!

> Stand therefore, having fastened on the belt of truth, and having put on the breastplate of righteousness, and, as shoes for your feet, having put on the readiness given by the gospel of peace. In all circumstances take up the shield of faith, with which you can extinguish all the flaming darts of the evil one; and take the helmet of salvation, and the sword of the Spirit, which is the word of God.
> – EPHESIANS 6:14-17

These are not fancy poetic metaphors; they are your weapons in the battle against the rulers and powers of darkness. This is your ammunition, which you take to the battlefield to overcome. Your place is the throne of God, safe in the arms of the Triumphant One. God is the army commander, not you. He is the Lord of heavenly armies.

The phenomenon of not being able to move or talk though you are awake is common, especially in young people. Science calls it sleep paralysis and says it is caused by stress, anxiety disorders or sleep apnea. I tell you that this is demonic and you need to address it at the root. The question is: Why is this demon able to attack you? With me, fear was the entry point. Ask God on which grounds the enemy has gained access and then deal with that access point. Make sure you find your safety in Jesus. When you feel the presence of the enemy, look for the table Jesus prepared. Sit at that table in full view of the enemy and fix your eyes on Jesus, who fought and won every battle. Listen to his voice; it changes everything.

> You prepare a table before me in the presence of my enemies (...)
> – PSALM 23:5

Prayer for cleansing your home or bedroom

Father in heaven, I thank You for Your Son, Jesus, and Your Holy Spirit. I invite You into this house, it is Yours and Yours alone. In the name of Jesus, I take authority over every demonic power present in this house and I bind you and command you to leave this house now. I cleanse this house with the blood of Jesus Christ of every iniquity that has taken place and been spoken here. I break every influence from the kingdom of darkness over this place in Jesus' name. Holy Spirit, fill this house with Your presence, send Your angels. For "as for me and my house, we will serve the LORD" (Josh. 24:15). Amen

Tip: The use of anointing oil is also powerful in conjunction with prayer.

Freedom in the Night

> You are a hiding place for me; you preserve me from trouble; you surround me with shouts of deliverance.
> — PSALM 32:7

Even though it may seem that darkness surrounds you on all sides, the truth is that you are always surrounded by God's presence. Whether you are awake or asleep, He sings a song over you (Zeph. 3:17), a song of freedom. God is your Shelter and Deliverer, during the day as well as the night. These are not just comforting words, they are reality. Robbie (speaker and teacher at Royal Mission, a Dutch ministry) experienced how God protected and delivered him from his bullies.

Robbie's story

When I was fourteen, I was threatened by a group of high school boys. At one point they said they would wait for me the next day after school to beat me up. That night I had a dream in which I was being chased by dogs. This, besides the bullies, was one of my biggest fears. The faces of the dogs were the faces of the boys and at the front was the biggest bully. At one point I couldn't hold out any longer and there was nothing I could do but give up the fight. Then a huge dog came and stood between me and the boys. At that moment He spoke to me, "You don't need to be afraid, I am with you." He chased the other dogs away and I was safe. Soon after, the biggest bully at school came to me to apologize. I was never bothered by him or the other boys again!

How extraordinary that God appeared in the form of a dog, the animal Robbie was so afraid of! God protected him from the bullies, but it didn't stop there. God gave him safety when he was faced with his greatest fear! And what God did there was so powerful that the bullies had to let go of Robbie in real life, too. Now, that's deliverance!

As I write this book, I regularly have this same dream. It's New Year's Eve. I see people going into New Year's Eve as a prisoner and starting New Year's Day as a liberated person, full of zest for life and joy. It is clear that God wants to speak about the possibility of receiving freedom in the night! Many people do not feel free. You may not know exactly where that feeling comes from, but you crave space and air, refreshment. God wants to give that, during the day, but also while you sleep.

You can see that in this wonderful story in the Bible. Maybe you hadn't noticed, but this particular turn of events happened at night:

> But the high priest rose up, and all who were with him (that is, the party of the Sadducees), and filled with jealousy they arrested the apostles and put them in the public prison. But during the night an angel of the Lord opened the prison doors and brought them out, and said, "Go and stand in the temple and speak to the people all the words of this Life."
> — ACTS 5:17-20

Maybe you ended up in a prison because of jealousy of others, like the apostles. Maybe there is some other cause. No matter the reason, your prison doors may open during your sleep. Your mind, soul and spirit are free when you wake up, and the Holy Spirit gives you insight in the night to further freedom.

Freedom is a great gift and God longs for you to accept it. I know a number of people who have received freedom in their sleep. Often this was accompanied by such a new and overwhelming sense of joy that their attention became focused on what was in front of them and no longer on what was behind them. That provided the right focus to keep walking in that new freedom.

It is not a problem for God to set people free in the night; it is not even a problem to set an entire people free! Jerusalem experienced this miracle. God delivered them from the attack of the king of Assyria. It happened in the night, while they were sleeping.

> "Therefore thus says the LORD concerning the king of Assyria: He shall not come into this city or shoot an arrow there, or come before it with a shield or cast up a siege mound against it. By the way that he came, by the same he shall return, and he shall not come into this city, declares the LORD. For I will defend this city to save it, for my own sake and for the sake of my servant David." And that night the angel of the LORD went out and struck down 185,000 in the camp of the Assyrians. And when people arose early in the morning, behold, these were all dead bodies. Then Sennacherib king of Assyria departed and went home and lived at Nineveh.
> – 2 KINGS 19:32-36

Surely they must have been surprised when they woke up and saw that the danger had passed! God wants to bring freedom to our minds and souls. He even wants to literally set us free. There is a miraculous testimony of a man named Liu Zhenying, better known as Brother Yun or "the heavenly man". He was captured in China and both his legs were broken during torture. God sent an angel who took him out of the prison. Even the guards did not see him as he walked right past them. The heavily guarded doors opened by themselves and a cab was waiting in front of the prison; he was able to get in immediately. He escaped by walking on his own legs, which had been healed by God. You can read this testimony in the book *The Heavenly Man*.[17]

God has not changed. He is able to do things far beyond our prayer or imagination. What He did for this man, He can do for others too. He can open doors so that prisoners can leave. Imagine God freeing people from captivity, prostitution and slavery in this way. For Him, nothing is impossible. Let us pray that God will do it again so that people can be set free who should be free.

A Surprising Awakening

> And to which of the angels has he ever said, "Sit at my right hand until I make your enemies a footstool for your feet"? Are they not all ministering spirits sent out to serve for the sake of those who are to inherit salvation?
> — HEBREWS 1:13-14

Angels are there to protect and serve us, but they do more. We regularly read in the Bible that an angel appears in a dream, or appears at night and gives a message. The person who sees the angel is surprised or startled by the visit of the heavenly being, but does not take off running. This person listens to what the angel has to say on behalf of God. Even today we can see, hear and interact with angels.

There is often some fear surrounding angels and apprehension when people say they have seen or met them. People can feel that attention placed on angels would steal the attention that is actually meant for Jesus. But angels of God do not do this. The Bible calls them "ministering spirits"; they serve God and not themselves. Consider the forty days Jesus spent in the desert. He did not eat, drank only water, and was constantly tempted by the devil. Then it says this:

> Then the devil left him, and behold, angels came and were ministering to him.
> — MATTHEW 4:11

A little further on it says again that Jesus received help from an angel when He drank the cup in the garden of Gethsemane with the sin of the world in it:

> And there appeared to him an angel from heaven, strengthening him.
> – LUKE 22:43

Jesus accepted the help and care of angels. If Jesus valued them and welcomed them during His life on earth, then may we follow his example.

The Bible tells us about huge angel armies, as the heavenly part of God's household. Jesus said He could call 72,000 angels instantly (Matt. 26:53) and that we are surrounded by huge numbers of angels from the moment we repent.

> But you have come to Mount Zion and to the city of the living God, the heavenly Jerusalem, and to innumerable angels in festal gathering...
> – HEBREWS 12:22

Whether you can see it or not, you are surrounded by angels. Earlier, I shared how afraid I was of the dark, and how God delivered me from that. Since then I have often seen an angel standing at the foot of our bed when I woke up at night. It has helped me tremendously to know who surrounds me.

> Oh, taste and see that the LORD is good! Blessed is the man who takes refuge in him!
> – PSALM 34:8

The following is a testimony of an encounter that I had with an angel.

An Encounter with an Angel

One morning I woke up to footsteps outside. We sleep on the first floor and our bed is next to the window. The footsteps didn't stop and came right in through the outside wall. They stopped next to my head. I felt overwhelmed. Then the presence of God filled our bedroom in a way I hadn't experienced before.

I can best describe it as "tingling". A sparkling, flashing, tingling presence with heavenly authority. The victory of Jesus could be felt in the atmosphere. I heard a voice saying, "Dite, what do you want?"

Immediately I began to talk about the dreams that were in my heart for my life and for the world. I didn't have to think about it and listed everything. They were God's desires in me flowing out of me. I closed by saying, "These are big things, aren't they?" To which the voice said, "Do you think so? This is just the beginning." And then the one speaking to me was gone. At that moment I knew it was an angel, a way maker. He was moving forward to prepare the way for the things I was telling him. It was amazing, awe-inspiring and at the same time not even strange, because God was there. Since that encounter not so long ago, several things I told the angel have actually happened, even though at the time it seemed impossible!

Angels often work in ways that are invisible to us. We can even give shelter to them without knowing it, as we read in Hebrews 13:2. But would that be because they are invisible to us, or because they can come in the form of a human being and we don't even recognize them as angels?

When Peter was freed from prison, he first went to his friends. When one of them opened the door, she was so startled by Peter that she closed the door again and ran to the others in the house. Then the following happened:

> They said to her, "You are out of your mind." But she kept insisting that it was so, and they kept saying, "It is his angel!" But Peter continued knocking, and when they opened, they saw him and were amazed.
> – ACTS 12:15-16

The disciples found it more believable that she saw Peter's personal angel than Peter himself! Apparently, people at that time were used to seeing angels. Not only that, but they seemingly knew that a guardian angel can take the form of the person to whom it belongs, because in their minds it could not be Peter, so then it had to be his angel in the form of Peter. Do stories like this make you just as curious and excited as I am about this? Here's another one:

Personal Angel

It was the middle of the night, about two o'clock. I was in the back of a tour bus with a group of people; we were on our way to go abroad for a mission trip. I was praying softly for the upcoming days. Suddenly I saw a clear picture of our bedroom. I saw my husband sleeping on his right side. I saw a man standing in the corner of the bedroom. He looked like an army officer. His face was serious and his posture was very straight. The clothes he wore were reminiscent of those of a high-ranking army officer. I knew it was my husband's personal angel, and marveled at his appearance, but perhaps even more so at his serious expression. He exuded tremendous authority. This angel clearly bowed to nothing but God alone. I asked myself why this angel was standing there, and immediately I saw my husband lying there again. I watched Jesus take him in His arms and rock him back and forth. It was so endearing to me that tears ran down my cheeks. My husband served fifteen years in the military and was deployed to all kinds of war zones. There he had experienced several times God's supernatural protection. Besides that, Joost has a great interest in history, especially that of the First and Second World Wars. All these personal characteristics of his I saw reflected in the angel that stood in our bedroom!

The Bible speaks regularly about the appearance of angels, and one thing becomes clear in the process—they really come in all forms. They are often quite impressive (Judg. 13:6) or excessively large (Rev. 10:5) and show up in the strangest places (Rev. 19:17).

You can talk to angels. The book of Zechariah, for example, is one big conversation between Zechariah and angels of God. They have emotions (Luke 15:10). They work at the bidding of God and not based on their own motives.

> For he will command his angels concerning you to guard you in all your ways. On their hands they will bear you up, lest you strike your foot against a stone. You will tread on the lion and the adder; the young lion and the serpent you will trample underfoot.
> — PSALM 91:11-13

Isn't it amazing that God lets us work together with angels? The Bible says that they move into action when they hear the words of God. As soon as we proclaim God's words, the angels start moving to make them visible on the earth. You can read this in the following verse:

> Bless the LORD, O you his angels, you mighty ones who do his word, obeying the voice of his word!
> — PSALM 103:20

I have had several encounters with angels, and my experience is that such an encounter does not make you primarily excited about angels, but rather makes you marvel at who God is and how He does everything He can to help, encourage and speak to His children. When we focus on Jesus alone, it is up to Him how He gives us a message—by His Holy Spirit, through an angel or in some other way.

Traveling While You Sleep

> And when he had spoken to me, I fell into a deep sleep with my face to the ground. But he touched me and made me stand up.
> — DANIEL 8:18

When the Bible refers to sleep, it quite often means something other than going to bed every evening and sleeping. Jesus said that Jarius' daughter was sleeping while everyone thought she was dead. If you look at the original text, it uses the word *katheudo*, which actually means sleep. Before Jesus called Lazarus from the tomb, Jesus said he had died. Here it actually says the word for die. When Isaiah wrote about the watchmen of Israel preferring to sleep and slumber, he used the word *haza*, which is the opposite of "seeing in the spiritual world". Here sleep means to be blind to God and focused on your own needs. As you can see, there is quite a bit of variation on the theme of sleep.

We will take a closer look at two different meanings of the word "sleep" from the original text because they say something about the different kinds of sleep we can experience. When Daniel received a vision of the end times, it says that he "fell into a deep sleep". The Hebrew word used here is *tardemah* and means deep sleep or trance. This is also the kind of sleep God put Adam into when He created Eve from Adam's rib. Daniel and Adam were completely out of this world during these touches of God, and perhaps that is just as well!

Let's look a little farther. Jesus regularly skipped a night of sleep because He was spending time with His Father. We see He had a different rhythm of sleep than we ourselves are used to. It would seem that Jesus as a human being did not depend on eight hours of sleep to function. This is probably because Jesus continually walked in God's will. Consider, for example, when He arrived at the well where He met the Samaritan woman. Jesus was tired and thirsty, but then He had the opportunity to reveal the Father to that woman. When the disciples returned from getting food, they found Him refreshed. Jesus said:

> My food is to do the will of him who sent me and to accomplish his work.
> – JOHN 4:34

Jesus lived by doing His Father's will. Perhaps you have experienced what it was like to lead someone to Jesus. It makes you feel very energetic! That's what I am reminded of when I read this Bible passage—Jesus was no longer tired, but He was revived by doing God's will.

When Jesus did sleep, it was sometimes during strange circumstances, like during the storm on the Sea of Galilee. The boat filled with water, but Jesus slept. Could He sleep peacefully because He did not experience the fear that the disciples did, or did Jesus fall asleep because of the rocking of the boat? Did He already know that the wind would die down when He commanded it to be silent? Or was something else going on?

> So they set out, and as they sailed he fell asleep. And a windstorm came down on the lake, and they were filling with water and were in danger.
> — LUKE 8:22-23

In the original text, the word *aphypno* means "sleep". It comes from the words *apo* and *hypnos*. *Apo* means to be detached from place or movement. The word *hypnos* means a state of sleep or spiritual sedation. This is similar to what we see when someone comes under the power of God and is seemingly unconscious for an extended period of time. This looks like sleep, but is something else. Could it be that Jesus walked fully in God's plan for the night and had an encounter with the Father during the storm?

God's Spirit is outside of time and place and can take your mind to other places even while you sleep. The Bible speaks of this extraordinary phenomenon. Paul said:

> I know a man in Christ who fourteen years ago was caught up to the third heaven—whether in the body or out of the body I do not know, God knows.
> — 2 CORINTHIANS 12:2

This is clearly talking about a person being moved from earth to heaven. Paul wondered if it was only his spirit or if his body was also taken up.

Elijah knew what it was like to be moved in the spirit by God:

> But Elisha said to him, "Was not my spirit with you when the man got down from his chariot to meet you?"
> – 2 KINGS 5:26a (NIV)

In this case, Elisha traveled with his spirit to another place on earth. John was taken to heaven:

> And he carried me away in the Spirit to a great, high mountain, and showed me the holy city Jerusalem coming down out of heaven from God (...)
> – REVELATION 21:10

And if that wasn't strange enough, God can also transport both our spirit and body. Philip experienced this:

> And when they came up out of the water, the Spirit of the Lord carried Philip away, and the eunuch saw him no more, and went on his way rejoicing. But Philip found himself at Azotus, and as he passed through he preached the gospel to all the towns until he came to Caesarea.
> – ACTS 8:39-40

Suddenly he is in another city, 75 kilometers away. None of these people had a desire to travel in the spirit, God just did it because He wanted to. Are you already in shock? If God is the same, He still can and does do these things today. The first time I heard a testimony about this, I was absolutely amazed.

A girl we will call Claire was to go on a missionary trip to Colombia with her class. Before she left, she dreamed several times about the planned trip. They were very realistic dreams in which she was in an orphanage and playing with the children.

She became very excited about going on the trip, and when it finally happened, the following occurred: Claire arrived at an orphanage with her class and was walking toward the door, when a group of children ran up to her and called her name. They hugged her as if she was an old friend who had returned. Stunned, she asked how they knew her name. The children replied that they had played with her several times recently. Because of the time difference, it was daytime for them when Claire dreamed of that place. Apparently she had actually been there! She herself had not experienced it as something that was really happening, but to the children she was apparently completely present. How incredible!

So it is possible for God to take you in your sleep, to disconnect you from your location. Now, don't think that this is unsafe or that you can get lost somewhere between planets or on another continent. God is a good Father who cares for His children. I long for these things—that God can bring us to places we could never normally go. The testimonies I heard on this subject have one thing in common—the person in question had a real-life dream in which all the senses were stimulated. Have you ever had a dream in which you can smell, hear, feel and taste the place you are in the dream? If so, it could be that you may have actually been there. The answer is up to God, but the idea of a journey with the Holy Spirit is great, right?

PART | 7

Dreaming in God's Family

> For this reason I bow my knees before the Father, from whom every family in heaven and on earth is named, that according to the riches of his glory he may grant you to be strengthened with power through his Spirit in your inner being, so that Christ may dwell in your hearts through faith—that you, being rooted and grounded in love (...)
> – EPHESIANS 3:14-17

Wonderful things can happen when we trust God more and more as the good Father He is. He takes us to places in His heart that we dare not even dream about! So far we've talked about the dreams you and I can have as individuals, but what happens when you awaken as a married couple or family to God's plan for the night? What does it look like when the body of Christ starts dreaming and living with what God gives while they sleep? There are endless opportunities to encourage and strengthen each other and bring heaven on earth together. Imagine everyone at home and everyone in the church receiving what they need at night—a good night's sleep *and* encounters with God! I believe that it is possible and that we may take back what has been stolen for years. Because what God wants to give on earth we can only receive with all the saints. How does God want to speak for others? And what are the areas in which we can expect this to happen? You will read more about that in the following chapters.

Family

> And above all these put on love, which binds everything together in perfect harmony.
> – COLOSSIANS 3:14

From the Garden of Eden until today, it has always been God's plan: God's household as one family. We have strayed far from that. Our society is so self-centered, so lonely. Vulnerability and honesty have become rare. Everyone lives on their own island, wearing their own mask, for fear of rejection.

The world screams in many ways, "Hear me, see me, know me!" Humankind, who have been created for relationship and real, honest connection have ended up in a prison. Long before social distancing was used to eradicate a virus, there was a tremendous distance. The distance between people that we see now is just a visible manifestation of what has been going on in so many hearts for a long time. There is only one solution, one vaccine. The antidote is family. We as God's children, the body of Jesus, have the key that can free the world from this prison. We need an injection of God's unifying love so that the Church can return to God's original plan and fulfill its task in the world.

God's love requires raw authenticity, great grace and great courage. Courage to fix things we would rather ignore. Authenticity to be honest about what's behind the mask so we can actually change. Grace for all those times we disappoint or are disappointed. We usually have the best intentions, but all of us are very different people. And we need to be! We don't become a family by all behaving the same, or even by everyone agreeing. It is not the similarities but rather the diversity and uniqueness of each person that shows God's multicolored and multifaceted beauty. God's plan for His family is for us to be a combination of vibrant differences, a colorful fountain of talents and a brilliant reflection of God's creativity, bound together with unconditional love. Together we may have one common goal—to make Jesus visible! Just look at the following verses:

> When I think of the wisdom and scope of his plan, I fall down on my knees and pray to the Father of all the great family of God—some of them already in heaven and some down here on earth— that out of his glorious, unlimited resources he will give you the mighty inner strengthening of his Holy Spirit. And I pray that Christ will be more and more at home in your hearts, living within you as you trust in him. May your roots go down deep into the soil of God's marvelous love; and may you be able to feel and understand, as all God's children should, how long, how wide, how deep, and how high his love really is; and to experience this love for yourselves, though it is so great that you will never see the end of it or fully know or understand it. And so at last you will be filled up with God himself. Now glory be to God, who by his mighty power at work within us is able to do far more than we would ever dare to ask or even dream of—infinitely beyond our highest prayers, desires, thoughts, or hopes.
> — EPHESIANS 3:14-20 (TLB)

When we look at how God speaks to his family at night, there are two things we can keep in mind—love reigns and God works through all different kinds of people and in various ways. He also works in ways we don't know yet, that we find exciting or strange, and yes, even through that brother or sister we don't like very much.

How wonderful it would be if we as a Church woke up to God's voice in the night and grew in the knowledge of dreams; that dreams would no longer be relegated to a place where people don't quite know what to do with them or are just afraid of such manifestations of God's Spirit. Imagine dreams and dream interpretation becoming part of the Christian life in a healthy way. And just as with testing a prophetic word (1 Thess. 5:20-21), many people would be able to interpret dreams of God. It would no longer be possible for a dream to be misused to manipulate and control. When church members received dreams related to the church, there would be room for them, and there would be knowledge to deal with them. Most importantly, God's will would become known on earth, people would walk in their God-given ministry, and Jesus would become visible through all of us. Because: "Now you are the body of Christ and individually members of it" (1 Cor. 12:27).

God wants His Church to grow and move in the gifts and ministries He gives. With God there is order, but it is not the same order that people have often made of it, order born out of fear of losing control (1 Cor. 14:33). Paul uses the word *eiréné* in this verse. This means that everything is in place and functioning as God intended, leading to peace and security. Godly order is a place where God can move optimally, and it brings peace. This may look different from what we have seen so far. Even different than what we are comfortable with. May we learn to trust Him more deeply and take steps toward a new way of understanding God and cooperating with Him (Eph. 3:17-19). It will make the Church of Jesus much more colorful!

I will not get into how the Church should function, that is simply too big a topic to cover in this book. We are going to look at God's plan for our sleep within the family, within God's household. For only together will we see more of God. That is a wonderful promise that may bring us closer to each other when we are hungry for heaven.

Dreams to Bring Encouragement

> For you can all prophesy one by one, so that all may learn and all be encouraged (...)
> – 1 CORINTHIANS 14:31

Sometimes God gives dreams about another person. The purpose of such a dream is usually not to share it, but to act on it. They are dreams that show how we can encourage and affirm the other person.

An important task for us as believers is to strengthen and encourage one another. Everyone needs encouragement, even those people from whom you would never expect it. We all struggle at times, with personal issues, or something that's going on in our lives. We are running the race ahead of us and need supporters to keep going. Encouragement is neither complicated nor even a deep prophetic message. When you encourage, you speak from the culture of heaven; not focused on yourself but on the other, not focused on what is not there but on what is and what is to come.

Joyce brings people before the throne of God through prayer and worship. She regularly receives dreams from God in which He gives her information for which she may pray and in which she can encourage the other. She shared the following testimony:

Joyce's story

I often experience connection with friends and family in my dreams. Sometimes I dream about the difficulty someone is experiencing, other times I dream about where a person is in their life or what they are going through. This helps me approach people with wisdom, deepen relationships or speak life to someone. Also, I sometimes dream very briefly that someone comes along in a dream and says something, or I see their facial expression or something they do. I will share an example. In a dream I saw a friend who looked very tired. I wondered what was going on. I was worried because she looked so exhausted. When I spoke to her the next morning, she told me how she felt. What I had seen in the dream was true. I pray for these things, asking God what I can do with them. Often God asks me to encourage people. An example of this happened in my family. Almost all of my relatives are very musical, including my sister. In a dream she told me that she wanted to quit music because she no longer had any hope of bringing something new. After all, everyone was already making such beautiful music. I dreamed she was singing beautiful songs, while playing her guitar, that she had composed herself. It sounded very authentic. I was amazed at how good it was, and was so happy about what I had heard. God wanted to restore her faith and hope and make her believe again in her talent to make music.

I started praying for her and sending her encouragement. At first she didn't respond very enthusiastically. But my enthusiasm was unstoppable and I kept praying it over her. A while later she called me and said she had renewed faith in her talent to make music. Now she is in her third year of a music course and making amazing and unique songs that praise God.

I dream more often about things that people no longer believe in, but for which God has called them. I love experiencing God's enthusiasm, and seeing what He gives come alive again and blossom in the people around me.

This is the heart of prophecy! God wants to make His loving heart known, even if someone no longer believes in it. This is how dry bones of death come to life and hopelessness is turned into hope. Prayer and encouragement are oil on the fire of God. And everyone can encourage, including you!

Dreams to Pray Through

> Upon a watchtower I stand, O Lord, continually by day, and at my post I am stationed whole nights.
> — ISAIAH 21:8

Increasingly people are becoming aware of the power of prayer. Prayer groups are being formed everywhere and people are meeting to pray God's will. The Bible encourages us to do the following:

> Praying at all times in the Spirit, with all prayer and supplication. To that end, keep alert with all perseverance, making supplication for all the saints (...)
> — EPHESIANS 6:18

We are called to pray, and God promises in His Word that powerful prayer accomplishes much (Jam 5:16). A prayer is made powerful by faith, faith that what you pray for is actually going to happen. Faith is the hope for the things you don't yet see (Heb. 11:1), but what if God wants to show you right now? Then your faith would only increase. God can give a dream in which you see His will. When you have a dream like that, to pray from it will give you great faith for powerful prayer!

When you receive a dream that includes a known or unknown person, God may not ask you to share it with that person, but rather to pray for them. God's eyes go over the earth (Prov. 15:3) to see who He can assist with power. Often God does this by placing intercessors around people to pray out His desires over that person.

For example, God gave me a dream about my sister-in-law. In the dream, I saw her walking to the water with her husband. Their two daughters were at the water's edge watching their parents walk into the water. I saw that my brother-in-law appeared very insecure, it was weighing heavily on him. My sister-in-law did not seem to suffer from doubt and was happy. Then I saw that my brother-in-law was baptizing his wife. I watched it from a distance and felt such joy at my sister-in-law's choice. I knew she had doubted baptism for years. When her husband was baptized a few years back, she doubted whether she wanted to do the same and was tossed back and forth by all kinds of opinions from other people. But now she was sure of her choice! I noticed that there were few people standing around the water, but their children were there, watching their mother choose to follow Jesus. What a testimony for those two girls!

When I woke up, I talked about the dream with the Holy Spirit. It was clear that I was not the main character in the dream; it was about my sister-in-law and brother-in-law. Yet I did not have the impression that I was to share the dream with them. Rather, I felt urged by God to pray for my sister-in-law's choice and my brother-in-law's uncertainty, so I did.

About six weeks later, I received word from my sister-in-law that she had been spontaneously baptized on Easter Sunday in the water near their home, by her husband! Their children were there. Her choice for Jesus was firm and she wanted to seal that with her baptism. When we spoke to them later, my brother-in-law told of the doubt he had suffered from before baptizing her. This gnawed away at him, but he felt supernatural power to get over the doubt and do it anyway. I am convinced that God's Spirit worked through the prayers I prayed for them. This is the impact of your and my prayers: they can turn things around and undo the works of the enemy. So let's witness together about the power of prayer so that many more people will pray again.

If you have a ministry of intercession, more often than not you will be given dreams to pray through about a person, organization or area. Perhaps you don't know if you have such a ministry, or on the contrary, you know that you have been given a very different ministry by God. Even then, God can give you such dreams. Perhaps God wants to teach you to pray persistently for another person, or He places an emotion in your heart that you didn't know before. Sometimes we can be so focused on what we know and what God has entrusted to us that we would almost forget that we can learn a great deal in other areas. I know several people who for a period of time were suddenly awakened at night by the Holy Spirit to pray for someone, or for a situation or place. Then you know for sure that it is important for you to respond to God's request at that moment, and you almost can't help but pray.

Bert, a street evangelist, experiences this on a regular basis.

Bert's story

When my wife and I came to faith, we immediately had a desire to serve God.

We became active in His Kingdom right away and held Bible studies in our home. New people joined us every week. We were somewhat overconfident and regularly cried out to the devil that he was losing people again and he certainly didn't like that very much. At that time, we regularly went through spiritual battles and suffered intimidation from the enemy.

One time I woke up at night with a strange feeling; something was not right. The grim feeling increased and suddenly I saw a dark apparition. It startled me violently and I broke out in a sweat. I dared not look at it and turned around. It was exactly three in the morning; I saw the time on the alarm clock. I began to punish the apparition, but he did not go away. I prayed even harder, but he remained where he was. I called Jesus for help and suddenly the darkness was gone and there was peace and tranquility in the room. I thanked Jesus, but was very upset about what had happened.

That morning I went to church. A sister in the Lord came to me asking, "Bert, what was going on last night? I was awakened by God at three o'clock and felt that I had to pray for you." I told her the story. I discovered that I had been praying out of fear and not authority. As a young believer, I had not yet fully understood that I should not challenge the devil, nor did I yet understand the authority we have received in Jesus. Fortunately, God wants to protect His children and sought someone through whom He could do that. God found my sister and woke her up in the middle of the night. She did pray from authority, which meant the devil had to go. Because of what happened that night and how my sister reacted to it, I learned something. I take it very seriously when someone is on my heart in the night. I know God is looking for people to break the devil's work so that His will happens on earth.

I am now regularly awakened in the night to pray for situations. Sometimes I hear later what the effect was of my prayers, sometimes I do not. I trust that God is working it out and that prayer is not in vain.

One night God woke me up at four o'clock and said, "I want you to walk your dog now." I thought to myself that it was rather early for a walk with the dog, but I took what God said to me seriously and left the house. As I was walking, I saw a boy sitting alone on a bench. I felt for him and spoke to him. I was able to tell him that God had awakened me especially for him. I shared the gospel with him and told him that God loved him. The boy was very touched by this nightly encounter. He told me that he wondered why he was on earth and what the meaning of life was. I was allowed to tell him that God has a good plan for him and that he was placed in the world for a reason. It changed his life and he met Jesus.

I love stories like this, they are a beautiful example of how much God cares about that one person. He wants to partner with you in that. Let the Holy Spirit inspire you. You don't need to be focused on what the devil is doing, rather focus on what God is doing! God is looking for you and me to pray for what is dear to Him, His children. Are you awake?

Healing in Families

> But the steadfast love of the LORD is from everlasting to everlasting on those who fear him, and his righteousness to children's children (...)
> – PSALM 103:17

If there is one thing God's heart is moved for, it is healing in families. The place where there is so much brokenness and where people are wounded is a mission field for God's goodness and healing. Earlier, I shared that God performed a great miracle in our family. That does not mean that this solved everything; our souls and minds need time and love from God the Father to be fully restored. But this miracle of God loosened something that had been stuck for generations. Many people recognize this. They don't seem to be moving forward within their family relationships, there is too much pain and brokenness. It takes a miracle, a heavenly intervention, to break through this. God wants to speak and give keys, even through dreams, to restore and bring our families back to God's heart and His original plan. I know people who have gone through a whole healing process with their families through dreams. Dreams are God's way of speaking to them in that moment, and they bring a tremendous flow of blessing!

Geralda also experienced God giving her insight about the mess in her family through a dream. It's a great testimony of what God wants to do for you, too.

Geralda's story

I attended a prophetic training, and at the end of the first evening there was an opportunity to receive prayer for specific prophetic gifts. Dite prayed over me that I would soon receive a dream that would bring healing to my family. I liked the thought, but had no idea that God would give me a dream with far-reaching consequences that very night. In the dream, I saw family members of mine who suddenly changed shape. They had blue circles around their eyes and became very aggressive. I rebuked the powers of the devil who did this in the name of Jesus, and saw how they changed back into my relatives. When I woke up, I knew this was more than just a dream, and I started to investigate. To make a very long story short, my ancestors turned out to be Freemasons. I thought my family had been serving God for generations, but this turned out not to be the case at all. Far into my ancestry, God gave insight in a special way about the unhealthy bonds that had been established by the devil. I saw the consequences of those ungodly bonds in my own life and family through all the depression and sickness we experienced. God wanted this to stop and for us to become free from the influence of my ancestors' choices. I asked forgiveness for my ancestors' sin in their stead and together with the Holy Spirit, I cut the ties and disconnected them from my life and that of my

> family and relatives. The wonderful thing was that we all immediately noticed the effect of this; reconciliation came between family members who had not spoken to each other for a long time. We were able to speak about Jesus to family members who did not yet know Him, family members chose to follow Jesus and were baptized. This had been unthinkable previously. Through this dream, a door had opened for all of us to deeper healing and freedom on many levels.

This is one of the many testimonies in which God exposes a family curse. Just think what would happen if every child of God were to attune their ears to hear what heaven is saying, receive these kinds of dreams *and* act on them. How many families would be released from generational curses and generational wounds! How many families would be brought back to the heart of the Father! When I read the Bible, I see hope, power and authority. I do not intend to lower my standard to that of the world or what we see with earthly eyes. Jesus' mission is to bring every person back into the safety and security of God's love, where redemption, healing and deliverance flows. Think of the impact when this starts flowing in families!

Dreams in Your Marriage

> Therefore a man shall leave his father and his mother and hold fast to his wife, and they shall become one flesh.
> — GENESIS 2:24

Have you ever experienced this? At breakfast, you tell your partner what you dreamt that night. To your amazement, they have dreamed the same thing. Or you both received part of a dream, or dreamed about the exact same subject, but in a different form. How is this possible?

Actually, it is not at all strange. In the words of Genesis, as a married couple you are "one flesh". As a married couple, you form a unit. Maybe it doesn't always feel that way, but spiritually speaking, you are fused together. Thus, if you are open to it, you could receive insight or answers from God together through dreams. Joost and I experience this regularly and it strengthens our relationship like a "threefold cord" (Eccles. 4:12). As a couple, you can simply reach out for this and ask God to meet you in the night.

Perhaps God wants to say something to you, an important message that concerns both of you. But also remember that God enjoys seeing His children enjoy themselves, even if it is during a dream. Ask Him for adventurous dreams just for the two of you—I guarantee you it will be fun! My husband and I regularly pray and ask if we can go on adventures together at night, meeting Jesus in new ways. It doesn't always happen the same night, but we have experienced how God responds to the desires of our hearts. He has given us the same dreams several times about important decisions.

A while back, I suddenly woke up in the middle of the night. I turned around and looked straight into my husband's open eyes. At that moment we were both filled with heavenly joy, we burst into laughter and laughed uncontrollably for at least ten minutes. I don't know about you, but I rarely have a fit of laughter when I wake up, let alone wake up at the exact same time as my husband. It was heavenly joy and it refreshed us immensely! I do believe that God is always happy to give us laughter, though; in His presence is "fullness of joy" (Ps. 16:11)! Just look: "He who sits in the heavens laughs" (Ps. 2:4).

As a married couple, you have another wonderful opportunity—you can ask God to reveal how He sees your partner in a dream. Your own view may be so clouded by all that you have been through that it is difficult to still see your partner from God's perspective. When God shows you that in a dream, you can see clearly again, without being colored by your past experiences. Sometimes you go through tough times as a married couple or you are looking for more depth in your marriage. Then it is so beautiful to hear from God how He sees your partner. There are even testimonies that God brings restoration to marriages through dreams! Who knows, maybe God wants to give you a dream through which you supernaturally begin to understand your loved one better. You can also ask the Holy Spirit to give your partner a dream about you. Marriage is precious to God and He wants very much to help us make it prosperous and vibrant.

Dreams in Friendships

> For in one Spirit we were all baptized into one body—Jews or Greeks, slaves or free—and all were made to drink of one Spirit.
> – 1 CORINTHIANS 12:13

In friendships, it makes sense if you regularly appear in each other's dreams. After all, you are part of each other's lives. God wants to use your friendship, and He can speak about your relationship through dreams.

When you have a close friendship with a brother or sister in the faith, you can also have the same dreams, or each have a different part of a dream. After all, we are one body in Jesus Christ. God's Spirit joins His body together, like the radiant bride for whom King Jesus is coming back. So it's not so crazy to talk to each other about dreams from time to time. Especially if a friend appears in your dream.

I regularly have dreams about friends. I have learned that I dream mostly about friendships God has given so that we can support and encourage each other in His Kingdom. The first time I experienced this, the following happened: I dreamed that I was cleaning up in my house with a friend.

There was a pile of junk that my friend and I were quietly sorting through, both fully focused. I thought my friend's dedication to cleaning out my stuff during the dream was remarkable. I knew God was trying to say something through that. The next day I asked her if she happened to dream. She told me that in a dream she was in my house and had cleaned up stuff with me. She had exactly the same dream, in other words! At the time we both had this dream, I was cleaning things up in my life. God wanted to make it clear to me that I could involve her in this, and ask her for help and prayer. He knows that we often prefer to figure things out on our own, but we are not made for that. It was a simple dream, with an important message. I didn't doubt I could trust her, and she didn't doubt she was the right person to help me. We had both heard it from God and saw the blessing of it when we started doing this.

For God there are unlimited possibilities to make Himself known. He can simultaneously give the same dream to different people to reveal Himself. Therefore, as friends and brothers and sisters, we can help each other with our dreams. The Bible says:

> To each is given the manifestation of the Spirit for the common good.
> – 1 CORINTHIANS 12:7

And there is something else we can help each other with as friends when it comes to dreams. Think about Daniel for a moment. In Daniel 2 we read that he told his three friends that he wanted to ask God the meaning of Nebuchadnezzar's dream. Daniel understood that we see more of God when we are together. He believed in the power of prayer, and as these four friends turned to God, their unanimous prayer drew the heavens toward them. This is an example for us as we start to work with our dreams. Also, ask your friends to pray with you for the meaning of a dream!

Keys for Deliverance and Healing

> The LORD your God is in your midst, a mighty one who will save (...)
> – ZEPHANIAH 3:17A

God wants to speak. He wants to work with us to bring His Kingdom to earth. His will is not limited to worldly frameworks or human-made boundaries. It is no problem for God to show something in the night that causes a breakthrough in a person's life. This is a great opportunity, especially if you regularly help or counsel other people. For example, do you give pastoral care or counseling, work in (mental) health care or pray for people regularly? Or do you not do these things yet, but long for God to touch people through you? Then God wants to give you keys, even during the night. He did that with Ananias:

> Now there was a disciple at Damascus named Ananias. The Lord said to him in a vision, "Ananias." And he said, "Here I am, Lord." And the Lord said to him, "Rise and go to the street called Straight, and at the house of Judas look for a man of Tarsus named Saul, for behold, he is praying, and he has seen in a vision a man named Ananias come in and lay his hands on him so that he might regain his sight."
> – ACTS 9:10-12

What an amazing passage! God gave Ananias the hometown, street name, house number and name of Saul. God showed him that Saul prayed and had a vision and that he was now blind, and what Ananias had to do to make him see again. This dream contains a whole range of words of knowledge! The word "vision" in this text is the Hebrew word *horama*. This means to receive a sight in a divine ecstasy or during sleep. It is not clear whether Ananias received this vision during the day or night, but it is a powerful example of how

God wants to speak to bring healing and freedom. At the same time, this Bible story shows that the one who needs help, Saul, also receives a message from God. God shows him in advance that he is going to be healed of his blindness. Are you in physical or spiritual need? Ask the Holy Spirit for dreams that show you the way to your healing or deliverance.

I frequently experience God revealing something during a dream or as I slumber. Then I receive a word or insight about the person I am going to meet or may help the following day. Sometimes it is abundantly clear, other times I need to go back to God with the information He has given me.

Like the time God gave a dream about Jaleesha. It was the night before the first evening of a course on freedom in which I was one of the mentors. God gave me a dream in which I saw the face of a woman I didn't know. I could not see her body because there were snakes swarming over her. Above her head, movies were playing of things that had happened in her life. I could see the pain and sorrow on her face, and she was trying to extricate herself from the snakes that held her captive. When I woke up, my heart was filled with compassion for this woman. I was sure God wanted to do something, but found it hard to know what because I didn't recognize the woman. I started praying and God made it clear to me that it would all fall into place. All I had to do was trust Him. That evening I saw the woman come in for the course. I knew immediately that it was her. It probably won't surprise you to hear that she was assigned to my group. She later told me that when she saw me, she became extremely anxious and wanted to run away. The demons in her knew that the time had come to release this woman. During the prayer moments, I listened carefully to the Holy Spirit and so was able to name something at the right time that I knew was holding her in darkness. This allowed us to work together and give Jesus the room to be her Deliverer. She went through a deep process of change in a short time.

I really love it when God does things like this. What a powerful Deliverer He is! We don't have to muddle through when we pray with people. He helps His children out of their prison. I often experience God showing me someone's face, which immediately gives me the right focus when I encounter that person. God also regularly gives a key to release someone from their prison. The devil lies, twists and hides, but the bright light of God's revelation exposes the works of the enemy. The Bible says that "we are not ignorant of his [satan's] designs" (2 Cor. 2:11). We can receive revelation about the enemy's plans through the Holy Spirit and nullify them.

We read how God delivers people from a literal prison several times in the Bible, but how many people today are trapped in a spiritual prison? Many struggle with depression and all sorts of other mental health issues. The mental health system cannot handle the demand and the success rates of treatments are low. People need Jesus, He is the only one who can free and heal them. What would happen if we asked God to speak in the night before we help others? Imagine if people who came for help or prayer asked God to give keys to the one helping them. Then what we do becomes much more powerful, we learn to destroy the enemy's work and make room for what God wants to do in the lives of others who are so precious.

A friend of mine works in a closed ward of a mental health institution. Here people are admitted who have psychological problems and need more help than a weekly meeting with a psychologist. She regularly counsels people who have been hospitalized many times and do not seem to be getting better. They have been stuck in an endless cycle, until God intervenes.

One night I had a dream in which I saw an unknown man. In the dream I saw the person's life history, with the struggles and moments in which he had been damaged. I also saw the talents God had given this man and some specific traits he had.

For example, I saw him playing a guitar; he wore a cap with green and yellow on it and moved his head to the beat of the music. This was a literal dream with accurate information about a person I did not know as of yet.

The next day, when I woke up, I saw that I had received a message from my friend. She asked me to pray with her for one of her clients. He had been hospitalized for the umpteenth time and was suicidal. My friend was moved by him and knew that Jesus could help him. I asked her if he happened to look like this and that, and told her that God had already spoken to him in a dream that night. I told her what God had shown and she was able to discuss this with the man. He was deeply touched by the fact that God knew him and was with him when he was struggling so much. He still had a way to go after this moment, but he had hope in his heart and faith for his life. He wanted to live, perhaps for the first time!

You see, God has keys for everyone who loves Him, both the one in need and the one helping. Reach out, ask God to speak and you will see heaven break through.[18]

Dreams in the Prophetic Ministry

> And he said, "Hear my words: If there is a prophet among you, I the LORD make myself known to him in a vision; I speak with him in a dream."
> – NUMBERS 12:6

Dreams are an indispensable part of the prophetic ministry Christ has given to us, His body. If God has given you a prophetic or leadership ministry, it may very well be that He will speak through dreams for your own congregation, your region, your country, or for the body of Christ. Such a dream then has a message that is of interest for many people because it is about something the Holy Spirit is doing nationwide or worldwide.

God is your Master; He makes sure that you gradually learn to recognize these dreams and distinguish them from other dreams. After all, not every dream is for the global Church, even if you have a prophetic ministry. You need wisdom and discernment, and God wants to give that. In addition, it is helpful if you can share with brothers and sisters who have experience with this.

I will give an example of a dream I received not long ago for the body of Christ. This dream is relevant to our time.

DREAM
Eagle

I was standing on the beach, along the waterline. I looked around, and no matter where I looked, there was water everywhere.

Then my attention was drawn to a spot about 5 meters from the shore in the water to my left. Although nothing could be seen yet, I knew I had to keep looking.

Below the surface of the water, a dark spot appeared and grew larger and larger. A mixture of wonder and fear came over me. Inside me there was a battle between the familiar and the new. The wonder won; the fear gave way to awe.

The surface of the water opened and a huge wing became visible. The sea water churned and murmured as if it were speaking with all voices at once. The wing was followed by the body and head of an eagle; the second wing also surfaced. Only for a brief moment could I see the giant eagle in its entirety as it began to move. The first wing disappeared underwater again, and the body and second wing followed. Then the eagle rose again from the water. Thus it passed like watermill blades in front of me through the water from my left side to my right.

Five times it dipped under the water and resurfaced. As I watched it, I knew it was God. Then He spoke to me: "I am going to show Myself in a whole new way to those who dare to look."

Behind me, a crowd of people had gathered on the beach. More and more people joined, until I could no longer see the end of the crowd. I pointed to the water. Everyone followed my finger with their eyes and they were silent with the wonder and awe of God.

When I woke up, I asked the Holy Spirit to help me understand the dream. He told me to let my eyes be led to the spot in the water. Letting your sight be led is crucial to seeing what God reveals. Fear arose in me, fear of the unknown and the unseen. Yet I dared to trust in the Father's goodness, so the fear did not win. I continued to look. This is important because many people dare not go beyond their last experience or most intense encounter with God. They dare not believe that there is more for them and something better to come. Fear causes them to avert their gaze and miss the new.

The Holy Spirit showed me that water in the Bible symbolizes Himself and the environment in which He moves. The eagle is a symbol of God. An eagle is supposed to fly; it is not supposed to be in water. Yet this eagle went completely under water up to five times. Five is the number of God's grace. This is how the Holy Spirit spoke: "A new grace is available to see God moving in a whole new way through the Holy Spirit. The new thing God gives is very surprising and not obvious. What you think you know, the logical and explainable, is shaken up. The new can only be seen if you lay down your own frameworks and dare to expect something new. Let your gaze, that which you see, be guided by the Holy Spirit, not by your own mind or previous experiences. And dare to keep looking and keep listening. Then you will see what no eye has seen and hear what no ear has heard.

> But, as it is written, "What no eye has seen, nor ear heard, nor the heart of man imagined, what God has prepared for those who love him" (...)
> — 1 CORINTHIANS 2:9

This was a prophetic dream with a message for the body of Jesus. This is the time of dreams and visions. These are no longer reserved for the few, they are for all generations, races and peoples. God wants to awaken and give hunger for that which He is about to pour out on earth. By sharing this prophetic word, He can prepare hearts and awaken desire. He can encourage, affirm and break down frameworks, if we allow Him to. Then we will see more and more of His goodness.

A prophetic word often has multiple layers and can reveal something different and deeper in different seasons. This was a word for myself; I was the one with the pointing finger through which many others began to see. I put this into practice by being active in my prophetic ministry by speaking, writing and training. This was how I got to take people into seeing with spiritual eyes.

I learned over time that dreams for the body of Christ have a different "tone", sometimes because of how many people I see in the dream and other times because I just know it is a message for our country or beyond. Often it feels like there is a certain "weight" on the message. Sometimes you need to wait a long time until you actually see what God has spoken in such a dream take place. Prophetic people recognize this; waiting takes a long time. Go pray out the dream. Your prayer is powerful and at the same time it gives peace in your own heart.

You can receive a dream for your country without being a prophet; at the same time, God can show you that you have more impact than you thought. God is the only one who can increase your mandate and grant supernatural power to your words. Trust Him and the path He is taking with you, and above all, don't forget to enjoy yourself along the way!

Receiving Messages

> Pursue love, and earnestly desire the spiritual gifts, especially that you may prophesy.
> — 1 CORINTHIANS 14:1

What do you do when someone comes to you with the message that God has given them a dream for you? You probably want to know what God wants to say, but may have trouble with the form. Many people have been disappointed in the past by a misinterpreted word or misuse of the prophetic ministry. They feel manipulated or lied to, and therefore have closed their hearts to any form of speaking from God. If the same is true for you, I want to say to you that this should never have happened. It is sad that someone has represented God in this way.

God is a God who speaks; it is His nature to communicate. We see that from the very beginning. God created humans, and walked and talked with them every day in the Garden of Eden. Right into the last book of the Bible, God shows that He speaks through people to proclaim His will on earth. In the verses before this chapter, Paul wrote about the importance of prophecy and the necessity of love. This combination is the key—the fuller we are of God's love, the more we will be like Jesus, think like Jesus and speak like Jesus. Jesus spoke words of life, blessing and absolute truth. He is the Word incarnate:

> All things were made through him, and without him was not any thing made that was made.
> — JOHN 1:3

Jesus speaks things into existence. Every word from His lips creates something new, something living. Prophecy is speaking on behalf of Jesus. First, by affirming and encouraging one another, but also by giving direction. Our words have unimaginable power: "Death and life are in the power of the tongue" (Prov. 18:21). When we live and speak from love, something special happens; we create a new world with our words.

The exchange of a prophetic word always involves two equally powerful people—the sender and the receiver. No matter how gifted the person who gives you a prophetic word is, the fact is that we only know and prophesy "in part" (1 Cor. 13:9). Therefore, God points out to us the responsibility we have as the receiver of a prophetic word. He says:

> Do not despise prophecies, but test everything; hold fast what is good.
> — 1 THESSALONIANS 5:20-21

Strangely enough, in this, people seem to hear the second command and conveniently forget the first and last. That's called selective listening—you hear what you want to hear. In this case, that is, try all things and if you don't like it, get rid of it. But that's not what it says here. This is a call to discernment. Do not despise what God speaks, even if it is brought with limitations and imperfections by a brother or sister; preserve the good. Or as the saying goes, don't throw the baby out with the bathwater. When God speaks to another through a dream, you are also dealing with their interpretation. In that, someone can go completely wrong, even though God really wants to speak to you through that dream. It takes patience and grace to deal with that. But you also need the gift of discernment (1 Cor. 12:10). Discernment of spirits is a gift—you can ask God for it. You will need this gift if you want to properly test a prophetic word. With this you establish the source of the words. Do they come from the Spirit of God, from the person, or are they spoken by a demonic spirit?

Not every word is edifying. There are also spiritual powers that are out to enchant, oppress and deceive you. The Bible warns us about this. This is not to create fear and division, causing everyone to look at each other as a potential deceiver. We are children of God, born of the Spirit of God. We may be wrong at times, but that absolutely does not make us false prophets. A false prophet speaks from the wrong source—the enemy. Jesus encourages us to stay close to Him; He *is* the truth. Moreover, Jesus says "each tree is known by its own fruit" (Luke 6:44a). So look at the fruit in the life of the one who gives you the word; you can tell a lot from that.

It is good to take a look at the word God speaks through another person. Ask the recipient to write down the dream for you, or do that yourself so that you can go to God with it. The bottom line then is this—do not despise the prophecies; make sure you have the dream on paper, or record it, test everything, keep the good. So go to God with the word and embrace what He wants to say.

How do you actually test a word (or in this case, a dream)? You don't do this by looking at your experiences or mindset, but by going back to God and His Word. A prophetic word is often outside of your own thinking and understanding. God gives it to take you out of your comfort zone and deeper into His plan for your life. He wants to draw you closer to His heart.

Ask yourself the following questions when someone tells you a dream they had for you. First: Is it in line with God's Word and His character? This does not always mean that the word is literally in the Bible; God's Spirit is not limited to the Bible. But a word from God never contradicts the Bible.

Next: Does the word click in your mind? Is the dream in line with the direction Jesus is already leading you, or is it going in a completely different direction? The latter can still be a message from God. You just didn't know it yet. But it seems like somewhere you already knew it. It clicks the moment you hear it; the Spirit of God in you confirms the word.

Third: Is the word being confirmed? When God speaks, you will find that He confirms it through those around you. Talk about it with your spiritual leaders and loved ones. God will also confirm the word to you Himself, perhaps through a dream, a Bible passage or in one of the many other ways He uses.

And finally, does it bring you closer to God? That should always be the fruit of a prophetic word. Does it build up or break down? Does it bring freedom or bondage? Does it bring you clarity or doubt? Does it bring joy or oppression? Does it give peace or turmoil? As you move along with the prophetic word, God's Spirit affirms you and encourages you. He has already paved the way for you!

This last question is so important. It is a good indicator of a prophetic word, both at the time you receive the word and when you start praying about it and acting on it. As I was writing this section, I "happened" to receive a question from a sister asking me to look at her dream. I sent her the interpretation God gave me. This was her response: "I have read your interpretation at least six times and each time I am deeply touched somewhere. It is as if the Lord is suddenly that much closer." This is the goal—to bring that other person closer to God. That is the most beautiful thing there is!

Sharing Dreams

> Pursue love, and earnestly desire the spiritual gifts, especially that you may prophesy.
> – 1 CORINTHIANS 14:1

If you suspect that you have been given a dream for someone else, there are a few things to consider.

If this dream is indeed for another person, you may assume that God is giving the meaning to you in addition to the dream. So go to God with the dream and ask for His guidance in what to share and how to share it. In settings where prophecy is normal, believers can become lax in how they pass on a message from God. Of course, you may practice and make mistakes, but that is no excuse for carelessness. Many people go straight to the person in question when they have received something. It is better to go back to God first, ask Him about the message He wants to give for the other person, and keep asking questions. You may receive more accurate information that strengthens the word, or a beautiful picture. It is affirming when you find that the Holy Spirit wants to say more to you, and the recipient is powerfully touched by God's clear message.

If you can't figure out the meaning of the dream, but you feel you may share it with the recipient, just do so. Share the dream humbly, and trust that the recipient is also filled with the Holy Spirit.

God's message goes through you; you are the filter, so to speak. This means that with the best of intentions you can still misinterpret the message or share it just a little awkwardly. Be aware of that and take responsibility for your "filter"; get it cleaned. But know that the Holy Spirit can also strengthen our imperfect words in many ways. He can still speak clearly even when we don't have the interpretation quite right. If you as the sender and the other person as the receiver are already accustomed to speaking within a prophetic culture, the receiver knows that they must test the word. If not, you can remind the receiver of the importance of testing. Love and a humble attitude are the key.

Perhaps you are tremendously excited about what God has told you about the person, and you cannot imagine that the other person is not as excited as you are. Still, it is important to ask for wisdom when sharing a dream. You may not know what that other person is going through. You may not even know if that other person is open to receiving a word from God.

Not that you should be reluctant, but you should be wise. That way God's message can reach that other person in the best way possible.

How do you share a dream? I'll give you a few tips. First, give the other person a moment to prepare for the message so that they can better receive what God is saying. For example, you can introduce your dream with: "I had a dream last night and you played a part in it. Is it okay if I share the dream with you?"

Second, keep it lighthearted. For example, you could say, "I have the impression that God wants to say this with this." That sounds very different from, "God says ..." This way you create space for the receiver. They can now receive the message freely and discern what God wants to say.

Then ask the receiver, "Do you have a click with this?" or "Does this mean anything to you?" Give the other person room to respond and give you feedback on what you have shared. The other person may also want to let it sink in and choose to come back to it later. That's fine, too. Give it time! Either way, it is instructive to hear the impact of the message.

Help the other person retain the message. Ask, "Do you want me to write it down for you? Or do you want to record it on your phone?" Prophetic words and messages from God are there to be treasured. Do try to stick to the core message when you do this.

Finally, point out to the recipient that they are supposed to test the message for themselves. Be focused on bringing the other person closer to God. You want to bring the other person into deeper connection with God, not make them dependent on you. You release that other person to God and can leave them in the care of the best Father there is.

When the other person becomes dependent on you to "hear from God", you get an unhealthy connection. That's how it was in the Old Testament. The people depended on that one prophet of God because they couldn't get to God themselves. That time is gone forever with the coming of Jesus Christ! He says:

> I am the way, and the truth, and the life. No one comes to the Father except through me.
> – JOHN 14:6

Even when people come back to you repeatedly for prophetic insight, point them to their own relationship with God. That is the best gift you can give another person.

Unexpected Response

> For all the promises of God find their Yes in him. That is why it is through him that we utter our Amen to God for his glory.
> – 2 CORINTHIANS 1:20

When you want to share a dream and the recipient reacts defensively or does not want to hear the dream at all, give the dream back to God. Ask Him to give that person the message. Or pray for another opportunity to still give the message. In this way, you remain free from blame and God can do what you cannot.

Below I share an example of a dream that did not immediately evoke the response I was hoping for, and how I dealt with it.

Several years ago, God gave me a dream about my brother-in-law, my husband's brother. In the dream, God showed that he would be free from a terrible generational disease that ran in the family. In the dream, I saw that his children would also be free from it. I thought this was a confronting message to give to him. I knew that he had not yet been tested for the disease and that he had symptoms that made him anticipate becoming ill in the future. This would mean that his children could also be carriers of the disease.

I found it difficult to deliver this message and made myself take three days to pray about it. In those three days, God only gave more confirmations, including through the Bible. I carefully gathered and wrote everything down and felt encouraged by God to share the message. With my heart pounding, I called my brother-in-law to ask if I could come over. I shared the message of the dream with him and his wife. They hardly seemed surprised or touched. They did find it extraordinary and said, "Time will tell." After three days of prayer, and the faith God had given me, that was not quite the reaction I had counted on. I thought they would be very happy. Despite their reaction, I was not discouraged and did not lose faith in the message. I had done what God asked of me.

In the years that followed, the Holy Spirit encouraged me to keep praying for my brother-in-law and his family. His faith in Jesus grew, and fortunately God commissioned another person to give him a message, this time to get tested for the disease. He did so, even though he thought it was very scary. And guess what? He was not a carrier of the disease! That means that his children are also not carriers and all the generations that follow are set free from this terrible disease. This is the kind of God we serve!

It was wonderful that God showed this to me in a dream, and with that gave me the faith to keep praying for him and his family in the years that followed. Sometimes people are not yet ready to receive a promise in their hearts, but when God says you can share the word, it plants a seed of faith. Their spirits have heard the promise, even if their ears can't or won't hear it yet.

This is not about whether I understood the dream correctly and get credit for that, it is about God's will being done in this family. Remember Abraham and Sarah? They received a word from God that they would have a many descendants. They then had to wait years for it and as a result even thought they had to help the promise out a little. Ishmael was conceived. But the promise was fulfilled after all, and Sarah had a son in her old age: Isaac. We can learn to trust God at His word, even if we don't get the desired response right away. God is not a man that He would lie (Num. 23:19) and His promises are always yes and amen (2 Cor. 1:20).

Dreaming Children

> See that you do not despise one of these little ones. For I tell you that in heaven their angels always see the face of my Father who is in heaven.
> — MATTHEW 18:10

Dreaming is for all ages, including children. How wonderful it would be if children learned at an early age that God speaks to them, even in the night. What a change would then take place: no more unnecessary sleepless nights for children and their parents, no more fear of the dark or of monsters under the bed. Children who have a personal relationship with the Holy Spirit and grow up to be strong, loving people who change the world! Below I share some keys that you can apply in your family. This is not meant to be a set of rules, but suggestions. It could also be that God is making you aware of things from your own childhood.

Think back to the chapter about the left and right hemispheres. In children, the functioning of these two is still quite balanced, which is why they are generally more open to dreams. In children, REM sleep lasts longer than in adults. In babies, REM sleep takes up to 60 percent of the night. In addition, children often dream in great detail and find it more difficult to distinguish dreams from reality.

Many think it is normal for children to be afraid of the dark and have scary dreams. One magazine for mothers said that children had nightmares because they had a room that was too hot, or because they were growing up. But it's high time that changed! Children live in the same spiritual reality as we do. This is nothing to be afraid of, but something to be aware of. The chances of your child getting nightmares from the room temperature are many times smaller than the chances of the enemy trying to exert influence. As a parent, you have a responsibility to protect your child from unhealthy influences, both natural *and* spiritual. Fortunately, you do not have to do this alone: God has given His Spirit and sends His angels to assist you; you can cooperate with heaven! The story of Helen and her mother shows this in practice.

Helen's story

When I was eight years old, I had a bizarre recurring dream. I dreamt that I came to work in a brothel where a woman was in charge. This woman was big and strong and darkness surrounded her. In that dream, my mother came to set me free. Every time I had this dream—this happened up to three times—I told my mother.

At the beginning of my adolescence, I began to desire to work as a prostitute. This desire was so serious that I even told my mother. My mother was greatly shocked by this and could still remember the dreams of the past. During that period, she visited a church regularly. At one point she was in a conversation with a woman there and told her about my desire to work as a prostitute. This woman became very upset by this and said she was going to intercede for this immediately, with some other women. They interceded for me for a period of time with my mother and dealt with the darkness that had a hand in this in the name of Jesus.

When I look back, I see that the devil tried to sow darkness and destruction in my life at an early age.

> He gave me these dark dreams as a young, open-minded child, trying to get me to offer myself as a prostitute. Fortunately, it never came to that and, in fact, I see that God completely reversed this plan of the enemy and used it for good. Years later I actually went to work for an organization that works among prostitutes. There I was allowed to share the love of Jesus with the many women who were going through life broken and bound by darkness. We experienced how many women got out of prostitution and started a new life with Jesus.
>
> Jesus is so loving! He placed His protection over my life, prompting my mother and several other women to pray for me and break every dark claim on my life. No plan of the enemy can stand against our great God!

Almost everyone I talked to about dreams in their childhood felt shame about going to their parents with it. Shame is one of the ways the enemy tries to silence children, so pay close attention to this! Helen's openness led her mother to pray for her daughter, which gave a breakthrough. Helen's incredible story shows the reality of the enemy's plans. If we know those plans, we can undo them in a tactical way.

Children often encounter stories of monsters under their beds and ghosts in the dark from an early age. TV and the internet are full of images and words that do not convey love, peace and life. Somehow, witches and zombies attract the attention of many children, unfortunately resulting in fear. You can see this reflected in the night. Be aware of what your children come into contact with.

Also, choose your words carefully. When a child is acting out, parents often threaten things like, "Tonight you're going to bed early." Although parents often have the best intentions, and a child needs adequate sleep, such statements can cause your child to associate night and sleep with stress, anxiety and punishment.

Help your children with a good preparation for the night and take time to put them to bed. The most precious thing you can give your children in parenting is to bring them into a personal relationship with Jesus. He is the only Person who is always with them. A friend of mine understands this principle. Even when things go differently than planned, she brings her children back to God's heart.

A teenager's story

> I had woken up several times during the night, always every twenty minutes. At 1:30 a.m. I called my mother. She asked what was wrong with me, and I said, "I kept waking up." My mom asked why that was, and then I told her what I had seen on social media that day. There I had read, if you wake up between three and four in the morning, ghosts are coming into your room. Actually, I don't believe that, but I still kept waking up and it did something to me. I didn't like it. My mother prayed for me and then I went to sleep. The next day we talked about it some more. It is important that you dare to tell your parents or other people who can help you when you see such things. I'm glad I slept well after that and it didn't bother me anymore.

This is a sobering story from everyday life. It is a fact that teens can come into contact with these things. How you handle it as a parent is critical.

Children and the Supernatural

> But when Jesus saw it, he was indignant and said to them, "Let the children come to me; do not hinder them, for to such belongs the kingdom of God."
> – MARK 10:14

From childhood, I was familiar with the supernatural. I knew it was as real as anything I saw around me on earth. Unfortunately, I did not know Jesus at the time and did not know that there were many spiritual beings in the heavenlies. Because of this, I did not have the ability to arm myself against the darkness. When God transferred me to the Kingdom of His light, I noticed a tremendous change. Suddenly it all became clear. When God took me into His principles of the supernatural; it was an advantage rather than a disadvantage that I had never doubted the existence of the spiritual world.

For many people, it's just the opposite. When you begin to reach out for more of the Holy Spirit, you find that you have often learned at a very young age to reason away the supernatural. It takes a long time to break free from such beliefs. But God made us as supernatural creatures and wants to give us so much more than we can understand with our earthly minds.

That places a responsibility on parents. Children believe what their parents say. Once you deny the spiritual world, perhaps out of fear, and teach your children that there can't be scary monsters in the room or in their dreams, you also shut your children off from beautiful, spiritual experiences with God. Of course, your children are not meant to focus on those monsters, but you can teach them that Jesus wants to give them beautiful things. Do not underestimate what children actually see and experience, even if you yourself do not see or feel anything at all. Denying doesn't help in this case, listening does. How you deal with spiritual things has a lot of influence on how a child learns to deal with the supernatural. Even if as a parent you have little experience with the spiritual world or understanding God's voice, you can still create an environment in which your child can grow in this.

The story of Samuel and Eli in 1 Samuel 3 shows this. Just take a look at Samuel's story! Samuel heard God's voice in the night. Eli heard nothing, yet he took Samuel seriously and told him what he should do if he heard his name again. Eli knew that God was speaking and wanted to give messages to his children. He asked Samuel the next morning to tell him what God had said to him. Eli did not let the fact that Samuel was a child hold him back.

We too may know that the same Holy Spirit who dwells in us also dwells in our children. They can meet God at any time and at any age, even before they are born. In Luke 1:41 we read that John the Baptist jumped in the womb of his mother, Elizabeth, when the latter greeted the pregnant Mary. He responded to the Holy Spirit because Mary was pregnant with the Savior of the world. The presence of God cannot be stopped or directed; His heart goes out to his children, great and small.

> (...) for he will be great before the Lord. And he must not drink wine or strong drink, and he will be filled with the Holy Spirit, even from his mother's womb.
> – LUKE 1:15

In the Bible we read that we are saved by faith (Eph. 2:8). When we are saved, we receive a guarantee of our inheritance, the Holy Spirit. Nowhere does it say that this is tied to an age. Nor do I read anywhere in the Bible that the Holy Spirit makes His dwelling in a person only after a certain age. Rather, Jesus warns us not to hinder children from coming to Him:

> And they were bringing children to him that he might touch them, and the disciples rebuked them. But when Jesus saw it, he was indignant and said to them, "Let the children come to me; do not hinder them, for to such belongs the kingdom of God."
> – MARK 10:13-14

In short, children have access to the Kingdom of God. Moreover, they do not have a smaller, childish Holy Spirit.

Through the Holy Spirit, they can connect with God and experience the supernatural. This is often easier for children because they are less bothered by unbelief and set ideas of thinking. The Bible speaks of this:

> In that same hour he rejoiced in the Holy Spirit and said, "I thank you, Father, Lord of heaven and earth, that you have hidden these things from the wise and understanding and revealed them to little children; yes, Father, for such was your gracious will."
> – LUKE 10:21

According to this verse, God makes truth known to little children. We as adults had better listen! The key is that we help and teach children to cooperate with the Holy Spirit dwelling in them. We may tell them what to expect: that they have authority in Jesus' name, and how to use it. But also don't underestimate what they themselves learn from the Holy Spirit. There are such great opportunities for children to meet God and hear from Him! When you put your child to bed, you may lay them in Jesus' loving arms. When you leave the bedroom, He takes over the care of your child. This gives you and your child peace of mind.

Teaching Children

> And these words that I command you today shall be on your heart. You shall teach them diligently to your children, and shall talk of them when you sit in your house, and when you walk by the way, and when you lie down, and when you rise.
> – DEUTERONOMY 6:6-7

There is a new outpouring of God's Spirit in our time. It is our responsibility as parents to guide our family in this and thus help build God's Kingdom. Your children are born "for such a time as this" (Est. 4:14) and need parents who will take them into the heart of God, into the movement of the Holy Spirit. But how do you do that, specifically in the area of dreams?

First, it is important to teach your children the truth about the dark and the night. Read a Bible text with them or make a beautiful drawing together to hang on the wall to remind them of God's words. In doing so, you can teach them these things:

- Jesus protects me during the night
- God's angels are always around me
- I don't need to be afraid, for I am safe in the darkness
- God speaks to me in a way I understand
- He always hears me when I talk to Him
- When I am afraid I call Jesus and tell Mom or Dad or whoever cares for me

Second, whenever possible, it is good to protect children from images and words that have a negative impact. Explain to children that the things you watch or listen to do not always have a nice effect. In this way, they will better understand why they should not watch certain things and will be more likely to make the right choices themselves. Now, paying attention to what fills your children, especially in our current society, is quite a task, but it helps if you yourself are also careful about what you allow into your life. What is your home filled with, spiritually speaking? What do you look at, what do you say out loud? And remember, what you do often speaks louder than what you say. You can be a great example of what it means to be a friend of Jesus and a child of God.

In addition, before bedtime, make sure your children have time to come to you with their concerns. Then bring the concerns to Jesus together. Teach them that Jesus is always close to them and wants to speak to them. Pray over them that they will have dreams of God and heavenly encounters that they can remember.

Then, a small light or soft, instrumental worship music is may make them feel safe. The tips for good sleep from Part 2 (The Original Plan for Our Sleep) also apply to children.

Make it a habit to ask about your children's dreams in the morning and tell them about your dreams too. Just by you asking questions, your child will begin to pay attention to what happens during the night, and in this way awaken to the voice of God and the dreams He gives. Then ask the Holy Spirit to help them understand their dreams; ask God to make Himself clear. If the meaning is not yet plain, write down the dream with your child and leave it for now.

Are you struggling with how to deal with this whole area with your child? Don't panic! God the Father knows what He is doing and has been a Father for a long time. He also knows your shortcomings as a parent and will not give more than you can handle. However, He will always challenge you to trust Him more and more, even in raising your children. You can teach your child the following prayer:

Dear Father in Heaven,
Thank You for being with me tonight
and protecting me so that I can sleep well.
I would like to meet You tonight
and hear what You want to say to me.
Holy Spirit, will You help me to remember
and understand my dreams?
Amen

Children are open to dreams of God. Let's take them seriously. Just read about one of the many wonderful dreams Mila (age nine) received:

Mila's dream

I had a dream that I got to know Jesus better. I saw Jesus with a girl (that was me). I was learning from Him and Jesus was playing with me. We played on swings, painted, sang and danced together. He taught me what it is like in heaven and told me that Moses, Noah, Adam and Eve have a good time there. They worship Jesus there in heaven. The angels go to people on earth; they have fun with adults and children. Also in the hospital ... There they give relaxation, so the sick are distracted for a while, for example, before an operation. I saw angels going to countries where you are not allowed to worship Jesus. The angels broke down the idols. These were pink angels, causing more trust in Jesus. I saw more confidence coming, people started cheering for Jesus.

Belonging

> Now Joseph had a dream, and when he told it to his brothers they hated him even more.
> – GENESIS 37:5

God has a plan for families, that they would be loving and colorful; that they would be one. Unfortunately, throughout history we see brokenness in families. Joseph's family in the Old Testament is an example of this. In Genesis 37 we read that twice he received a dream from God and shared it with his family. The reaction was not exactly positive. How would things have turned out if Joseph had been able to fulfill his dreams with his family? If they had not allowed jealousy and envy to rule their hearts? It's difficult to say, but worth thinking about.

But that's not what happened. Joseph's journey was a lonely one. No doubt that shaped him, and God used it for good (Gen. 50:20). However, if our natural or spiritual siblings tell us that God has called them in a dream, I imagine God would prefer us to react differently to how Joseph's brothers did! What do you do when a brother or sister comes to you and tells you that they heard God's voice in the night? Do you tell them they are crazy or do you listen to them? Do you encourage them when they struggle with doubt?

God has no favorites. He has a unique plan for each of His children. You do not need to fear missing out on God's goodness!

> For God shows no partiality.
> — ROMANS 2:11

You may know this verse from the King James Version, "For there is no respect of persons with God." But I like the translation of English Standard Version better, because it shows that for God everyone is equal. Let's look at each other in the same way. We are cleansed, sanctified and justified. Chosen, called and set apart. Competent, fit and anointed to do the impossible with Jesus Christ. God has more than enough room for each of us; we don't have to fight for a place in His Kingdom.

> For you did not receive the spirit of slavery to fall back into fear, but you have received the Spirit of adoption as sons, by whom we cry, "Abba! Father!"
> — ROMANS 8:15

Not slaves but children. No distance but access. No punishment but blessing. Let us continue to remind one another of this truth! When God asks you to encourage and affirm another, perhaps in hearing God's voice, that is a wonderful thing.

God trusts you to encourage one of His children. It may be entirely in God's plan for you to walk with someone for a while, to help that person along their way. That doesn't mean that person is better than you or has a more important calling. It means that God thinks you are suitable for the job.

Maybe you feel more like young Joseph, and could use some help and encouragement. I understand that very well. As a newly converted believer, I thought it was perfectly normal to hear God's voice and have dreams and visions. (Don't get me wrong, I still believe that!) I found out that many people did not respond positively when I boldly shared what I was experiencing with God. People would say things like, "You have just started out!" and "What would you know about that?" Or worse, "I was as enthusiastic as you are at the beginning too; that will disappear soon enough!" I quickly learned that many Christians were used to keeping expectations low, rather than expecting God's glory. But that was not how I had come to know my Father!

I never doubted that God was speaking to me, but the reactions from those around me caused me to lose some of my boldness and joy in witnessing about God's great deeds. But what God gives, He protects and cares for. That is why I am writing this to you who recognize my story. Understanding God may sometimes seem like a lonely road, but you are being trained by the Master, who guides you in His ways. He understands you like no other and draws you close to His heart. This is not lost time, but rather precious time.

> And after you have suffered a little while, the God of all grace, who has called you to his eternal glory in Christ, will himself restore, confirm, strengthen, and establish you.
> – 1 PETER 5:10

God gave me great people who supported me. From the beginning there was always someone who had my back and encouraged me. Sometimes it just doesn't look the way you expect. Perhaps God gives a grandpa, an aunt or acquaintance you don't see very often. These people say just the right thing, allowing you to move forward. Ask God for a father or mother figure, spiritual brothers and sisters who push you forward and guide you. Ask Him to open your eyes to these people. He will not abandon you. Keep your heart open to other people; you were not born to be alone. Remember Joseph—he didn't get the immediate support he might have hoped for, but God took care of him *and* kept His promise. Despite everything, Joseph arrived at the exact place God had promised him in the dream. Won't God do the same for you?

PART | 8

Walking in God's Dreams

> What I tell you in the dark, say in the light (...)
> – MATTHEW 10:27a

God's Kingdom does not break through on earth without a fight, but the outcome of the battle is already certain—the whole earth will be full of God's glory (Hab. 2:14). Justice will prevail and love is the only thing that will endure, because the Word of God says so.

Every knee will bow before King Jesus. The Father's house will be full and every seat at His table will be occupied. The expansion of Jesus' Kingdom is not a mission for the next generation, but something God wants to do today through you and me, regardless of our age, race or origin. We are made for victory and stand strong on the rock, Jesus Christ. God fills us with His glory and allows us to walk in His will so that through us heaven can come on earth.

Receiving dreams is great, but you need more to come to the fullness of what God wants to give you. You need an awareness of your place in God's body. People who are on the same mission as you. A guide to walk in your dreams, and a push to wake up. Because what you receive in the night can change the world!

Wake-up Call

> How long will you lie there, O sluggard? When will you arise from your sleep? A little sleep, a little slumber, a little folding of the hands to rest, and poverty will come upon you like a robber, and want like an armed man.
> — PROVERBS 6:9-11

These straightforward verses, written by Solomon, sound a little funny. God says to us, "Get up, sleepyhead!" But wait ... aren't we allowed to sleep in for once from our Father? Of course we are! Yet this verse holds a serious key for us: God is warning us here not to fall into a slumber. This is a state that makes us lukewarm and in which life passes us by. In fact, this state brings poverty into our lives, spiritual lack.

God has so much to give us. He does not want us to "lie dormant" but to rise up in faith and strength. He wants us to be awake to what God's Spirit is doing, in us and around us. He wants us to follow Him and be awake to what He is doing on earth. Finding a place of rest is necessary to receive what God is speaking and wants to give us. But we are not supposed to remain lying down.

Jesus died not only for our salvation, but to recover the authority God gave in the Garden of Eden:

> So God created man in his own image, in the image of God he created him; male and female he created them. And God blessed them. And God said to them, "Be fruitful and multiply and fill the earth and subdue it, and have dominion over the fish of the sea and over the birds of the heavens and over every living thing that moves on the earth."
> — GENESIS 1:27-28

Grasp the gifts God gives so that you become fruitful. Distribute what you have received so that you multiply. Get to work on plans He gives you so that you reign with Jesus. This is the model through which heaven comes to earth.

God is faithful and all His promises are yes and amen (2 Cor. 1:20). You have access to His throne. There you may boldly meet God and ask Him what you need to take your place on earth. Heaven has the answers, all the answers, for the earth that is in travail and sighing and groaning as it looks forward to the children of God taking their place:

> For the creation waits with eager longing for the revealing of the sons of God.
> – ROMANS 8:19

So wake up! Being a dreamer is great, but a dreamer who puts their dream into practice will change the world!

Your Life is a Set of Keys

> But as it is, God arranged the members in the body, each one of them, as he chose. If all were a single member, where would the body be? As it is, there are many parts, yet one body.
> – 1 CORINTHIANS 12:18-20

In this book you have been able to read about all kinds of areas in which God wants to speak through dreams and nightly encounters. Some types of dreams you will get more often, and others less often. The types of dreams you receive will also vary with the season of your life. If you want to focus more on dreams and hear what God wants to say, it is important to know that God gives dreams to make something of His heart known on the earth. Dreams have a function; they bring you or another person closer to God. Whether it's a dream that brings deeper healing to your soul or a dream with an insight, or a plan, it's great to receive dreams. And when you act on your dreams, it will have an impact on the earth.

God wants to reach every person with the good news and establish His Kingdom on earth. When you consider that the earth has an area of 510 million square kilometers and that there are around 7.8 billion people, it takes a lot of workers to do that! That's why God created the body of Christ, the Church. When Jesus walked the earth 2,000 years ago, He could only be in one place at a time. But because of the body, His Church, He is now everywhere in the world.

You have a place in the body of Christ. You don't have to fight for that place. Nor do you have to envy someone else's place—your place fits you perfectly. By the hand of God's Spirit, you may explore what your position entails; what God has given you to live in your destiny. Part of that is to break free from the old and learn to trust God in the new. Do not be afraid, you are doing well, and you are right on time.

You were made by God to move with Him in His master plan. Throughout the Bible you see God using ordinary people to carry out a supernatural mission with Him. God gives a calling for a place or a group of people and He makes a simple person competent to fulfill the calling. A good example of this is Moses. When he meets God at the burning bush, God says this:

> "Come, I will send you to Pharaoh that you may bring my people, the children of Israel, out of Egypt."
> – EXODUS 3:10

After forty years in the desert, this is a huge turn of events for Moses. His sphere of influence is now suddenly the people of Israel. What an assignment from God for a man who for the past forty years had been herding a flock of sheep, living largely alone! We all know how Moses balked and doubted himself. Moses needed to break free from his old way of thinking. But Moses' story shows that God supernaturally gifted him in a short time to lead a large number of people out of slavery. God made Moses strong and courageous, and gave him the compassion for the people to persevere no matter how difficult and contrary the people were at times. God assisted him with extraordinary signs and wonders. We don't know for sure, but Moses would probably never have seen such works of God if he had chosen to remain a shepherd.

God used the staff in Moses' hand, a simple piece of wood, and made it a key to deliver the people and show the people that God lives.

> The LORD said to him, "What is that in your hand?" He said, "A staff."
> – EXODUS 4:2

God is asking you the same question: "What do you have in your hand?" He has given you keys that fit the lock of a particular area, a particular audience. Such a key is specifically and uniquely formed so that it fits that particular lock. In the same way, you are uniquely and very specifically shaped. Your life, your ministry, carries a key that can open an area so that heaven comes to earth through your life. As Christians, we can be overwhelmed by all the suffering of the world. Then we start carrying that suffering on our shoulders. This is impossible and paralyzing. Although we have the answer for the world in need, it is only manifested when each one operates in their own sphere of influence. No one can get there the way you can. It is a wonderful, wondrous plan of God in which everyone is needed—from small to great.

If you feel that you don't have keys, I want to remind you that God is the Giver of good gifts. You have no doubt been given heavenly keys. Your challenge is to find the locks that can be opened by your keys. Ask yourself: "What would I do if I had no fear?" What social problems do you have compassion for, what situations in society attract your attention and cause deep dissatisfaction or indignation in your heart? What are your thoughts about these things and what would you like to see transformed by heaven? You have these feelings for a reason; they show you that you have a specific key to unlock these areas for God's glory.

Suppose you've been praying for your workplace for years and you notice that God gives you a desire to keep doing that. Then you could say that your work is an area of authority over which God is putting you. He gives you entrance into the spiritual world to make a difference there in particular. Of course, we may make a difference if we tell someone the gospel on the street; spreading the gospel should always be the focus point for every believer. But your workplace, for now, is one of the still closed areas in which the Holy Spirit wants to work with you. He wants to draw your co-workers to His heart through your life.

So, how do you know if your key fits? Try it out—what happens? When the resistance disappears and freedom comes, when God's Spirit can flow where it first seemed impossible, you have your answer! God can work mightily when you get to work in that particular area. Doors open, healing comes, miracles happen and heaven touches earth. The key fits!

The problem is that we often don't recognize our impact because it is so close to us that we see it as that simple piece of wood, like Moses' staff. You might think that you can't make a change. But did you know that you often make the most impact by simply being yourself? You plus God is a glory bomb!

We need each other to know what our sphere of influence is. One of the ways God does that is through the prophetic ministry. It was instituted by God to form His body, to assign each one their place and empower them. At the same time, God can even speak through a donkey (Num. 22:28)—He speaks willingly and through anyone who is open to it. So feel free to ask those around you what kind of power they see in you. Where do they see the impact of who you are? Do you work best with children, or with the elderly, or in business, or in the field of mental health or creativity? It could be anywhere! In what ways will your light shine? Perhaps through music you create, lyrics you write, words you speak, hugs you give, art you create, or business insights you apply? All of these things are important and necessary. Talking about this is instructive; we need to encourage each other to share what we see. In addition, it binds people together as we look at each other from heaven with the Father's love, encouraging and affirming.

Remember that there are keys especially for you. You can pick them up or lay them aside, but they don't go away; you are the owner of the keys. Even if you don't have people around you who recognize your keys, they are yours. Just read this text:

> Every good gift and every perfect gift is from above, coming down from the Father of lights, with whom there is no variation or shadow due to change.
> – JAMES 1:17

What God gives you, He does not take away again. His gifts are specially made to bless others. They are precious instruments of love, deliverance and life. What will you do with your keys? Ask God's Spirit to help you recognize and use them. Ask Him for people with whom you can cooperate and who will affirm and encourage you. And last but not least, don't think too little of yourself; you were made to change this world with Jesus!

Maybe your keys are not for as vast an area as Moses', but you can be sure that you are capable of using them. And when you do, God promises that He will multiply and enlarge your territory (1 Chron. 4:10). It is a heavenly principle—what you are faithful in, grows, and what you share, becomes more.

Your life, your marriage and family are always your area of authority. That is where your feet are and that is where God wants heaven to come to earth. When we all begin to take that area seriously, we can expect great things. When heaven touches earth in you, in your marriage and in your home, your fire also sets others on fire for God! You have the authority to be a huge spreading fire for God's glory.

Solomon's Lessons

> For wisdom is better than jewels, and all that you may desire cannot compare with her.
> — PROVERBS 8:11

God wants us to excel in ways far beyond what is humanly feasible. He wants to give us wisdom during the day and the night. What is the end goal? It is transformation in your own land, and worldwide. That is also exactly what He did for Solomon. Therefore, let's look at his life a little more closely. Besides the wisdom Solomon received in the night, there is more we can learn from this man. Or should I say "boy"? Solomon may not have been older than fifteen when he experienced the night encounter that changed everything. He knew he had a nation to lead and was aware of his incompetence. He had seen his father reign and may have dreaded leading the battles that were constantly taking place. Does this aversion to war have anything to do with his name? In the Bible, names are significant. Solomon means "peace", and it must be that peace in his DNA that causes him to reach out for something other than war for his people.

We can tell a bit about this young king's character by looking at what he wrote:

> Keep your heart with all vigilance, for from it flow the springs of life.
> — PROVERBS 4:23

> Let not steadfast love and faithfulness forsake you; bind them around your neck; write them on the tablet of your heart.
> — PROVERBS 3:3
>
> The fear of the LORD is the beginning of wisdom, and the knowledge of the Holy One is insight.
> — PROVERBS 9:10
>
> Iron sharpens iron, and one man sharpens another.
> — PROVERBS 27:17
>
> My beloved is mine and I am his; he browses among the lilies.
> — SONG OF SOLOMON 2:16 (NIV)

These statements hold deep keys for us. They show Solomon's heart; it is full of integrity and wisdom. He knows God's tangible love and even writes a passionate book about it: Song of Solomon. At the same time, he is in awe of God. When God visits him in the night and asks him what he wants, Solomon says this:

> Now, LORD my God, you have made your servant king in place of my father David. But I am only a little child and do not know how to carry out my duties. Your servant is here among the people you have chosen, a great people, too numerous to count or number. So give your servant a discerning heart to govern your people and to distinguish between right and wrong. For who is able to govern this great people of yours?
> — 1 KINGS 3:7-9 (NIV)

Reading between the lines, you can hear his doubt and fear of his calling as king. At the same time, he did not act out of fear, but looked at it from God's perspective. He knew the state of his heart was important for how he functioned. He must have learned that from his father, David. Both men had troubled and far from perfect lives, but each time we see their sincere hearts to serve God. Solomon longed to bring justice to his people. During this heavenly encounter, he said, "I cannot do it, but You can; I need You to perform this task."

That night is the gamechanger, not only for Solomon but for the entire nation of Israel. The heavenly wisdom he received became apparent when he had to administer justice. Two women came to him, both laying claim to a baby (1 Kings 3:16-28). What did Solomon do? He did not consult the books of the law—which was the usual way in those days—but he used God's wisdom to resolve this. Since his encounter with God, he has had access to the wisdom and thoughts of God. Solomon himself must have been amazed to see heavenly wisdom turn his life upside down. He knew that wisdom was not a gift to keep for himself, but to bless the people with.

As Solomon did this, you see how the other promise of God takes effect: Solomon became rich, richer than anyone on earth. But wisdom was dearer to Solomon than wealth. He knew that money and possessions alone would not bring justice to the land, but wisdom from God would. That wisdom influenced Solomon's life. Even kings of other nations came to visit him to see for themselves how he ruled the land!

Solomon's wisdom came from heaven, and was therefore accessible to every believer since the sacrifice of Jesus and the coming of the Holy Spirit. Imagine, God gives heavenly wisdom to His children for every part of society—politics, education, faith, family, economy, media and art. The Holy Spirit knows every person on the planet, is the greatest Genius of all, the best Doctor and Inventor. He is supernaturally brilliant, and according to Paul, we have His thoughts (1 Cor. 2:16). When we live, work and move from that wisdom, everything changes! And in such a way that other nations will come to know Jesus! It brings to mind the text from Isaiah that describes God's call to his people:

WALKING IN GOD'S DREAMS

> Arise, shine, for your light has come, and the glory of the LORD rises upon you. See, darkness covers the earth and thick darkness is over the peoples, but the LORD rises upon you and his glory appears over you. Nations will come to your light, and kings to the brightness of your dawn.
> — ISAIAH 60:1-3 (NIV)

God wants to do extraordinary things through our land. For centuries, people from around the world have come to see how we do certain things. Our country is small, but it has a big influence on the world. The Netherlands is known worldwide for trade and innovation. So imagine what happens when these things are inspired by God's Spirit! We will build, renovate and bring to life what God wants because we move in what He has given. We can then walk in His footsteps and do what He does:

> The Spirit of the Sovereign LORD is on me, because the LORD has anointed me to proclaim good news to the poor. He has sent me to bind up the brokenhearted, to proclaim freedom for the captives and release from darkness for the prisoners, to proclaim the year of the LORD's favor and the day of vengeance of our God, to comfort all who mourn, and provide for those who grieve in Zion —to bestow on them a crown of beauty instead of ashes, the oil of joy instead of mourning, and a garment of praise instead of a spirit of despair. They will be called oaks of righteousness, a planting of the LORD for the display of his splendor. They will rebuild the ancient ruins and restore the places long devastated, they will renew the ruined cities that have been devastated for generations.
> — ISAIAH 61:1-4 (NIV)

The Spirit of Lord is upon you. He has anointed you to spread the gospel. He has sent you to heal broken hearts and set captives free. He makes you cry out that the time has come for God to turn everything around; the time for a jewel instead of ashes, joy instead of mourning and a mantle of praise instead of a distressed spirit. You will rebuild devastated places with Him. In the spiritual and natural you will renew desolate places. In the small things and in the big things you will bring renewal from generation to generation, so that the earth may know that Jesus is alive.

Step-by-step Plan: From Dream to Reality

> For the revelation awaits an appointed time; it speaks of the end and will not prove false. Though it linger, wait for it; it will certainly come and will not delay.
> – HABAKKUK 2:3 (NIV)

You know you've been given a dream from God, but what do you do with it? Here I share some steps that can help.

Step 1 - Write down the dream. Write down every detail of it. Pay extra attention to writing down your emotions during your dream. Describe what you felt when you woke up and when the meaning dawned on you. Do you get immediate ideas for applying the dream? If so, write those down as well. Make sure your dream has a title that contains the core message. That way, even after years have passed, you will still have a clear record of your dream.

Step 2 - Give the dream back to God. A dream from God can have tremendous impact on you. You may be upset or experience restlessness. This is quite normal. The Creator of heaven and earth has made something known to you, given you something; perhaps a world-changing plan. This is extremely precious. Put the dream back in God's hands; it is safe where it came from. This way you give God space to speak further and work out what the dream means and what you can do with it. Let yourself be filled with peace again. Now you are in a position to hear what He continues to speak without feeling like you are the main person responsible. Remember, what God gives, He works out as you cooperate with Him.

Step 3 - Pray out your dream. Sometimes you receive a dream that touches you deeply, but time passes and little seems to happen. That can discourage you and even cause disbelief about what you have received. Pray out your dream, speak out what you have received and proclaim that it will become visible. Your words have power, even for yourself. By speaking it out, you are prophesying about yourself. Your dream comes from God, and what comes from Him always brings new life. Sometimes it takes a little longer for your dream to become visible, but don't give up. There is a key in your persistence.

Step 4 - Ask for confirmation. When your mind fails you or when you doubt what you have received, you can ask God for confirmation. He is happy to give it. This is also how He confirmed Pharaoh's dream:

> The reason the dream was given to Pharaoh in two forms is that the matter has been firmly decided by God, and God will do it soon.
> — GENESIS 41:32 (NIV)

He can give that affirmation in many ways. For example, by giving the dream again. He can also speak through His Word, or through another person, or in other ways. It is important to have open ears and eyes. You can simply ask the Holy Spirit for that: "Holy Spirit, open my eyes and ears and enlighten the eyes of my heart, so that I may not miss anything You have to say to me."

Step 5 - Take action. Ask God what you can do. What steps, big or small, can you take to walk in this dream? Perhaps you can write a plan, draw the dream, or figure out what it will take to make your dream a reality. The moment we take a step of faith, the heavens move. You will find that God opens doors as you walk toward those doors. And sometimes He closes one door and shows you a new one.

Step 6 - Share the dream. Take the step, talk about your dream with someone you trust, someone who builds you up and encourages you. That way the dream becomes more and more of a reality for you, and that person can remind you of it. Often God wants to work more in us than just the outcome of the dream. He may want to teach us to cooperate and trust other people. Do think carefully about who you share a dream from God with; you want to avoid having your faith and enthusiasm broken down. But even if that happens, there's no harm done, because what comes from heaven is not lost.

Step 7 - Work together. Look for people who can help you make your dream practical. The Kingdom is a collaboration. Firstly with God, but also with your brothers and sisters. You may have received the idea, the solution or something else, and someone else has received another piece, so you complement each other and can accomplish much together. Ask God to bring those people into your path. He knows exactly who you need!

Our Father in heaven remains the same yesterday, today and forever (Heb. 13:8). He is always near and He is willing to help you with anything. He is immensely interested in you, He has time for you, and He is God. Stay close to Him in the little things and the big things, in what you see and in what you don't yet see. He wants to meet you now and hear from you. The dream He has given you has no expiration date. He is faithful in what He promises. In the end, you will be amazed at its effects!

God's Fire Over Your Nights

> For the LORD your God is a consuming fire, a jealous God.
> – DEUTERONOMY 4:24

When you walk with Jesus, you are continually renewed by His life in your life. He is the Source that washes you. Endless streams of fresh water cleanse you from every iniquity. He wants to bring every part of you that is not yet in line with God's thoughts about you, to the surface, and turn it to the truth. He straightens everything that is crooked and cleans what was once dirty. Not because God doesn't think we aren't good enough now, but He loves us so much that He can't stand to see us walking with baggage that Jesus has long since carried, or believing in lies that keep us away from an abundant life with Him. God wants us completely. He wants to change us from glory to glory (2 Cor. 3:18). God wants to make us fully visible, as He had in mind before the foundation of the world. But God is not only a Source of living water, God is also a cleansing fire.

Where God is like a fire, He burns away everything that does not belong to us. And it doesn't stop there. He makes us healthy and whole, exactly as we should be. Whether you have only just come to know Jesus or have been doing what He has called you to do for years, we are all on our way to becoming the real version of ourselves. When we look at the bigger picture, it becomes clearer. Jesus is coming back for His bride. The Bible says:

> (...) so that he might present the church to himself in splendor, without spot or wrinkle or any such thing, that she might be holy and without blemish.
> – EPHESIANS 5:27

The Church, the bride for whom Jesus, the Bridegroom, returns, is "without spot or wrinkle". She is magnificent, whole and in complete unity. She is full of color because of all those unique people, full of strength, full of love, pure and holy. The bride of Christ must be a dazzling spectacle by the time Jesus returns! That means she must be cleansed. She is made clean not only on the surface but also inside. Stains disappear by the water from the Well, Jesus, and the cleansing bath of God's Word. Wrinkles disappear through the heat of God's fire.

This is also who God is: He is holy and cannot allow His bride, with whom He merges, to be unholy. Just think what those spots and wrinkles might be—mutual hatred, jealousy, envy, sin and division, pain, sorrow and trauma, rejection and self-hatred. All of these things you might recognize within the body of Jesus; perhaps also in your own life. Can you imagine God in His fiery love wanting to cleanse this?

You and I are part of the bigger picture. God sees you as holy and at the same time He says, "Be holy, for I am holy" (1 Pet. 1:15-16). When we allow God's cleansing fire into our lives, a piece of the bride is made spotless and pure. If you look closely, this process has long since begun; the Church of Christ is under pressure today. Many Christians experience this as a challenging or even difficult time. But you don't have to see this only as negative; the cleansing process is in full swing. The bride of Jesus is being born!

> "Shall I bring to the point of birth and not cause to bring forth?" says the LORD; "shall I, who cause to bring forth, shut the womb?" says your God.
> – ISAIAH 66:9

When you are under pressure, your deepest motivations come up to the surface. All the dregs are brought up. Your walls of false security crumble and your mask of perfection can no longer be worn. This is necessary—we very much need God's cleansing.

> You are my Lord; I have no good apart from you.
> — PSALM 16:2b

This Bible text is a fierce message for our self-righteous flesh. But it is true, the only thing good about us is what God has made of us. We cannot add anything to that ourselves, no matter how much we would like to. It is actually a relaxing message: God creates it in you and me. He simply asks us if we want to give our whole life to Him, so that He can make something wonderful out of it:

> Humble yourselves, therefore, under the mighty hand of God so that at the proper time he may exalt you.
> — 1 PETER 5:6

Surrender is like a magnet for God's fire on your life. When you put your life on the altar, God's fire can get to work. It is a partnership in which you get to choose what you want to keep for yourself and what you want to give to God. Worldwide, more and more people are willing to lay down their lives for God so that He can cooperate with them wherever and however He wants. This is God's work on earth. This is what His Spirit is doing among us now, and He also wants to touch you with His fire so that you will be on fire for Jesus.

God's fire demands awe. We are not resistant to it and can do nothing but surrender to it. Many people struggle to surrender because they don't want to lose control, but in fact, you have never been in control. God is your only security and your only Source of life. He is looking for people who are willing to lay themselves down before Him and be cleansed and sanctified for His glory. God even attaches a tremendous promise to it:

> Blessed are the pure in heart, for they shall see God.
> — MATTHEW 5:8

Through your pure, honest heart you will see God. Isn't that a glorious promise? You will see Him, He who looks at you with eyes like flames and wants to set you on fire. The eye contains a hole in the middle—the pupil—which is like the opening in a camera. It acts like a window. The source of fire is not Jesus' eye, but his heart. He has a fire burning deep in his soul (Luke 12:49) and desires it to be kindled in each of us.

The eye also has a clear lens covering the cornea. It acts like a mirror. When you look into someone's eyes, you see your own image reflected. When we look into the eyes of Jesus, the fire that is in His soul flows out of Him, through our eyes, into our souls. This transfer of energy does not involve the physical eye, but the spiritual eyes (Eph. 1:18).

Some people run from conference to conference, trying to receive the fire of God. But there is direct, personal access to the fire of God, the fire that is available to us at any time. All you have to do is this—close your physical eyes, focus on Bible verses that describe the fire in the eyes of Jesus, imagine Him looking you in the eye—face to face—and that flame will begin to flow from His soul into yours.

You may wonder, what does this have to do with the night and dreams? When God cleanses you, this happens in every part of you. Your mind, soul and body, your speech and your actions, during your days as well as your nights. Streams of living water from within you (John 7:38), heavenly life in your bones and God's fire on your life. I believe it is possible for children of God to receive full salvation and cleansing for our nights—nights of deep rest and refreshing, a sweet sleep with encounters and dreams of God. The fuller your thinking is with truth, the cleaner your soul is, and the more righteous and loving your actions and walk are. Then you will no doubt see this reflected in your nights. What a wonderful promise: God's plan, His blueprint for the night, will become fully visible in your life!

ADDENDUM | 8

Testimonials

> For the testimony of Jesus is the spirit of prophecy.
> — REVELATION 19:10b

In this book you will find all kinds of testimonies from my life and from the lives of others. Some are exceptional, others just taken from everyday life. Witnessing what God does is a powerful weapon against hopelessness and discouragement. For if God did it then, He is going to do it again! When we witness about what Jesus did for us, it helps to focus on the God of the impossible. That sets faith free for supernatural breakthrough. Through testimony, God's Spirit speaks over the listener and says, "I want to do this, even for you!"

Not everything God does seems to have a use in our eyes, but to Him it apparently matters. These are invitations from a good God; we won't always be able to understand Him, but His plans are always good and full of hope. "Even if you do not see, I am good. Even if you do not understand Me, I am working to pave a way and give My abundance to you." We may discard the boundaries we have made for God. To help you do that, below you will read more wonderful testimonies of an unimaginably good Father.

Co's Story: Treasure hunting with God

It was a Sunday evening. All afternoon I had been out and about with my metal detector. This has been a big hobby of mine for a few years now, and I've found a lot of beautiful things. I have been making videos about my finds for about a year, and share them on YouTube. But on that night I was in great doubt about whether I should continue this. I asked God what He thought: "Wouldn't You rather have me do important things for You? That metal detector is really just a useless thing that I use only for my own pleasure." As I prayed, I actually felt like a selfish person. I concluded my prayer by asking God to speak and was already preparing to say goodbye to my hobby.

That night, Dite had a dream about me. She saw me walking in a meadow and strangely, I left my metal detector at a fence. She looked me over and saw that I was slumping my shoulders and did not look cheerful. What I didn't see in the dream, but she did, was that there were special eggs in the meadow. She knew I wanted to find those eggs because I love treasure hunting, and she called me back. Then she saw a snake gliding through the grass hissing, "Doubt, doubt, doubt." Dite herself, however, did not hesitate for a moment. She grabbed the metal detector, hit the snake on the head, and the snake disappeared.

The next day, not yet knowing that Dite had had this dream about me, I received a call from a man. He asked me to come over with my metal detector. He had found an old coin. I went to the man and started looking. Within ten minutes I pulled six old coins out of the ground. I continued searching all evening and to my amazement

I found a treasure hoard![19] I spent a total of three evenings getting all the coins out of the ground. I stood there laughing and marveling at God's involvement in my hobby. He knew all along what was in store for me and granted it to me to find this treasure. By giving the dream and thus allowing Dite to pray for my doubt, I made the find of a lifetime!

Vanessa's story: Heavenly air conditioning

Spring has tried very hard to pretend it's summer the last few years, not to mention the heat later in the year. My apartment is on the second floor, with the living room and bedroom facing south. With the sun on it all day, it gets hot quickly without air conditioning or awnings.

As soon as the sun goes down, I open my doors and windows to catch a cool breeze, and leave them open all night. Early in the morning when the sun rises, I close everything again. One morning I wanted to close the windows, when I felt a cool refreshing breeze filling my living room. What I had been trying to accomplish all night happened in one moment. I breathed in the fresh air and said, "Praise the Lord." I went upstairs to close the bedroom window, and there, too, a coolness began to enter the room. My hands and feet got cold, just like what happens when you turn on an air conditioner. The only difference is: I don't have an air conditioner!

I felt the furniture and found that it too had become cool. I even walked over to the thermostat, expecting it to drop a few degrees, but it didn't. I stood in the middle of the room and felt God's presence around me. Suddenly it dawned on me: God was providing the cool breeze in my home. It was Him! I prayed so often for cooling so

I could sleep better during hot spells, and there He was! Nothing is impossible or too much trouble for God the Father. Now, that is exuberant love!

Marlien's story: Favorite instrument

I have been making music, singing and writing songs for years. I also love string instruments immensely. Never before had I written or played a piece of music for a string orchestra, until one morning I woke up with an entire string orchestra piece in my head! Still half asleep, I almost wanted to turn over again, but I decided to sing the melody into my phone, with my cracking morning voice. When I listened to the melody later on, I could recall several layers in the music. Not playing a string instrument myself, I decided to record the layers in a program on my laptop. Gradually, the entire orchestra from my dream became complete. The dream also contained a message to myself about what would happen in the next season of my life. Every time I hear the melody, I am reminded of this! It is so nice to create music in this way, and remember what God said![20]

God's heart created dreams

Dreams are a particularly strange phenomenon. You can dream about the strangest things, and you can dream very normal things. No matter how I try to make dreams as understandable as possible, it remains a strange subject, and perhaps we should leave it that way. It's also wonderful, isn't it, to be able to do things during your sleep that you can't actually do when awake? Flying on a golden bicycle, walking the streets of Jerusalem, standing on the edge of the earth, or floating among the stars; dreams can be one big celebration! They are a creative expression of a God without limits. God could have left them out when He made humankind. But in His endless love for us, He created an opportunity to reach out to us in those hours of sleep, when we are physically absent. God's heart thoroughly enjoyed conceiving dreams! I can imagine how He looked forward to all the encounters during the night, when for a moment our mental processes do not set the standard for our lives. He could show Himself in other ways. What a magical idea. First and foremost, remember to enjoy and rejoice in all that is to come. Jesus saves the best wine for last (John 2:1-12) and it will surpass our finest dreams!

> Your mouth [is] like the best wine. It goes down smoothly for my beloved, gliding over lips and teeth. I am my beloved's, and his desire is for me.
> – SONG OF SOLOMON 7:9-10

Notes

1. You can read my sister Charlotte's testimony in Kamp, W. van der, *Waarom grijpt God niet in*. Aalten: Vrij zijn, 2016, pp. 36-39.
2. *Skotizo*, G4654 in Strong's Greek Lexicon.
3. *Chosek*, H2822 in Strong's Hebrew Concordance.
4. *Layil*, H3915 in Strong's Hebrew Concordance.
5. YouTube: *Stars and Whales singing How Great is Our God (Chris Tomlin) – Louie Giglio – 9min version* https://youtu.be/helxFeG-OnO
6. *We'areba*, H6147 in Strong's Hebrew Lexicon.
7. More on this can be found on embryo.asu.edu/pages/roger-sperrys-split-brain-experiments-1959-1968
8. See Proverbs 3:20 and Hosea 14:6.
9. Sozo is a Christian Restoration Program, see https://www.bethelsozo.com.
10. Dissociation is a term from psychology. This word literally means "disintegration". A person is temporarily detached from themselves, so to speak; thoughts, emotions, perceptions or memories are temporarily inaccessible.
11. You could consider Sozo.
12. See for more testimonies: Doyle, T. (2012), *Dreams and Visions*. Nashville: Thomas Nelson.
13. A recording of this moment can be found on "Real Angel Choir", https://youtu.be/UiDP2hcAjBw
14. You can find this song on YouTube or Spotify: "All eyes on You", https://youtu.be/tTtMY-RvxwE
15. You can see this painting on my website, ditecoumou.com.
16. Such a door is open due to deliberate sin or sin in your ancestry.
17. Hattaway, P., Yun (2002). *The Heavenly Man*. London: Kregel Publications.
18. A reading tip for those longing for more healing is Wal, T. de (2020), *Jezus aanraken*. Werkendam: Frontrunners Ministries, 2020. The English edition is currently prepared.
19. You can find a video of this treasure at YouTube, https://youtu.be/urEfZmHDPtl
20. The album *Hartsverlangen* by Eden Worship can be found on Spotify and YouTube.

Acknowledgments

The acknowledgment part of a book may seem like a compilation of flattering words, but nothing could be further from the truth. Writing a book is a complicated process that cannot be done alone. Those around me have made a huge difference. That is why I want to thank several of them.

Joost, my darling, thank you for your sacrificial love. You led me to Jesus and support me as I chase after Him, regardless of the cost. You not only helped me to start this book, but also to complete it. You encouraged me as I wrote God's words, held me tight when I was discouraged, helped me to focus when I needed it and you reminded me again and again of the reason why I was writing this book in the first place—that the Father's heart would be revealed to many and the Kingdom of heaven would come here on earth.

Heleen, you have stood by my side like a Jonathan. You have done that from the moment God called me and have tirelessly pointed me to His promises. Thank you for never giving up.

My dear friends, thank you for your prayers, how you have spurred me on and helped me as this book was written. It is an honor to walk with you and to receive what you pour into my life.

My family, thank you for believing in what God is doing in and through my life. From the horse-girl to a vessel for God's glory has been a bumpy road, but you have always stood by my side.

Finally, my *I AM* family, thank you for your love for each person, both young and old, and the space you have given me to grow. Surrounded by so many people who chase after God's Kingdom on earth is glorious and an honor!

It makes me realize my insignificance.

How great You are, Lord, that You need every person and every generation to show yourself. Above all, I thank You, God, that You found me, called me and sent me. You have been with me every step of the way, even in the darkest of nights. You give me all I need, and more, and your goodness brings me to my knees again and again.

Thank You that You have given me this opportunity to show your heart to the world. Take it and use it as You see fit.

About Dite Coumou

Dite met her Savior, Jesus, when she was in her mid-twenties. He gave her life a radically different direction—from a background of occultism to a life completely dedicated to passionately following Jesus and building His Kingdom.

During a personal encounter with God, He called her into a prophetic ministry. Since that time, she has been speaking in various congregations, training, creating podcasts and writing. Her ministry aims to awaken and equip the body of Jesus to hear God's voice, understand it and practically walk in what He says.

Her desire is to connect people to the heart of God, where a stream of revelation is available day and night. This is the place where transformation happens, where we find healing and freedom. The place where we truly come alive. She has a deep desire to see this transformation in every layer of society until God's love is known worldwide.

Dite is married to Joost and together they are affiliated with the church *I Am* in Hendrik-Ido-Ambacht. Would you like to invite her to speak or contact her? Or would you like to share with her what God has done in your life through this book? Then go to ditecoumou.com

On her website you will also find podcasts teaching about dreams.

On the Bible app YouVersion, you will find Dite's reading plan "God's Plan for the Night".

IMPACT
Prophesy and Change the World

Prophecy transforms people's lives, but it is meant for more. God is ready to transform every segment of society, and He reveals strategies to accomplish it.

Arleen Westerhof shows us how to work with prophetic revelation. She describes how to give prophetic words, test prophecies, and how apostles and prophets can work together to accomplish breakthrough. She shows that character development, inner healing and deliverance are essential for anyone building a prophetic ministry.

This practical book proves that prophecy can have an amazing impact on every aspect of the world around us!

TRADE PAPERBACK
192 PAGES
8.5 X 5.4 X 0.4 IN
ISBN ITP: 9781951014018
ISBN EBOOK: 9781951014025
RRP $15.99

DR. ARLEEN WESTERHOF is the founder and director of the Netherlands Prophetic Council. She initiated the Living in Your Destiny Schools of the Prophets and founded Women on the Frontlines in the Netherlands. Arleen regularly speaks at conferences all over the world. Together with her husband Dick, she leads God's Embassy Amsterdam, a church and apostolic center. Her passion is using prophecy to equip people to bring transformation to the different areas of society.

Cutting-Edge Materials for Radical Followers of Jesus

Visit us at
arrowz.org

For questions and bulk discount orders
please contact us at info@arrowz.org

www.ingramcontent.com/pod-product-compliance
Lightning Source LLC
Chambersburg PA
CBHW030147100526
44592CB00009B/156